## Praise for Ephesians

"Grant Osborne's *Ephesians Verse by Verse* is a commentary written by a churchman, for the church. Lucid and engaging, the exposition helpfully unpacks Paul's letter in such a way that dense logical arguments become clear and hard-to-understand theological concepts are made accessible. Especially praiseworthy is the way Dr. Osborne walks the reader through sometimes divisive passages, summarizing and explaining clearly various interpretive positions. His arguments are consistently fair-minded and balanced, instructive as well as applicable to modern life. Here pastors and other students of God's word will find a rich resource for navigating Paul's Ephesians."

—**George H. Guthrie**, Benjamin W. Perry Professor of Bible, Union University

"As a pastor, I have often turned to Osborne's work not only for sermon preparation but personal study. Osborne has a way of balancing academic work and an emphasis on practical application from the biblical truth he is expounding. This truly is a great resource for all Christians wanting to study Ephesians."

—**Cody Kargus**, senior pastor, Maranatha Evangelical Free Church (Rice Lake, WI)

"A clear and powerful exposition of Ephesians. This commentary has succeeded in explaining how the Triune God works to bring about our salvation and how Christians are to live individually and as a church under the lordship of Christ. The last section on our spiritual warfare is described very vividly and practically. A must-have for Bible study and sermon preparation."

—**Janson Chan**, executive director, Timothy Training International

"Dr. Grant R. Osborne is well-known to have invested his entire life in the study and explication of the New Testament. His many writings reflect the detailed breadth and depth of his involvement with the text, but in this series, he seeks to complement much of his other work by removing the complexity of many modern commentaries. Here, he provides an easy-to-read explanation of Ephesians and applies its teachings to our lives today. Anyone interested in the mission and writings of the Apostle Paul will find this work to be personally enriching and refreshing indeed."

—**Barry J. Beitzel**, professor of Old Testament and Semitic languages, Trinity Evangelical Divinity School

T0327010

## Praise for the Osborne New Testament Commentaries

"For years I have found Grant Osborne's commentaries to be reliable and thoughtful guides for those wanting to better understand the New Testament. Indeed, Osborne has mastered the art of writing sound, helpful, and readable commentaries and I am confident that this new series will continue the level of excellence that we have come to expect from him. How exciting to think that pastors, students, and laity will all be able to benefit for years to come from the wise and insightful interpretation provided by Professor Osborne in this new series. The Osborne New Testament Commentaries will be a great gift for the people of God."

—**David S. Dockery**, president, Trinity International University

"This is a set of commentaries by one of the premier New Testament commentators of our day—a reputation earned over many years of teaching, preaching, and writing. Dr. Osborne brings a full understanding of the Old Testament and Second Temple literature to bear on a careful and profound reading of the New Testament. In this series his previous exegetical commentary writing comes to a full expository expression that will be of great benefit to students, preachers, and teachers alike."

—**Richard E. Averbeck**, director of the PhD program in theological studies, professor of Old Testament and Semitic languages, Trinity Evangelical Divinity School

"One of my most valued role models, Grant Osborne is a first-tier biblical scholar who brings to the text of Scripture a rich depth of insight that is both accessible and devotional. Grant loves Christ, loves the Word, and loves the church, and those loves are embodied in this wonderful new commentary series, which I cannot recommend highly enough."

—**George H. Guthrie**, Benjamin W. Perry Professor of Bible, Union University

"Grant Osborne is ideally suited to write a series of concise commentaries on the New Testament. His exegetical and hermeneutical skills are well known, and anyone who has had the privilege of being in his classes also knows his pastoral heart and wisdom."

—**Ray Van Neste**, professor of biblical studies, director of the R.C. Ryan Center for Biblical Studies, Union University

"With this new series, readers will have before them what we—his students— experienced in all of Professor Osborne's classes: patient regard for every word in the text, exegetical finesse, a preference for an eclectic resolution to the options facing the interpreter, a sensitivity to theological questions, and most of all a reverence for God's word."

—**Scot McKnight**, Julius R. Mantey Chair of New Testament, Northern Seminary

# EPHESIANS

*Verse by Verse*

# EPHESIANS

*Verse by Verse*

GRANT R. OSBORNE

LEXHAM PRESS

*Ephesians: Verse by Verse*
Osborne New Testament Commentaries

Copyright 2017 Grant R. Osborne

Lexham Press, 1313 Commercial St., Bellingham, WA 98225
LexhamPress.com

Print ISBN 9781577997726
Digital ISBN 9781577997733

Lexham Editorial Team: Elliot Ritzema, Abigail Stocker, Joel Wilcox
Cover Design: Christine Christophersen
Back Cover Design: Brittany Schrock
Typesetting: ProjectLuz.com

*Printed and bound by CPI Group (UK) Ltd, Croydon, CR0 4YY*

24 iv / UK

# CONTENTS

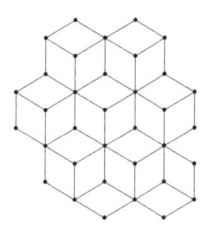

# SERIES PREFACE

There are two authors of every biblical book: the human author who penned the words and the divine Author who revealed and inspired every word. While God did not dictate the words to the biblical writers, he did guide their minds so that they wrote their own words under the influence of the Holy Spirit. If Christians really believed what they said when they called the Bible "the word of God," a lot more would be engaged in serious Bible study. As divine revelation the Bible deserves, indeed demands, to be studied deeply.

This means that when we study the Bible we should not be satisfied with a cursory reading in which we insert our own meanings into the text. Instead, we must always ask what God intends to say in every passage. But Bible study should not be a tedious duty we have to perform. It is a sacred privilege and a joy. The deep meaning of any text is a buried treasure; all the riches are waiting under the surface. If we learned there was gold deep beneath our backyard, nothing would stop us from getting the tools we needed to dig it out. Similarly, in serious Bible study all the treasures and riches of God are waiting to be dug up for our benefit.

This series of commentaries on the New Testament is intended to supply these tools and help the Christian understand more deeply the God-intended meaning of the Bible. Each volume walks the reader verse-by-verse through a book with the goal of opening up for us what God led Matthew or Paul or John to say to his readers. My goal in this series is to make sense of the historical and literary background of these ancient works, to supply the information that will enable the modern reader to understand exactly what the biblical writers were saying to their first-century audience. I want to remove the complexity of most modern commentaries and provide an easy-to-read explanation of the text.

But it is not enough to know what the books of the New Testament meant back then; we need help in determining how each text applies to our lives today. It is one thing to see what Paul was saying to his readers in Rome or Philippi and quite another to see the significance of his words for us. So at key points in the commentary I will attempt to help the reader discover areas in our modern lives that the text is addressing.

I envision three main uses for this series:

1. **Devotional Scripture reading.** Many Christians read rapidly through the Bible for devotions in a one-year program. That is extremely helpful to gain a broad overview of the Bible's story. But I strongly encourage another kind of devotional reading—to study deeply a single segment of the biblical text and try to understand it. These commentaries are designed to enable that. The commentary is based on the NIV and explains the meaning of the verses, enabling the modern reader to read a few pages at a time and pray over the message.

2. **Church Bible studies.** I have written these commentaries also to serve as guides for group Bible studies. Many Bible studies today consist of people coming together and sharing what they think the text is saying. There are strengths in such an approach, but also weaknesses. The problem is that God inspired these scriptural passages so that the church would understand and obey *what he intends the text to say*. Without some guidance into the meaning of the text, we are prone to commit heresy. At the very least

the leaders of the Bible study need to have a commentary so they can guide the discussion in the direction God intends. In my own church Bible studies I have often had the class read a simple exposition of the text so all can discuss the God-given message, and that is what I hope to provide here.

3. *Sermon aids.* These commentaries are also intended to help pastors faithfully exposit the text in a sermon. Busy pastors often have too little time to study complex, thousand-page commentaries on biblical passages. As a result it is easy to spend too little time in Bible study and thereby to deliver a shallow sermon on Sunday. As I write this series I am drawing on my own experience as a pastor and interim pastor, asking myself what I would want to include in a sermon.

Overall, my goal in these commentaries is simple: I would like them to be interesting and exciting adventures into New Testament texts. My hope is that readers will discover the riches of God that underlie every passage in his divine word. I hope every reader will fall in love with God's word as I have and begin a similar lifelong fascination with these eternal truths!

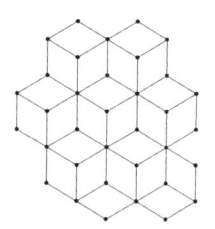

# INTRODUCTION TO EPHESIANS

Ephesians is one of the most difficult books in the New Testament. The material, dealing with the mystery of the gospel, the exalted nature of Christ, the **apocalyptic** events of the last days, and the spiritual warfare against the powers of darkness, boggles the mind. The sentences are complex, the background elusive to uncover, and the theological issues discussed as deep as any in Scripture. As we work our way through this treatise, we often have to stop and meditate for some time to make sense of the points Paul is making. In this commentary I hope to help the student of God's word perform that difficult task and to explain some of the complexities so we can assimilate the book's message.

## AUTHOR

This letter claims to have been written by the apostle Paul (1:1; 3:1), and this was accepted until modern times. Several church fathers (Ignatius, Polycarp, Clement of Rome) admitted that it is very different from Paul's other writings but said it demonstrates the very heart of Paul and therefore should be regarded as authentic. However, beginning in the nineteenth century critical scholars began to doubt Paul's authorship, and today the letter is widely considered non-Pauline—a pseudepigraphical (falsely ascribed to Paul) letter.

There are several reasons its authenticity is doubted. Its language and style are quite different from those of Paul's other letters, with 125 words not found in any of the others. There are also several unique phrases, like "in the heavenlies," "spiritual blessing," "the mystery of his will," "the father of glory," and "the desires of the flesh." The lengthy sentences and impersonal tone (there is little interaction with readers or presentation of the author's own situation) cause many to conclude that the author is not really acquainted with the Ephesian situation. Finally, the close connection with Colossians makes many think the author has copied parts of that letter.

In response to these concerns, there is no doubt that Colossians and Ephesians share language, themes, and even structural similarities. However, this does not necessarily mean that a later writer copied portions; it may be that the same author wrote the two letters at close to the same time. It is also not true that there is no personal material in the letter. The author reflects in 3:1–6 on the meaning of his ministry and his calling to proclaim the mystery and then presents himself in verses 7–13 as a "servant of the gospel." Moreover, he prays for the Ephesians in 1:15–19 and 3:14–21, showing his pastoral heart. I doubt that a later writer is making up all of this to make people think he is Paul.

Moreover, the theological themes of this letter (see below) are wholly consistent with Paul's in other letters, and there is no evidence the writer merely copied Colossians in order to look Pauline. In short, both Colossians and Ephesians stem from the hand of Paul himself. There is no reason an author writing two letters at virtually the same time would not include a great deal of material in common between them. Moreover, the two cities were in the same province and not far from each other, so the churches would have shared many of the same issues.

## DATE

It is generally accepted that Ephesians is one of the Prison Letters, along with Colossians, Philemon, and Philippians. Paul calls himself "I Paul, the prisoner" in 3:1 (also 4:1). But the question is which imprisonment? Paul was imprisoned at Philippi (Acts 16:19–34), Caesarea (23:23–26:32), and Rome (28:11–31), as well as in Ephesus (implied) at the end of his third missionary journey (Acts 19:35–41; 1 Cor 15:32). Two can be dismissed; the Philippian and Ephesian imprisonments were too brief to be likely.

The choice, then, is between Caesarea and Rome. At Caesarea Paul waited in limbo for two years while the governor, Felix, waited for a bribe and the Jerusalem leaders lobbied for Paul's execution. Since very little happened during this time, the kind of involvement in the ministry of the gospel in the region that we find in the Prison Letters clearly did not take place while Paul was in prison at Caesarea. The details of the situation fit Rome much better. Paul was in prison in Rome from AD 60–62, and Philippians was written at the end of that time, just before Paul learned his fate (Phil 1:20–23; 2:23–24). It is debated which of the two—Colossians or Ephesians—was written first, but it is more likely that Ephesians expanded the material in Colossians than that Colossians abbreviated Ephesians. So it is best to date Ephesians in AD 61–62, after Colossians, perhaps at the midpoint of the trial in Rome. Paul gave the letter, along with Colossians and Philemon, to Tychicus. So while the three letters (Colossians, Philemon, and Ephesians) were written over a period of three or four months, they were likely sent via Tychicus at the same time.

## RECIPIENTS

There are not many local issues addressed in this letter, which may mean that Paul intended it for a general audience. "In Ephesus" in 1:1 is missing in several important early manuscripts, and the consensus position is that Ephesians was a circular letter written to the churches in the Roman province of Asia (including the seven churches of Rev 2–3, Hierapolis, and Colossae). The letter was likely sent first to the mother church of Ephesus and then circulated to the other churches.

Asia occupied the western third of modern-day Turkey. It was a very pro-Roman province and quite wealthy as a result. Pergamum was the capital, but Ephesus was the leading city and center of Christian activity. It was one of the largest cities in the Roman Empire (behind Rome and Alexandria), with about a quarter million in the city and its environs. It was the major port city of the region and a trade center for the whole province and was home to one of the seven wonders of the Roman world, the temple of Artemis (her Greek name; her Roman name was Diana). Because of this temple it was the religious center of the province; it also boasted three temples to the emperors, making the imperial cult (the worship of the emperor as a deity) especially prominent. Magic was also prominent there, as attested by the interconnected stories of the sons of Sceva and the burning of the magic books in Acts 19:13-20. Because of this fascination with the occult, the war against the cosmic powers was especially relevant to Ephesus.[1]

There was also a strong Jewish presence in the city. While the Romans generally allowed the Jews to practice their religion freely, there is evidence of persecution and disfavor in Ephesus and the region. This is reflected in persecution against the church, which was initially assumed by the Romans to have been a Jewish sect. This situation of pressure and oppression continued into the 90s, as seen in the book of Revelation.

Paul spent more than two years in Ephesus at the end of his third missionary journey (Acts 19). By the time he wrote Ephesians it had been six years since he had left to go to Jerusalem for Passover. He had stayed in touch, though; we know this because of the number of letters he wrote and the fact that he met with the leaders of Ephesus every time it was possible, as, for instance, in Acts 20:7-37. A good portion of his

---

1. See below under "Theology of the Book."

ministry team in Rome was also from the province of Asia. He is addressing the situation in the province as he knows it.

## PURPOSE

Paul's knowledge of what was going on in the churches of Asia at this stage was secondhand. While in prison in Rome he learned of key problems there and felt he had to address them in writing. The readers knew of Paul and his trial and were waiting for news, which would come via Tychicus (6:21–22).

As Ephesians is a general letter that does not deal in detail with local problems, it is difficult to be specific about its purpose. In writing this letter Paul deals with issues linked to the universal church, with a few aspects, like Jew-Gentile tensions, that were concrete problems in these particular churches. I see four purposes at the core of the letter, dealing with the following broad subjects:

1. Soteriology (doctrine of salvation): Paul wanted to help those who came from pagan backgrounds to understand their reconciliation to God via the atoning sacrifice of Christ. Atonement stems from the image of the cover of the ark of the covenant in the holy of holies. God's throne was above that cover, and when sins were forgiven they were pictured as being placed under it, and so "covered" or "atoned for" by the sacrifice. So Jesus' death as a sacrifice covered or atoned for our sins, leading to our forgiveness by God.

2. Christology: The exalted Christ in his universal lordship fills believers with power to live victorious lives.

3. Ecclesiology (doctrine of the church): God in Christ has brought together Jew and Gentile in a new humanity (2:15) made possible by the new creation in Christ (v. 14), resulting in a united church.

4. Spiritual warfare: Christ has defeated the cosmic powers and given his mighty power to the church to be victorious over these evil forces.

## LITERARY FEATURES

Ephesians is one of Paul's letters (see above on authorship), but it has some features that set it apart from the others. Because of its high theological content and lack of concern with local problems, some have labeled it as more of a homily, treatise, or word of exhortation. It looks less like a pure letter than, say, 1 Corinthians or Philippians, but it is still a letter—it has the opening and closing of **Hellenistic** letters and in this resembles Paul's other writings.

One of the interesting features of Ephesians is its lengthy sentences. For instance, Ephesians 1:3-14 constitutes the longest sentence ever discovered in the Greek language, and several other portions are also extensive, complex sentences (1:15-23; 2:1-7; 3:1-13; 4:11-16; 6:14-20). But this is not unique to Ephesians, for Colossians also has a few of these (Col 1:3-8, 9-20, 24-29; 2:8-15; 3:5-11), as do other letters (Rom 11:33-39; 1 Cor 1:4-8; Phil 1:3-7; 2 Thess 1:3-10). Paul, in his exuberance over these incredible dogmatic truths, simply kept writing one subordinate clause after another in his desire to get his point across. He was so enthralled with his subject matter that, in staccato fashion, he moved from one point to another, ostensibly without even taking a breath. At times it is difficult to put it all together and make sense of the complex relationships, but Ephesians is altogether rich in its theological substance.

Paul also uses an at-times bewildering array of styles. The whole of 1:3-14 constitutes a benediction of praise, what Jewish writers called a *berakah* or "praise cry," in which God is thanked for the blessings he has poured out upon his people. There are two prayer passages (vv. 15-23; 3:14-19) in which Paul sums up the things he wants his readers to know and prays for God's blessing on the process of coming to understand. There is a wide array of catechetical and liturgical material throughout, including vice and virtue lists in the ethical section of 4:17-5:20, the **Haustafeln** (social code) passages of 5:21-6:9, and the creedal material of 4:4-6. The summary of the doctrine of sin and salvation in 2:1-10 is an extremely concise version of the same material covered in Romans 1–8. There is no question that Paul is flexing his theological muscles in new and ever-deeper ways in this letter.

Finally, it has been common in recent scholarship to look at Paul through the eyes of Hellenistic rhetorical conventions that originated in Aristotle's *The Art of Rhetoric* and were developed further by Cicero and others. These scholars assume that Paul was trained in rhetoric and exhibits this in his writings. Several have put Ephesians into the category of "epideictic rhetoric," centering on shame vs. praise/honor, and vices vs. virtues. This would fit the ethical emphases especially of 4:17–5:21, but I doubt Paul was doing anything like this. In 1 Corinthians 2:1–5, to a church enamored with such rhetoric, Paul says, "I did not come with eloquence or human wisdom"; his preaching was not "with wise and persuasive words." Then in 2 Corinthians 10:3–6 he states, "The weapons we fight with are not the weapons of the world" but have "divine power to demolish strongholds"—"to take captive every thought to make it obedient to Christ." Paul eschewed secular rhetoric and preferred Spirit power. This is not Hellenistic rhetoric but a Jewish homily and letter, since Paul as a Jewish Christian used Jewish methods of reasoning and Jewish style in his writing.

## OUTLINE

It is critical to understand how the arguments of a letter develop, how an author has structured his argument and organized his thoughts, before trying to read all the details. The structure below will enable every reader to see the map of the developing plot and catch the flow as she tries to follow the logic of the literary presentation.

I.  Introduction: the blessings of salvation (1:1–14)
    A.  The salutation (1:1–2)
    B.  Prologue: the blessings of salvation enumerated (1:3–14)
        1.  Spiritual blessings in the heavenlies (1:3)
        2.  Blessing 1: predestination (1:4–6)

1. Contrasting the old life with the new (4:17–24)
2. Vices and virtues that define life in the new community (4:25–5:2)
   a. Practical exhortations regarding the old and the new (4:25–30)
   b. A catalogue of sins and virtues (4:31–32)
   c. The supreme virtue: love (5:1–2)
3. The movement from darkness to light (5:3–14)
   a. Warning against the deeds of darkness (5:3–7)
   b. Encouragement to live as children of light (5:8–14)
4. Living in the Spirit (5:15–21)
   a. Not walking unwisely and with ignorance (5:15–17)
   b. Walking in the Spirit (5:18–21)

C. Submission in household relationships (5:21–6:9)
1. Husband-wife relationship (5:21–33)
   a. The key attitude: mutual submission (5:21)
   b. The submission of the wife (5:22–24)
   c. The sacrificial love of the husband as head (5:25–27)
   d. Culmination: the reasons for the husband's love (5:28–30)
   e. Conclusion: the nature of the husband-wife relationship (5:31–33)
2. Parent-child relationship (6:1–4)
3. Slave-master relationship (6:5–9)

D. Concluding summary: putting on the whole armor of God (6:10–20)
1. Opening admonition: be strong in the Lord (6:10)
2. The need for strength: the opposing powers (6:11–13)
3. The pieces of armor described (6:14–17)
4. Prayer, the binding force of the armor (6:18–20)

E. Conclusion of the letter (6:21–24)

## THE THEOLOGY OF THE LETTER

### THE WORK OF THE TRINITY IN THIS WORLD

Nowhere in the New Testament do we find a discussion of the meaning of the Trinity, but the Trinity often functions together in its pages, and the reality of the Three in One is assumed throughout. In Ephesians, God is clearly Creator and sovereign over all there is, and the Spirit is the empowering presence of the Godhead in this world. In the prologue (1:3-14), God is the one who pours out spiritual blessings to us, but he does so "in Christ" (v. 3). He has adopted us as his children, but has done so "through Christ" (v. 5). Moreover, all of this has been guaranteed to us via the Spirit as the seal of our salvation (vv. 3-14). All three members of the Trinity are featured in the two intercessory prayers of 1:15-19 and 3:14-19. It is the "God of our Lord Jesus Christ" who has sent us "the Spirit of wisdom and Revelation" (1:17); it is the Spirit who gives us access to the Father through Christ (2:18); and it is God who pours out his riches through his Spirit, leading to Christ indwelling us (3:16-17). Finally, in 4:4-6 the blessings we have are presented in three sets of triads, with each triad centered in turn on the Spirit, the Lord Jesus, and the Father. The work of the Triune Godhead is central to this book.

### THE EXALTED CHRIST

No other New Testament letter does more with the glory and exaltation of the risen Christ than do the sister letters of Ephesians and Colossians. "Lord" (*kyrios*) occurs twenty-five times in Ephesians, the vast majority of the appearances referring to Jesus; even those that seem to speak of the Father probably include Jesus as Lord with him. Christ is cosmic Lord, raised to the right hand of God (1:18-20) and exalted to lordship over the cosmic powers (vv. 21-22). His victory over the evil forces (4:8) is passed on to his followers via the armor of God (6:10-17), so that the fallen angels are already defeated in the lives of those who are truly dependent on the exalted Jesus.

He stands alongside the Father as sovereign over creation and "head over everything" (1:22). It is he who defeated sin through his blood sacrifice on the cross and he who made possible reconciliation with God (2:16) by removing the dividing wall and making a new creation and a united church of the formerly divided humanity (2:14-16). The key phrase along with "Lord" is "in Christ," for it is in him that every single aspect of salvation has come to God's people (e.g., in 1:3-14 or 2:14-18).

## THE GIFT OF SALVATION

There is a wonderful blend of the realized and the final aspects of our salvation in this letter. The great gift of redemption is quite evident in 1:3-14 in all of its wondrous, multi-hued glory. There Paul describes the "spiritual blessings" (1:3) or "the riches of God's grace" that he has lavished upon us in Christ (1:7-8)—the fact that he has chosen and predestined us (1:4-5, 11), redeemed us (1:7), given us the mystery of a united humanity (1:9-10), and sealed us with the Spirit (1:13-14). And not only have we been raised in Christ, but we are seated *right now* with him in the heavenly regions (2:6-7). In a later remarkable passage Paul relates how Christ has broken down all the barriers separating a fractured humanity and created a new humanity in which sinful people can be reconciled first to God and thereby to one another (2:14-18). This cosmic redemption has now produced an earthly counterpart: a new harmony that can solve racial and social disharmony and produce a true unity of people groups in Christ.

## THE CHURCH AS THE BODY OF CHRIST

In Ephesians there is a rich depth regarding the doctrine of the church that is unmatched elsewhere in Paul's writings. Paul's purpose is to help these believers realize the reality of the corporate blessings they have in Christ. They are a part of a brand new creation that has produced a new humanity comprising of diverse people groups united in Christ (2:14-15). The cross has removed the dysfunctional results of sin, and a new peace has come to humanity via the reconciling work of Christ. The old has passed away and the new has come (4:22–24), and every believer has the opportunity to grow and mature into that new unity in Christ (4:13). Christ has become the head and the church is his body (1:22–23), which is growing to maturity and becoming like its head. Believers are united to him and then to each other as they use the gifts given them as members of his body to build up one another (4:15–16).

## THE DEFEAT OF THE COSMIC POWERS

Ephesians and Colossians are at the center of Paul's doctrine of spiritual warfare. In Acts 19 it is clear that Ephesus, with its incredible temple of Artemis, was an epicenter of sorcery and the occult in the Roman world.[2] In this letter Paul wants his readers to be aware of the dangers that the principalities and powers pose to the people of God, and of the triumph over these powers made available to us in Christ. At the outset they need to understand that Christ has already conquered these evil forces, for he has been exalted "far above" them all (1:21–22). As in Colossians 2:15, at his death Christ disarmed these powers and led them shackled in his victory procession through the heavens. While these believers used to worship and follow "the ruler of the kingdom of the air" (2:2), as the children of God they actually make known his victory to the demonic realm (3:10). The war itself is depicted in 6:10–17, where we are told of the forces arrayed against us (6:10–12) and the armor that will enable us to defeat these powers of darkness (6:14–17). Christ has clearly defeated these forces of evil, and his victory is re-experienced by his followers when they put their trust in him.

---

2. See above under "Recipients."

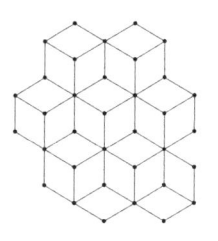

# THE BLESSINGS OF SALVATION
## (1:1-14)

Paul's letters follow conventional lines of **Hellenistic** letter writing, moving from writer to recipient to greeting and then to a thanksgiving and prayer-wish. In this letter Paul saves the latter two aspects for the end of his prologue (1:16–19) and in so doing frames the first half of his letter with prayer (1:16–19; 3:14–19). As in all his letters, he begins by extending to the Ephesians the covenant blessings of grace and peace.

### PAUL GREETS THE EPHESIAN CHRISTIANS (1:1-2)

As in Romans, Paul here names only himself as the sender of the letter (in most of his letters he names one or two associates as well). Elsewhere in the Prison Letters Timothy is named with Paul, perhaps as co-author (Phil 1:1; Col 1:1; Phlm 1). Here Timothy may have been busy with other ministry matters. As in Colossians 1:1 (and 1 Cor 1:1), Paul designates himself as "an apostle of Christ Jesus by the will of God." The title "apostle" can at times be used to designate a messenger sent by a church (like Epaphroditus in Phil 2:25 or Paul's coworkers in 2 Cor 8:23). Here it has a technical sense, referring to those designated by God to lead the church, called "apostles" by Christ (of the Twelve) in Mark 3:14 and including Paul, as well as Barnabas (Acts 14:14) and Apollos (1 Cor 4:9). The emphasis is on Paul's authority as one sent (inherent in the Greek term *apostolos*) as the special envoy of Christ to lead the church.

The true authority behind Paul is seen in the added "by the will of God," meaning that the Lord placed him in his office and stands behind him in his ministry. This especially looks back to the Damascus road experience of Acts 9, when Jesus called Paul to himself and gave him his commission to the Gentiles (see especially Acts 26:17-18). So Paul writes as Jesus' commissioned ambassador, speaking with the authority of Christ Jesus behind his words.

Paul is writing this letter to "God's holy people in Ephesus, the faithful in Christ Jesus." Paul often addresses his readers as "saints" or "holy people" (Greek *hagioi*; see Rom 1:1; 1 Cor 1:1; 2 Cor 1:1; Phil 1:1; Col 1:2), building on the frequent Old Testament designation of the Israelites as "God's holy people" (Exod 19:5-6; 22:31; Lev 11:44; 19:2; Ps 16:3). This meant that God had chosen them out of all the people of earth and set them apart to belong to himself. Paul's words indicate that the church is now the new covenant community that carries on the legacy of these people of the old covenant as the special possession of God, called out to exemplify his holiness and character to a lost world.

These believers are not only called to be holy but are also mandated to be "faithful" (Greek, *pistos*). This refers not so much to their lives of faithfulness as to their spiritual faith in Christ Jesus. In other words, they are set apart for God on the basis of their faith response to his Son. Because of their commitment to Christ they are also committed to his spiritual and ethical mandates; they are faithful in their lifestyle as a result of having faith in Christ.

Most likely the "in Ephesus" of 1:1 was not in the original letter but was added later on. It is missing from the third-century papyrus $\mathfrak{P}^{46}$ (one of the most reliable), the codices Sinaiticus and Vaticanus (also reliable, this time from the fourth century), and several other ancient manuscripts. It is commonly accepted, therefore, that this letter was a general or circular letter written to all the churches of the province of Asia.[1] It is still valid to keep "in Ephesus" in the text, however, as this was the mother church of the province (see the letters of Revelation 2–3), and the letter would likely have been circulated from there. I will use "Ephesus" or "Ephesians" throughout the commentary to refer to the recipients.

The greeting (1:2) follows Paul's regular practice in his letters, that of combining the Greek greeting (*charis*, "grace to you") and the Jewish greeting (*shalom*, "peace to you"), yet at the same time theologizing both into **eschatological** promises. Here he is saying in effect, "What you have been hoping for in your very greetings—divine grace and peace—is now being offered to you in Christ Jesus." For these believers these sacred promises from God have been realized. They already have God's grace and divine peace in their lives. This is called "inaugurated eschatology," the view of the early church that in Jesus the future has been brought into the present. Here future hope (for God's eternal grace and peace) has become a present reality in Jesus.

The reason such incredible blessings can take place is their source. They don't stem from Paul or just from the church but come "from God our Father and the Lord Jesus Christ." The fatherhood of God and the lordship of Christ undergird these heavenly gifts and guarantee their reality. The "Abba" (intimate Aramaic word for "father") theme stresses the love and care of God, and "Lord" stresses the sovereign power of the exalted Christ exercised on the believers' behalf.

## PAUL LISTS FIVE BLESSINGS OF SALVATION THAT STEM FROM GOD AND CHRIST (1:3–14)

This section is the prologue of the letter, introducing key themes that will guide Paul's discussion throughout and tracing all the blessings that God's salvation has provided for believers. It is

---

1. See "Recipients" in the introduction.

unique in Paul's letters, coming as it does before the thanksgiving and prayer that normally are part of the opening greeting. It is clear that he wants his readers at the outset to understand and rejoice in all that the Triune Godhead has done for his children. This comes in the form of a benediction, what the Jews called a *berakah* or "praise cry." The *eulogētos* ("blessed be"/"praise") of verse 3 governs the whole of 1:3-14. Each section could be translated with "praise": "praise God for predestining us" (1:4-6), "praise God for redeeming us" (1:7-8), and so on. This will guide the outline of this section. Such eulogies appear often in both the Old Testament (Gen 24:27; 1 Kgs 8:15; Ps 41:13) and the New Testament (2 Cor 1:3-4; 1 Pet 1:3-6). Here Paul is stressing the blessed results of the fatherly love of God and the sovereign work of Christ from verse 2.

### Introduction: Spiritual Blessings in the Heavenlies (1:3)

Praise language occurs three times in this section (1:3, 12, 14), the latter two instances providing a refrain ("to the praise of his glory") that frames the whole prologue in praise. "Praise be" asks God to receive the blessing or praise of his people for all he has done for them. In verse 2 God is "our Father"; here he is "the God and Father of our Lord Jesus Christ." The idea of Yahweh as the "God of Jesus" centers on his incarnate reality as the God-man; this will be explored further in verse 17. Jesus is the Son of God, we the children of God. This reenacts Romans 8:14-17, where we, the adopted children of God, are identified as "joint-heirs" with Christ. As in verse 2, Christ is "Lord" or exalted sovereign over this world and over the redemption that God has effected for us.

The basis for our blessing God is that he "has blessed us with every spiritual blessing." This is the theme verse, and the rest of the section enumerates these blessings one by one. The term "bless" occurs three times here in Greek: "Bless the God who blesses us with every blessing." There are two qualifications: it is *every* blessing, and each one is *spiritual*. God holds nothing back as he lavishes all his riches (1:7-8) upon us. Everything we need is poured out on us by divine generosity. When we shower God with our praise, it is our natural response to the God who has poured out his blessings on us.

These blessings are spiritual because they come to us on the spiritual plane and because they come through the Holy Spirit in the sense of Ezekiel 36:26–27 ("I will put a new spirit in you" and "put my Spirit in you"). The blessings of the **eschaton** (the end) that has been inaugurated are experienced spiritually by us right now. These spiritual gifts encompass the fruit of the Spirit in Galatians 5:22–23 and the spiritual gifts of 1 Corinthians 12:4–11, 27–31, but are not restricted to these. What are intended here are the salvific blessings of this section—indeed, everything God has for us as his people.

We experience these blessings "in the heavenly realms," referring not to heaven itself but to the spiritual realm that is now our true home (see also Eph 1:20; 2:6; 3:10; 6:12). In this world we are "foreigners and exiles" (1 Pet 1:1, 17; 2:11), and we are now citizens of heaven (Phil 3:20) rather than of any earthly nation. We are members of a new family and belong to a new country. In this new spiritual reality we experience all the blessings God has for us.

Moreover, we have all this "in Christ," a major Pauline theme that expresses both union with Christ and the resulting membership in his body, the church. Some form of "in him" occurs in nearly every verse in this section, and this is a dominant theme throughout this letter. Everything we are and have is ours only "in Christ."

## BLESSING 1: PREDESTINATION (1:4–6)

### Chosen to be holy and blameless (1:4)

The first blessing Paul enumerates is closely related to the idea of "God's holy people" in verse 2. God "chose us in him before the creation of the world" to be his special people and thus to be set apart for him. This is presented as the reason ("for/because") we praise God. Since he has blessed us by choosing us before this world was even created, we must bless him for it. Divine election involves an eternal choice, worked out originally in his choice of Abraham (Gen 12:1–3, whom God blessed to be a source of blessing to the nations) and of Israel (Deut 14:2, to be God's "treasured possession").

That choice was based not on Israel's worthiness or strength or place among the other nations but entirely on God's love for them. Throughout Ephesians the emphasis is on divine love and not human worth. God's electing mercy and grace are unmerited and undeserved (Rom 9:11–12; Eph 2:8–9—by grace, not works), the product entirely of love (Rom 8:35–39—nothing can separate us "from the love of Christ" or "the love of God"). Note that God chooses us "in him," centering on the "in Christ" motif discussed in the last verse. Every part of our salvation, including our election, is made possible by and takes place in Christ. Moreover, the choice was made in eternity past. God had plans for each of us from the beginning, and our special nature "in him" is especially precious.

Some have taken the choice here to be corporate—that is, God chooses the church as a corporate entity, and individuals enter it by faith decision. While this makes a certain sense, it is probably incorrect. In truth, God's elect will is both individual and corporate. This is in keeping with the "in him" that qualifies "chose us," for the "in Christ" motif has two dimensions—union with Christ (the individual dimension) and membership in his body (the corporate dimension). Each of us has been chosen from eternity past to be part of Christ's messianic community, the people of God's kingdom. The believer is chosen by the preexistent Christ to be God's child, part of his family, and a joint heir with Christ. We are first joined with Christ and then joined with each other as members of the messianic community.

The fact that this choice was made in eternity past, even before this world was created, is startling. God knew that Adam and Eve would fall into sin and that I would be born into a sinful world and live my life in sin (Rom 5:12), and he still decided to create this world and me! The depth of his love can never be truly understood. The key, of course, is that God had already decided to come, become incarnate, and die on the cross for my sins before he performed the act of creation. The possibility of my salvation was ensured before the decision to create had been made! My only response can be, "Wow! Praise God from whom all blessings flow!"

The purpose of our election is "to be holy and blameless in his sight." In the greeting the Ephesian Christians are called "God's holy people" (1:1), and now they are called to live up to that name. The Christian life contains both privilege (the gift of salvation) and responsibility (the demand to live life God's way). This reflects the **Holiness Code** of Leviticus 17–26, whose central theme is "be holy, because I am holy" (Lev 11:44; 19:2; 20:7, 26; see also 1 Pet 1:16). It is important to realize that believers are chosen not just for salvation but for sanctification as well. Those who belong to God are mandated to live lives of holiness. The "carnal" Christian is mentioned only once in Scripture (1 Cor 3:3); elsewhere this same adjective speaks of material or worldly things. Such a person is considered an aberration, a contradiction to all that is Christian. Yet in our time this has become almost accepted in our churches. It should not be so!

It is essential that God's true followers actually *follow*— that is, live lives that refuse the ways of the world. To be holy is to be blameless; this phrase is echoed in 5:27, where Christ presents the church to himself as "holy and blameless." Also, in the sister letter of Colossians 1:22, God presents his people as "holy ... without blemish"—the same Greek term as here— "and free from accusation." In the Old Testament the second term was used of the sacrificial animals that were "without blemish" (Exod 29:1; Lev 1:3). The term later came to be used of moral purity (Ps 15:2; Prov 10:9), and that is how it is used here. "Before him" or "in his sight" means that God is watching and will decide how blameless each person actually is. It is easy for Christians to be satisfied with appearing to live faithfully. We must remember that we will ultimately give account not to each other but to God (Heb 4:13).

## Chosen for sonship (1:5)

In verse 5 Paul reiterates this central truth and provides further detail. It is debated whether the phrase "in love" belongs with verse 4 ("holy and blameless before him in love," so KJV, NET, NLT, NRSV or verse 5 ("in love he predestined us," so NIV, ESV, NASB). If it is the former, we are to anchor our holy lives in love; if the latter, God's acts of creation and election stem from his great love. In my opinion the phrase fits better with verse 5 and God's elective action. In spite of knowing what creation would entail and the agony of heart that creating us would produce, his unfathomable love led him to choose to create us and make us his own.

The result of this great love is that he "predestined us for adoption." God's action in choosing us is now further defined as predestining, an unusual verb that occurs not at all in the **Septuagint** (the Greek Old Testament) and only six times in the New Testament. It means to "foreordain" or "predetermine," and it is done only by God in the New Testament (see Acts 4:28; Rom 8:29–30; 1 Cor 2:7). Clearly this means that before he created the world God determined whom he would adopt as his children.

The word for "adoption" (*hyiothesia*) means "sonship," and it refers to the process in the Roman world by which a child was brought into a new family, receiving all the rights of a natural child and taking the name of the new family. No doubt in Paul's mind also are the many passages in which the people of Israel are designated the sons of God (for example, Deut 14:1; Isa 30:9), as well as the Davidic covenant of 2 Samuel 7:14: "I will be his father, and he will be my son." The messianic community is a special adopted child of God.

The choice to adopt the believer takes place "in accordance with his pleasure and will," which further points to the depth of his love. It is not a cold, dispassionate choice but a joyous one. The term for "pleasure" (*eudokia*) connotes the delight and joy that attend an action and here pictures the intense satisfaction of God as he elects a former sinner to become his adopted child.

God's will is uppermost as he chooses the individual and calls them to be his own, and this brings him great pleasure.

The question of the exact meaning of this election of the believer has engaged theologians throughout the history of the church. The concept of predestination has to an extent defined the ministries of Augustine, John Calvin, Jacob Arminius, Jonathan Edwards, John Wesley, and others. It has proven incredibly divisive, but there has also been a great deal of fruitful dialogue, which I want to continue. The difficulty is in determining the balance between divine sovereignty and human free will. Do all Christians believe entirely because God has predestined them and brought them into his kingdom? Or does the Spirit convict all people and enable them to choose to accept or reject Christ on the basis of their faith decision? Can we find a biblical balance between the two sides?[2]

Let me provide a brief survey. The Calvinist opinion is named for Calvin, the great sixteenth-century French Reformer and theologian who developed what came to be known as the Reformed position. The Arminian opinion is named for Arminius, the late-sixteenth-century Dutch scholar who opposed some aspects of Reformed theology. Both positions believe that humanity is steeped in sin (called "total depravity") and that therefore the nonbeliever will always reject Christ when given a choice.

So how can anyone be converted to Christ? This is where the two sides diverge. The Reformed position is that, on the basis of his mysterious will, God "elects" or chooses certain individuals, reaches down, and with his irresistible grace brings them to Christ. His work of predestination is always efficacious. The Arminian position is that the Holy Spirit "convicts" every person, overcomes their depravity, and enables them

---

2. An excellent multiple-views book on this is Andrew David Naselli, ed., *Perspectives on the Extent of the Atonement: 3 Views* (Nashville: B&H Academic, 2015).

to exercise their will and make a decision. The issue is the exact meaning of "predestination" and the extent to which the human will is involved in the process.

Reformed theology teaches that:

1. Christ died exclusively for his people, the elect. Reformed Christians see this in Matthew 1:21 ("save *his people* from their sins"); John 10:11, 15 ("lays down his life for *the sheep*"); Romans 8:32, 39 (gave him up *for us all*").

2. Christ died to effect atonement, which is always efficacious. This is anchored in Romans 5:10 ("while we were God's enemies, *we were reconciled* to him through the death of his Son"); 8:29–30 ("those God foreknew he also predestined ... called ... justified ... glorified"); Ephesians 1:3–5 (the passage we are studying here); 1:7 ("in him we have redemption"); Philippians 1:29 ("It has been granted to you on behalf of Christ ... to believe in him"); 2 Timothy 1:9–10 ("He has saved us ... because of his own purpose and grace").

3. Jesus died only for the elect, and his intercessory work is limited to them. They find this in John 6:39–40, 44 ("this is the will of him who sent me, that I shall lose none of all those he has given me"); Romans 9:13, 22–23 ("prepared for destruction ... prepared in advance for glory"); 1 Thessalonians 1:4 and 2 Thessalonians 2:13–14 ("loved by God ... he has chosen you"); Hebrews 7:25 ("able to save completely ... always lives to intercede for them"); John 17:9 ("I am not praying for the world, but for those you have given me"). They conclude that, while "God loves the world," his special salvific love is reserved for the elect, and Christ died only for them.

Arminian theology teaches that:

1. The Spirit does convict the whole world. Arminian Christians see this in John 16:8–11 ("convict the world of sin, righteousness, and judgment"). Also, God wants all to be saved; they see this in John 1:4, 7, 9 ("gives light to

everyone"); 2 Peter 3:9 ("not wanting anyone to perish, but all to come to repentance").

2. Atonement has universal implications and cannot be limited to the elect. They see this in Ezekiel 33:11 ("no pleasure in the death of the wicked, but rather that they turn from their ways and live"); John 8:12 ("I am the light of the world"); Romans 5:18 ("justification and life for all people"); 1 Timothy 2:3–4 ("God our Savior ... wants all people to be saved") and 4:10 ("Savior of all people, and especially of all who believe"); Hebrews 2:9 ("tasted death for everyone").

3. Universal atonement stems from universal love. They find this in John 3:16 ("God so loved the world"); Romans 5:8 ("while we were still sinners, Christ died for us").

The conclusion is that the atoning sacrifice of Christ was sufficient and intended for all, but efficient only for those who respond with a decision of faith.

My own conclusion is that a moderate Arminian position best fits all the biblical data. Christ died for sinners as well as saints, and God sends his Spirit to shed God's light on all human beings and convict them of their sins. Still, since only believers are the elect, how do we find a balanced position? For me, the key is divine foreknowledge (1 Pet 1:2), which I do not believe is synonymous with predestination. As in Romans 8:29, it is "those whom God foreknew" that he "predestined." God knew who would respond with a faith decision to the Spirit's convicting work and chose them to be "conformed to the image of his Son." I believe God's elect will and human choice work together, with God uppermost in the process.

### Purpose: for the praise of his glory (1:6)

God's purpose in the process of election is "the praise of his glorious grace" (1:6). In essence, this says that in bestowing his salvation on undeserving sinners God is showcasing his glorious grace for all to see. "The praise of his glory" is possibly the central theme of this prologue, occurring also in verses 12 and 14.

Our only viable response to all the blessings God is bestowing on us is praise, and in all we do we seek to glorify him as he has glorified us.

Here it is his grace that is praised—that grace he exemplified in electing us to his family and adopting us as his children. The Greek says literally, "the grace with which he graced us." It is both a divine characteristic and a divine action, and it is "glorious"—that is, filled with his glory. It is a grace beyond our understanding, and we can only cry out our praise when we contemplate how wondrous it is. His grace flows through this letter, associated with our election (here), redemption and forgiveness (1:7), salvation (2:5, 8), the kindness expressed in Christ (2:7), the inclusion of the Gentiles (3:1-2), Paul's calling and ministry (3:7, 8), gifts given to the church (4:7), benefiting others (4:29), and the closing benediction (6:24). It is fair to say that the grace of God permeates virtually everything Paul has to say.

This grace flows to us and is experienced by us "in the One he loves," a title used of Israel in the Old Testament (Deut 32:15; Isa 44:2) and of Christ by God in his baptism (Mark 1:11 and parallels) and transfiguration (Mark 9:7 and parallels). God's grace is mediated to us via his beloved Son (Col 1:13, "the Son he loves"), referring to the extension of the love between Father and Son to the adopted children who are now added to his family. It is "in Christ" that all the spiritual blessings noted in verse 3 become realities for us.

### BLESSING 2: REDEMPTION (1:7)

Paul's thought moves from election to redemption, from God's past choice to the present act that brought us into his kingdom. Redemption is at the core of Paul's doctrine of salvation, as seen in Romans 3:21-26, where he moves from justification to redemption to atoning sacrifice in his presentation of the process of salvation.

The imagery of redemption is very strong. Let us begin with the terms of Romans 3:21-26 in reverse order. Christ gave him-

self on the cross as an "atoning sacrifice" for our sins. His blood
sacrifice became a ransom payment that purchased us from
the bondage of sin and from the curse of the law (Gal 3:13), producing our salvation and effecting the forgiveness of our sins.
This payment was made "through his blood," the ransom price
paid on the cross (see Heb 9:12; 1 Pet 1:18-19). Seeing Jesus' death
in this way began with Jesus' own use of "ransom" as a metaphor to describe his sacrificial service ("to give his life a ransom [*lytron*] for many," Mark 10:45). "Redemption" (*apolytrōsis*)
builds on this, picturing a ransom payment made to bring about
freedom from bondage, whether from slavery or for a prisoner
of war. It refers both to the payment made and to the deliverance from bondage it produced. Christ's blood sacrifice on the
cross became a ransom payment that purchased us from the
bondage of sin and from the curse of the law (Gal 3:13), producing our salvation and effecting the forgiveness of our sins.

As a result of this, God "justified" us; that is, from his *bēma* or
judgment seat he pronounced us innocent in his sight because
Christ gave himself as our substitute on the cross. In the Old
Testament the image of redemption was used of the exodus
that freed Israel from bondage to Egypt (Exod 6:6). Ours is a
far greater exodus—a "new exodus"—from the bondage of sin.
Our freedom has been purchased by the blood of Christ, our
substitute on the cross whose sacrifice brought about the forgiveness of our sins. Christ died in our place, bearing the payment for our sins himself. When God justifies us he applies the
blood of Christ to us, forgives our sins, and declares that we
are right or righteous in his sight. The Greek word for "sins"
is *paraptōma*, "trespasses," looking at sin as a transgression
of God's laws. We receive the divine pardon even though we
belong in prison.

### BLESSING 3: THE MYSTERY OF HIS WILL (1:8-10)

The following passage is one of the most beautiful statements
in the Bible about God's love, as it speaks of the "riches of God's
grace" being "lavished on us" (1:7-8). We can only marvel at

the depths of his mercy and love. God is not a penny-pincher who dribbles out his blessings to us a tiny bit at a time. All the riches of heaven are available to us, who are "kept by the power of God" (1 Pet 1:5). This pouring out encompasses not only the salvific riches that lead to forgiveness of sins but also the spiritual blessings of 1:3. God's wealth cannot be exhausted, and it is always available to his children (see also 1:18; 2:7; 3:8, 16; Col 1:27; 2:2). When we get to heaven we will be shocked by how little of the divine largesse we have actually used; we depend on ourselves far more than we should.

One of the primary blessings lavished on us is knowledge—God's "making known" (*gnōrisas*) the "mystery of his will" (1:9). Some have taken the "all wisdom and understanding" of verse 8 with what precedes, meaning that God has lavished his grace on us "with wisdom and insight." However, it is best to take it with what follows, further defining the process of "making known" the divine mysteries to us. Wisdom and revelation are closely intertwined throughout Scripture, and God's wisdom determined the "fullness of time" (Gal 4:4) when it was best to reveal the truths he had kept hidden throughout the old covenant period.

From eternity past God had decided how he would bring humanity back to himself through the death of his Son (see 1:5) and how he would bring history to an end, but he kept many of the details hidden until he determined the time was right. Paul's point was that the time of fulfillment had arrived (see Mark 1:15), and the mysteries have now been made known. "Mystery" is connected in meaning with "**apocalyptic**," referring to the process by which God reveals hidden truths (*apokalypsis* is the Greek title of the book of Revelation) and to the content of these truths.

All of this proceeds from God's will—that which he determined long ago to do in order to redeem sinful humanity, bring this evil world to an end, and replace it with the new heavens and new earth. It is incredibly comforting to know that God's sovereign will is ultimately behind the progress of history.

This is called "salvation history": God's control of human history to end evil and bring about final salvation. Here, the mystery is the unification of the cosmos in Christ at the eschaton (the end of history). In 3:3, 4, "mystery" refers to the coming of Christ, in 5:32 to Christ and the church, and in 6:19 to the gospel of Christ. In Colossians 1:26–27 it is the inclusion of the Gentiles, and in Revelation 10:7 it is the events of the eschaton. In general, then, the mystery is the progress of God's salvation from the coming of Christ to the end of this evil world and the arrival of the eternal reign of God.

This all takes place "in accordance with his good pleasure," which demonstrates further the love of God for his redeemed people. He is pleased and filled with delight to see his salvation worked out in human history (as in 1:5) and to reveal to his followers the plan he has formed for accomplishing this. Note that this plan has been "purposed in Christ," meaning that the Father and the preexistent Son devised this plan in union with each other. It was designed to be carried out by Christ in his coming to earth to become the atoning sacrifice on the cross (Phil 2:8).

In verse 10 we are told that this plan, devised by the Godhead "before the creation of the world" (1:4), was intended to "come into effect in the fullness of times," a phrase paralleled in Galatians 4:4, which speaks of the birth of Christ in "the fullness of time." This is similar to the summary of Jesus' teaching in Mark 1:15, "The time is fulfilled," meaning that God's plan has now completed the old covenant period and begun the new covenant with the arrival of the kingdom in Jesus. One could say here as well, "The time is up; God has arrived!" The term used for "plan" connotes the idea of administration, so one could translate this "come into effect when God administers and brings his plan of salvation to a close in history." These days have initiated the end times, as God's people will see (1) his purposes fully realized in history and (2) this world come to an end.

The final point of this section shows the true goal of his plan: "to bring unity to all things in heaven and on earth under

Christ." The Greek can be translated "to sum up all things in Christ," but there is a difference of opinion as to the exact meaning of the verb. It includes the verb *kephelaioō*; some link this with *kephalē* ("head") and translate "bring under one head, Christ." However, the verb here does not connote headship but denotes "summing up" an argument. So it is best to interpret this as God summing up or unifying all creation in Christ.

The primary theme, "in Christ," appears twice in the verse—"sum up all things in Christ, things in heaven and earth in him." Christ will bring together all aspects of God's diverse and disparate creation in himself. In 1 Corinthians 15:27-28 and Ephesians 1:22 God will place everything under Christ; in Colossians 1:20 God will reconcile all of creation to himself through Christ; and in Philippians 2:10 all things in heaven, on earth, and under the earth will bow at his feet. This passage in a sense brings together all of these. Every part of creation— including the cosmic powers (Eph 3:10; 6:10-16)—will submit and pay tribute to Christ.

## Blessing 4: His Divine Plan (1:11–12)

There is considerable debate as to the meaning of 1:11-14. Many believe that the "we" of verses 11-12 are Jewish believers and the "you" of verses 13-14 are Gentile believers, signifying the unity of the two groups in Christ and the church. Others feel it is stylistic, with the emphasis on all believers ("we") and then the specific readers of this letter ("you"). This is a difficult decision, and either is viable. However, while I spent most of my teaching career opting for the first view, since I do not see the Jew-Gentile issue addressed until 2:11 I now think the latter view is more likely. Paul is continuing his emphasis on God's salvific gifts and recapitulating the blessings to all Christians he mentioned earlier.

Paul returns to the themes of 1:4-6, centering on the glorious grace of God as he chose and predestined us to be part of his family. There is some question as to the connotation of "chose," since the Greek word Paul uses is not the normal term for choosing. It is *klēroō*, which contains the idea of "choosing by lot" and so is translated by many as "made heirs" or "obtained/ received an inheritance" (NRSV, KJV, NKJV, NASB, ESV, NLT). This is viable and would be similar to Colossians 1:12, where Paul calls for "joyful thanks" to God, "who has qualified you to share in the inheritance of his holy people in the kingdom of light." However, here the idea is not that we *receive* an inheritance but that we *become* God's inheritance, as in the NET Bible: "claimed as God's possession." The idea is similar to that of 1 Peter 2:9: "You are a chosen people ... God's special possession." So it may be best to translate "chosen to be God's special inheritance." The church is the new Israel, the chosen people of God and his special possession, echoing Exodus 19:5 and Deuteronomy 14:2 ("treasured possession").

We are "predestined according to the plan of him who works out everything in conformity with the purpose of his will." God's actions are not contingent on historical developments on earth. He is in absolute, sovereign control and has a plan of salvation that guides history in accordance with his will. The forces of evil are powerless against the divine plan and purposes, for he is in the process of working out everything according to this providential purpose; this applies especially to his predestined choice of every believer. We belong to God as his inheritance (Zech 2:12), and he will protect each one of us. In verse 5 Paul stated that the Christian has been predestined "in accordance with his pleasure and will," and this restates that truth. The emphasis here is on the pleasure God takes in seeing his will worked out in the lives of his children. Paul wants his readers to realize how incredibly blessed and privileged we are to have the God of all creation care so deeply and work so mightily for us!

The purpose (1:12) of God's sovereign action on our behalf is that we might exist "for the praise of his glory." This whole section centers on the praise God deserves for all the blessings he has poured into our lives, as seen in the opening statement of verse 3, "Praise be to the God ... who has blessed us ... with every spiritual blessing," and then again in verse 6, "to the praise of his glorious grace." Here it is the very meaning of our existence: We exist as his children and heirs, blessed with his lavish riches (1:7-8) and the recipients of his mighty work (1:11). This praise is due his *doxa*, "glory," stated here to sum up all his magnificent generosity and gifts on our behalf. The "glorious grace" of verse 6 stems from the God of glory, and all our blessings come from him. We can only stand in awe of his magnificent glory and be filled with wonder that we are allowed to share in it.

In this verse Paul brings out another aspect of those blessings and joy, describing the readers as those "who were the first to put our hope in Christ." This has produced a debate, for some interpret it as referring to Jewish believers who turned to Christ before the Gentiles. While this is possible, the instances of "we/us" in verses 3-10 have referred to all Christians. The verb *proēlpikotas* ("first to put hope") could well be emphatic—"put our hope completely"—rather than referring to time—"put our hope beforehand"; that would make better sense in this context. If so, Paul is celebrating the further blessing that in Christ we who are the chosen children of God are enabled to place our hope entirely in him.

### BLESSING 5: BEING SEALED WITH THE SPIRIT (1:13-14)

We come now to the fifth and final blessing of this opening section, all of which come to us "in him"—that is, as a result of our union with Christ. Here Paul addresses his readers directly, switching to the plural "you" to remind them of their direct participation in these blessings. All five have come to the believer at conversion, here "when you heard" and "believed." The source of this was the gospel, described as both "the message of truth" and "the gospel of your salvation."

Like today, the first century featured a bewildering kaleidoscope of competing religious claims, and it was critical to realize that the Christian claim alone is the true message. Now there are even more religious alternatives, and apologetics (defending the truth of Christianity) is more important than ever. We must remember that Christianity is an exclusive religion, and there is no hope for eternal life apart from Christ. This is clear in John 14:6 ("No one comes to the Father except through me") and Acts 4:12 ("Salvation is found in no one else, for there is no other name under heaven given to mankind by which we must be saved"). Those Christians who in the name of tolerance think pious people from any religion can be saved by following different paths are tragically wrong. There is only one gospel, only one truth claim that can be the source of salvation!

Those of Paul's readers who have heard this gospel and believed have received God's salvation, and the proof of this is that they "were marked in him with a seal, the promised Holy Spirit." In the ancient world a seal was often a glob of wax with the mark of an official signet ring to designate the authenticity of the document and the authority behind it (as in the seals of Revelation 5–6). With property it could be an inscribed stone or a precious jewel to indicate ownership, and slaves or followers of a patron deity often had a tattoo to indicate ownership and allegiance (as in the "mark" of the saints in Revelation 7:4 and of the beast in Revelation 13:16–17). So the Holy Spirit is our "mark," showing that we belong to God, who has marked or sealed us as his treasured possession (see the commentary on 1:4, 11) and both watches over and protects us.

The Spirit who seals the believer is "the promised Holy Spirit," meaning the Spirit promised in the Old Testament (Ezek 36:26–27; Joel 2:28–30). This Spirit was "poured out" by Christ both during his resurrection appearances (John 20:22) and at Pentecost (Acts 1:8; 2:1–11), as in Acts 2:33: "Exalted to the right hand of God, he has received from the Father the promised Holy Spirit and has poured out what you now see and hear." So the Spirit as our seal is an eschatological gift from God anchoring our present salvation; indicating that we belong to him; and guaranteeing our future, final redemption (Eph 4:30).

The Spirit is not only our seal but is also a "deposit guaranteeing our inheritance" (1:14). This is a commercial metaphor that functions here much as it does today, referring to a down payment that guarantees the future full payment of the amount promised. God has promised an inheritance to every believer, and the Spirit is a first installment or payment that anchors completely the full amount in the future.

But the inheritance is not entirely in the future. The Spirit is part of that inheritance, so God is initiating our end-time inheritance now. The full inheritance will be received in heaven at the eschaton, and the Spirit both initiates the process and guarantees full payment in the future. Paul sees the idea of an inheritance as the fulfillment of the promise given to Abraham (Gal 3:16–18) and the natural result of our adoption as God's children and Christ's joint-heirs (Rom 8:14–17). The promised inheritance is central in Hebrews (1:14; 6:12; 9:15) and in Revelation 21:7. God's people will inherit the final kingdom (Matt 25:34; Eph 5:5) and eternal life (Matt 19:29; Titus 3:7).

The time of final reward is described as the day of the "redemption of those who are God's possession." Virtually all the imagery of this section has centered on the metaphor of the saints as God's treasured possessions, and this culminates that emphasis. In verse 7 "redemption" spoke of Christ's ransom payment that led to the forgiveness of our sins and to our salvation. Here Paul is talking about our final redemption at the end of history, at the second coming. As in verses 3, 6, and 12, the purpose of God's redemptive work and now his gift of the Holy Spirit is "to the praise of his glory." The God who has blessed us "with every spiritual blessing" (1:3), including the Holy Spirit, deserves our praise. In fact, the connotation here may be that he receives praise from the entire cosmos, his whole creation, for his redemptive work. His glory has been shown, and all believers will share in it for all eternity—praise is the only proper response!

This section (1:3–14) has provided an incredible summary of all the spiritual blessings that a generous and loving God has heaped upon his children. Paul wants us to bask in delight as we contemplate the divine riches lavished on us by our gracious

Father. In the midst of all the pressures and difficulties life throws at us, we need to ponder our true heritage and realize all that is awaiting us from the God who has chosen us and redeemed us through the atoning sacrifice of his Son. We have all these blessings "in Christ," and we must live lives appropriate to our union with him.

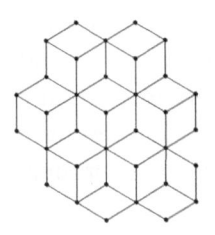

# A PRAYER FOR KNOWLEDGE
# AND POWER
## (1:15-23)

M ost of Paul's letters follow **Hellenistic** letter-writing practice in including a thanksgiving and a prayer. Although
this was usually perfunctory, for Paul it was detailed and generally introduced major themes in his letters. That is certainly true here, though in this case he will develop themes already introduced in the prologue (1:3-14). As in that section,
Paul writes a single lengthy sentence here. The prayer is closely tied with the introductory blessing of verses 3-14, as seen in
the opening "for this reason," showing that Paul is praying that
the blessings of the opening section might come to full fruition
in the lives of his readers. Several of the themes are continued,
especially that of the divine blessing of revelation and knowledge bestowed on us (v. 9 = vv. 17-18) but also the trinitarian basis of the gifts and the emphasis on wisdom (v. 8 = v. 17), fullness
(v. 10 = v. 23), and the powerful work of God (v. 11 = v. 19). This is a
prayer that the readers will grow in knowledge and experience
God's power in ever-new ways in their lives.

## PAUL GIVES THANKS FOR THE GOOD NEWS
## ABOUT THEIR SPIRITUAL STATE (1:15-16)

The reason for Paul's prayer is to rehearse all the blessings God
has "lavished" (v. 8) on the Ephesian saints. Moreover, Paul has

received a good report on the spiritual progress of their church and is rejoicing over them. He needs some encouragement in the midst of his own difficult situation in prison in Rome, and he has heard comforting news regarding their "faith in the Lord Jesus." Does this mention of faith refer back to their conversion, as noted in verses 13-14, or to the present vitality and growth of their faith and trust in Christ? The added "and love for all the saints" makes the latter more likely.

Paul is thrilled with their spiritual state, both in its vertical (faith in Jesus) and horizontal (love for the saints) aspects. They are growing spiritually in every area of their Christian walk, and this moves Paul to prayer. It had been five to six years since Paul had last seen the Ephesian Christians (a time period including his trip to Jerusalem, arrest, two-year stint in Caesarea, and at least a year so far on trial in Rome), so such good news would have been very heartening to Paul.

The language is much the same as that in Colossians 1:4, and these are sister letters. It is possible Paul had received the same report regarding all the churches in the province of Asia. These churches, including the seven addressed in Revelation 2-3 as well as several others, like those in Colossae and Hierapolis, were all evangelized while Paul was in Ephesus during his third missionary journey (see Acts 19:10), and they considered each other sister churches. Paul is stressing the lordship of Christ, and this relates to his emphasis on the power of God and the exaltation of Jesus in 1:18-20. The sovereign power of God and the lordship of Christ together constitute the basis of the Christian faith. Christian love for one another is the natural result of this newfound faith. We have entered a new family, the family of God, and what can be more natural than love for our brothers and sisters in him (see 1 Pet 1:22)?

So Paul has "not stopped giving thanks" (1:16) for the faithful at Ephesus whenever he remembers them in his prayers. This is undoubtedly a two-pronged thanksgiving, expressing gratefulness both for their spiritual growth and for the work of God in their lives. There are also two aspects of prayer theology here from which we can learn. First, prayer is meant to be unceasing—meaning not that it goes on day and night but that it is regular and frequent. As in Jesus' parable of the persistent widow (Luke 18:1–8), God responds to ongoing prayer. Second, prayer involves reflection and memory. We, like Paul, need to keep people and their needs in our thoughts. That is an essential component of true prayer. People who pray seldom for others show that they care little for them.

## PAUL PRAYS FOR WISDOM AND KNOWLEDGE FOR THE EPHESIANS (1:17–19A)

Here Paul turns from thanksgiving to intercession, reflecting on the gifts God has poured out on the saints according to the eulogy (praise section) of verses 3–14. He prays that God will give them the Spirit, who will fill them with wisdom to understand and grow in all that he has accomplished in their lives. There is a strong trinitarian emphasis, as the glorious Father of the Lord Jesus sends the Spirit to illumine their minds. There is also stress on the Christian triad of faith (v. 15), hope (v. 18), and love (v. 15), magnified by the incomparable power of God (vv. 19–21). There are two major parts to this prayer: requests for the Spirit of wisdom to illumine their hearts (vv. 17–18a) and for the knowledge the Spirit will give them, which comes in three parts—the realization of a deeper hope, more abundant riches, and greater power (vv. 18b–19).

### WISDOM FROM THE SPIRIT (1:17)

At the outset Paul's language prompts us to think deeply about the God to whom the request is given. He is "the glorious Father," drawing upon Old Testament depictions of him as "the God of glory" (Ps 29:2–3). This emphasizes not only his incomparable splendor but also his sovereign power and majesty. As stated in Ephesians 1:6, 12, 14, we have the joy of showering him with praise for his glory and grace. He is also not only our God but "the God of our Lord Jesus Christ," repeating the designation that began the eulogy in verse 3. The stress here is not only on the relationship between God and his incarnate Son (as the God-man, his Father is also his God) but also on the critical role Jesus plays as Messiah (translated into Greek as *christos*) and Lord of all. Jesus at one and the same time is subordinate to his Father and Lord over all!

After meditating on the kind of God and Father who heaps his blessings upon us, Paul specifically asks that God give his readers wisdom and understanding. There is a difference of opinion whether *pneuma* ("spirit") here refers to the human spirit or disposition (KJV, NKJV, NASB, ESV, NLT, NET) or to the Holy Spirit (NIV). While most versions take it as referring to the human spirit, most recent commentators take it as a prayer for the Holy Spirit; I heartily concur with the latter understanding. It is the Spirit who illumines the heart and gives new revelation. It is not the human spirit but the Holy Spirit who reveals truth.

There is a twofold thrust to Paul's request: The Spirit (1) has divine wisdom and reveals the mysteries (Eph 1:9; 3:5) and (2) channels these divine gifts to believers, as in John 14:26 ("teach you" and "remind you" of all things). This alludes to Isaiah 11:2—"The Spirit of the LORD will rest on him—the Spirit of wisdom and of understanding"—which depicts the Spirit resting on "the stump of Jesse," the messianic Branch who was to come. Here this Spirit rests on us, the messianic community.

The Spirit who seals us (Eph 1:13) is the same Spirit who reveals to us the mysteries of God. The meaning here is similar to that of 5:18, "be filled with the Spirit." Paul isn't suggesting that the Ephesian believers do not have the Spirit, for in Romans 8:14–17 and Ephesians 1:13–14 he refers clearly to the Spirit being given to the believer at conversion. Rather, he means that the Spirit, who is already within them, will fill every part of their being and enlighten them more fully in the truths of God.

The purpose of the Spirit's illumination is an increase "in the knowledge of him." The goal of all Spirit-given wisdom and enlightenment is to know God, as Paul writes in Philippians 3:10: "I want to know Christ." To know God is both to know about him and to come to know him experientially as Father and God. This includes obedience and worship, as well as mental awareness.

## God's Rich Gifts (1:18–19a)

The goal of the Spirit's work, Paul says, is "that the eyes of your heart may be enlightened" (v. 18), with the illuminating work of the Spirit internalized in the lives of the saints. There are two ways to understand this. The enlightening of the Ephesians' hearts could refer to their current spiritual state rather than being a prayer request ("the eyes of your heart being enlightened, I pray that you may know," so KJV, NRSV, ESV, NET), or it may be part of the request ("I pray that the eyes of your heart may be enlightened so that you may know," so NASB, NLT, NIV). Either reading is possible, but I believe it makes more sense to take this as part of the request. Paul prays that God will give them two things: the Spirit of wisdom, and through him an enlightened heart. Putting together verses 17b–18, Paul prays that when God pours out the Spirit of wisdom into the Ephesians' lives, their hearts will be illumined so that they will know the new hope and the riches of God made available to them.

What does it mean to have one's heart illumined? In the ancient world the heart did not refer to the emotions in distinction from the intellect—that is a more modern view. Rather, the heart referred to the whole person, but especially to the mind; the intellectual side was one with the spiritual. So "the eyes of your heart" are the thinking processes, and the "Spirit of revelation" will illumine believers' minds so they can understand all that God has for us. This is spiritual insight into the things of God.

Paul then mentions three specific areas of spiritual enlightenment that can apply to all believers:

1. "The hope to which he has called you." This refers to the final hope in our eternal inheritance but also to the hope expressed in our present salvation and the Christian life that ensues. This must be understood in terms of what is

called "inaugurated **eschatology**," the tension between the already and the not yet. The *already* refers to our present blessings in Christ and to the fact that our future on earth will entail our walk in Christ and the glory and joy of knowing we are being "kept by his power" (1 Pet 1:5). The *not yet* refers to the culmination of all God's promises in our final heavenly home. Moreover, it is a "living hope" (1 Pet 1:3), not a secular hope, which is an ephemeral and completely uncertain yearning for a future that is virtually unattainable. Ours is a Christian hope resulting from God having called us to be his own (see Eph 4:4)—the certainty of the "new heaven and new earth" (Rev 21:1) and of the crown of life that awaits us (Jas 1:12; see also 2 Tim 4:8; 1 Pet 5:4). Our near future is secure, and our eternal future is guaranteed.

2. "The riches of his glorious inheritance in his holy people." This needs to be understood in the same light as verse 14. This is not speaking of the inheritance that we will receive from God. Rather, it is speaking of us as God's inheritance, as his special possession. This was the message of several passages in the Old Testament that described Israel as God's inheritance and treasured possession (Deut 9:29; 1 Kgs 8:51–53; Isa 47:6), and Paul describes us as God's riches and glory. This is a wonderful turn of phrase: God shares his riches and glory with us (Eph 1:7–8), but to him we constitute his riches and glory! This demonstrates his great love and the extent to which he truly treasures us. God has placed us in his creation to display for the cosmos his glorious riches. That shows how much he loves us!

3. "His incomparably great power for us who believe." Believers must realize that in the midst of our powerlessness in this world God's incredible might is available and operating on our behalf. We may be marginalized and beaten down in the short run, but God guarantees our ultimate vindication and victory. Paul stresses the greatness of this power exerted on our behalf; it is "incomparable"

or "exceedingly great." He goes on in verses 19b–20 to demonstrate what he means by this "incomparably great power" by stating that this is the very divine power that raised Christ from the dead. This prepares us for 6:10–12, where believers are seen to be engaged in a terrible holy war against the cosmic powers and are told to "be strong in the Lord and his mighty power" (v. 10). Here we learn that this mighty power is already at work in and for us.

## GOD'S MIGHTY STRENGTH IS SEEN IN THE RESURRECTION AND EXALTATION OF CHRIST (1:19B–20)

Paul's desire to communicate God's wondrous power on our behalf is so strong that he suspends his prayer in order to retell the single most important event in human history: the resurrection and exaltation of Christ. Paul is clearly struggling for words to describe the stupendous nature of God's "mighty strength." He used the imagery of its "incomparable greatness" and "exceeding power" in verse 19a; now he turns to three terms, literally rendered in English "the working of the might of his strength." The term "working" (*energeia*) has given rise to the English word "energy." That is apt for the idea here, describing God's energetic work in the lives of his people. This stresses both the presence of power in God and the powerful energy he exerts as he works on our behalf.

The extent of this divine strength is beyond our ability to comprehend, so Paul piles up multiple terms to help us understand what God is doing for us. It is as though the greatest offensive line in the history of football is clearing the path for us as we run the race of life. Note that this power is exercised "for us who believe." Paul wants us to realize our part. God makes his power available and exerts it for us. We, however, must have the faith to put his power into operation in our lives—that is, to trust in him rather than in our own selves to live the Christian life.

The language of verses 19b–20 emphasizes the operative side of God's might. It can be literally translated "the working (*energeia*) of his might … which he worked (*energēsen*) in Christ when he raised him from the dead." The stress is on God's power, actualized first in Christ's resurrection and then in our lives. To Paul everything in Christianity is derived from the implications of the resurrection. If there is no resurrection, "our preaching is useless and so is your faith … your faith is futile; you are still in your sins … [and] we are of all people most to be pitied" (1 Cor 15:14, 17, 19). But Paul knows that Christ was indeed raised, so the Christian claims are the central truths that bring meaning to life in this world. The incomparable divine power was unleashed at Jesus' resurrection and continues today for all the saints.

The resurrection power also continues to operate in the life of the exalted Jesus, and the rest of 1:20–23 flows out of this idea. Paul illustrates this by elucidating the areas in which the divine power is operating. God's "mighty strength" seated Jesus at the right hand of God (v. 20b); exalted him above all other created beings, especially over the cosmic powers (v. 21); placed all of creation under his feet (v. 22a); made him head over all things (v. 22b); and made him the source of life, filling all creation (v. 23). The resurrection of Christ is the basis for our resurrection hope and guarantees our future (1 Cor 15:20–21; Phil 3:20–21). This event turns a mere wish that the future might turn out well into a "living hope" (1 Pet 1:3). Our future is now certain and our final victory guaranteed.

God exercised his power not only when he raised his Son from the dead but also when he "seated him at his right hand in the heavenly realms." This statement is derived from Psalm 110:1: "Sit at my right hand until I make your enemies a footstool for your feet." It is the most often quoted Old Testament passage in the New Testament (over thirty times) because it provides the Old Testament basis for the exaltation of Christ (Mark 12:36; Acts 2:34–35; Rom 8:34; Col 3:1; Heb 1:3; 8:1; 1 Pet 3:22). This was a Davidic coronation psalm, and at times Jews understood it as referring to the messiah. The early church understood the psalm to have been fulfilled in Jesus, anchoring his authority, power, and glory. For us this means that Christ is now in the place of power, and the entire Godhead is at work in this world on behalf of God's people. The heavenly realms, as we saw in 1:3, refer to the arena in which believers now dwell spiritually. Here this includes heaven itself, as Christ dwells alongside his Father in glory.

## GOD'S MIGHTY STRENGTH IS SEEN IN JESUS' AUTHORITY AND DOMINION OVER ALL (1:21–22A)

In his exalted state Jesus is "far above all rule and authority, power and dominion, and every name that is invoked." Paul uses a rare double preposition (*hyperanō*, "up above" or "high above"), possibly drawing upon the idea from Psalm 8:1, as translated into Greek in the **Septuagint**, "You have set your glory in [*hyperanō*] the heavens." While the terms "rule and authority, power and dominion" seem to refer to all created beings and were often used in Jewish circles for the angelic realm, both good and evil angels, there is general agreement that here Paul has in mind the "principalities and powers," the cosmic forces that are the enemies of Christ and the church. Paul is not using these terms technically, as though there were four classes of demonic powers. Rather, he is multiplying terms to designate the cosmic forces as a whole. Some think this includes malevolent earthly powers as well, such as wicked emperors, governors, and generals. That is possible, but it is more likely that Paul uses these terms in Ephesians and Colossians for the cosmic forces of evil.

These fallen angels (Rev 12:7–9) operate "far above" in the heavenly realms (Eph 3:10; 6:12), follow "the god of this world" (2 Cor 4:4), and so are rulers and authorities in this earthly realm. However, their "power and dominion" are restricted to this world and their followers. They have no power over Christ, for he has entered their stronghold, bound them (Mark 3:27), and given authority over them to his followers (Mark 3:15; 6:7). Yet while Christ has defeated them, their final subjugation is future, at the end of history. Satan is still a "roaring lion" wanting to devour every one of God's created beings (1 Pet 5:8), and he is still filled with frustrated rage (Rev 12:12) and can create all kinds of havoc. Paul spends a great deal of time in Ephesians and Colossians on the cosmic war with the demonic powers. The war is serious and very real, but the final victory is certain.

Paul stresses the universality of Christ's exalted authority in the added "every name that is invoked, not only in the present age but also in the one to come." Some think that "every name" means every type of cosmic power, but it is more likely that this is intended to echo the idea behind Philippians 2:10: "at the name of Jesus every knee should bow, in heaven and on earth and under the earth." Paul is describing every created being, good and evil angels as well as all humanity.

Christ has "the name above every name" (Phil 2:9), so the whole created order must bow before him—not only in Paul's day but for the rest of human history and beyond. The "age to come" is an idiom that describes both future history under God's control and the final consummation and onset of the eternal order. Every being that has ever lived or will live is subservient to Christ.

This section concludes with "God placed all things under his feet" (v. 22). The focus in verse 21 was on created beings, and "all things" here means that creation itself is subject to Christ. This is taken from Psalm 8:4–6, the passage regarding humanity quoted in Hebrews 2:6–8: "What is mankind that you are mindful of them ... you put everything under their feet" (see also 1 Cor 15:27). The psalm uses "son of man" for humanity, but the fall marred the image of God in human beings. It is the true Son of Man, Jesus, who has returned dominion to humanity (as stated in Heb 2:9). Ephesians 1:21–22 moves from Christ's lordship over the demonic realm to his lordship over all created beings and finally to his lordship over all of creation itself. He is indeed Lord of all!

## GOD'S MIGHTY STRENGTH IS SEEN IN JESUS' HEADSHIP OVER ALL FOR THE CHURCH (1:22B-23)

In verse 22a we learned that God has subjected all of creation under Jesus, and here we see that God has done so for the benefit of the church. In fact, God's people are in mind throughout verses 20–23. Jesus was raised from the dead as the firstfruits that guarantees the future resurrection of every believer (1 Cor 15:20), and he is exalted to the right hand of God as intercessor for the saints (Heb 7:25).

There is double meaning in the verb *edōken* ("gave, appointed") in verse 22b. The thrust is that God gave Jesus to the church as his gift. At the same time the word contains the idea of God "appointing" Jesus, installing him as head or sovereign over everything, especially over the demonic powers he has rendered powerless (see v. 21). It is from this place of authority that Christ guides and empowers the church.

The use of "head" as a metaphor stems from Hellenistic medical theory, in which the head was seen as the source of the body's life, as well as its ruler. As the head was the life force supplying the body and controlling it, so Jesus is the source of life and sovereign over all of his creation. This verse emphasizes that everything is subject to Jesus (v. 22a), with the flip side that Jesus thereby becomes the head over everything (v. 22b). Moreover, the primary recipient of this life and power is the church, the body of Christ. The head of the church is the head over all creation, and his life and power fill the church with divine life and power. This is of profound significance for us. We so often feel powerless in this world as the forces arrayed against us seem to overwhelm us. Paul is saying that in the ultimate sense this is not true. There is a power at work in us and for us that will take us through all our afflictions and tragic circumstances.

Verse 23 further defines the church as the beneficiary of Christ's headship over creation. The church is "his body," gaining from the life-giving power of the head (so also Col 1:18). Paul's body-life theology is fully expressed in Romans 12:4–8 and 1 Corinthians 12:12–27, centering on the idea that the head supplies energy and power to the body. As the members of the body use the gifts supplied by the head (Christ and the Holy Spirit in 1 Cor 12), this produces growth and spiritual strength. Moreover, all these passages emphasize the unity of the church. It is only when all the members of the body function together in unity that the body can flourish and succeed. Paul uses the Hebrew motif of corporate solidarity, that "we, though many, form one body, and each member belongs to all the others" (Rom 12:5). The many become one in Christ. This will be developed further in Ephesians 4:15–16.

Paul closes this section by saying that the church as the body of Christ becomes "the fullness of him who fills everything in every way." This is a very complex statement, and scholars have wrestled over it for centuries. There are three views, and I will take them in increasing order of likelihood.

(1) It is possible, but not likely, that this means the church fills or completes Christ, and together they fulfill God's purposes. However, it is difficult to see in what way Christ is incomplete without the church.

(2) More viable is the interpretation that there is a two-step process: the church is filled up or made complete by Christ, who then is filled up or completed by God. Both make a great deal of sense, but again it is hard to see how "fills everything in every way" can mean that God is completing Christ.

(3) The best view in light of the context of verses 20–23 is to say that the church is filled by Christ, who then also fills or completes all of creation. Both aspects culminate themes already developed in this section. As the head of the body, Christ both fills and fulfills his followers. Yet he is the head over the cosmos as well as the church; he completes every part of creation, which is subject and subservient to him. But while Christ fills his created cosmos, only the church is his body. Most likely Christ (and God) fills his body both with the gift of the Holy Spirit and with "every spiritual blessing" from verse 3. He fully lavishes his gracious riches on his people (vv. 7–8), and the created universe in this sense exists to fulfill his followers.

Paul's prayer in 1:15–23 combines with that of 3:14–21 to frame the doctrinal section of Ephesians with prayer. Paul's rehearsal in 1:3–14 of all the spiritual blessings Christ has lavished on believers provides the content for the prayer. He is so thankful for their spiritual progress and prays that the Spirit might anchor in their lives an even greater realization of the riches and power God has made available to his people. They need not allow their present difficulties to mar the great hope of their certain future, for they are God's treasured possession, and God is pouring out his mighty power into their lives (vv. 17–19). To enable them to understand more deeply this mighty strength made available to them, Paul reminds them that this power has already entered this world in Christ's resurrection and exaltation to the right hand of God. He is absolutely supreme over the demonic forces, and indeed over every part of his created order. He is the head or ruler over creation and exercises his sovereignty for the sake of his body, the church (vv. 20–23). The church already has the victory because it is united with *Christus Victor*, the victorious Christ.

This is just as important to us as it was for the Ephesians. In the midst of all our struggles and all the difficulties that face us, it is incredibly comforting to know that Christ has already won the victory for us, and we like him will in the end stand in glory and see this world of evil end forever. We cannot lose, but we must wait for God's chosen time and have patience in our present trials.

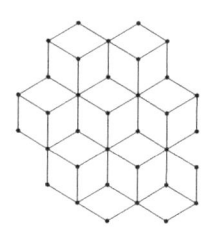

# SUMMARY OF THE BLESSINGS OF SALVATION

## (2:1-10)

Ephesians 1 concludes with a description of the mighty power of God exerted in the resurrection and exaltation of Christ and made available to the church. In Ephesians 2:1-10 this power is illustrated by the greatest gift given to God's people: their salvation and resurrection from spiritual death. Paul wrote his great theological portrait of sin and salvation in the incredible chapters of Romans 1:18-8:39, penned in AD 57 during a three-month stay in southern Greece (Achaia) on his way to Jerusalem (Acts 20:1-3). Now, about five years later, he summarizes that material in ten short verses. In them he succinctly explains our rescue from our former enslavement to sin by the death of Christ and the new life we have in him. The truths of this passage provide the basis for the spiritual blessings of Paul's first chapter and establish the means by which the problematic issues discussed in the rest of the letter may be solved.

## SIN LEADS TO BONDAGE AND DEATH (2:1-3)

### THEIR TERRIBLE PREDICAMENT: DEAD IN SIN (2:1)

After discussing the present power of God at work in the believer's life, Paul turns in this section to the problem of the believer's past: the effects of sin on the unregenerate. His purpose is to demonstrate the effects of God's power by showing how it has overcome the bondage of sin. It has overcome death and raised those who have turned to Christ to newness of life. Unbelievers are under the control of their "transgressions and sins." As mentioned at 1:7, "transgression" or "trespasses" looks at the legal side of sin—that it contravenes God's laws and brings condemnation on the sinner. The result of this spiritual death, which entered the world through the sin of Adam (Rom 5:12, 17), is death to all humanity (Rom 6:23). Spiritual death is a total separation or alienation from God, and the spiritually dead are the enemies of God.

### Their Terrible Predicament: Bondage to Sin and the Flesh (2:2–3)

This death or alienation characterized the Ephesian believers' previous state or way of life (v. 2) and constituted a bondage to evil. Paul describes this state in three ways:

(1) They "followed the ways of this world" (literally, "walked according to the age of this world"). This means that they conducted their lives under the control of the evil ways of this world. In the Roman world Aion was a deity, but Paul uses the Greek word (*aiōn*) here in its Jewish sense to mean an era or age. This refers to the present age of sin, in contrast to the new era of Christ and salvation. In Romans 1:18–32 Paul expands on the depravity of humanity, showing that in their capitulation to sin fallen human beings have "suppressed the truth," with the result that their "foolish hearts were darkened" (Rom 1:18, 21). The believers were controlled by the mindset and self-centered decisions of this age rather than by God.

(2) They were under the power of "the ruler of the kingdom of the air," referring to the control not only of this age but also of the cosmic powers. This ruler, of course, is Satan, the great red dragon of Revelation 12:3–4 who seduced a third of the heavenly host into rebellion and was cast out of heaven to earth with them (Rev 12:7–9). This world is their prison (2 Pet 2:4; Jude 6), but in it God has allowed the evil powers some authority. Thus

Satan is "god of this world" (2 Cor 4:4) and "prince of this world" (John 12:31; 14:30; 16:11), and in Matthew 9:34 and Mark 3:22 he is called "the prince of demons." This is the same term used here; Satan is "ruler" or "prince" of his domain. His sphere is "the kingdom of the air," reflecting a common Jewish idea that the cosmic powers operate in the heavens. In Ephesians 3:10, 6:12 they function "in the heavenly realms." They, like their counterparts the good angels, are spirit beings at work in the spiritual realm.

(3) Satan's control of the spiritually dead is further explained by describing him as "the spirit who is now at work in those who are disobedient." The term for "is at work" is *energeō*, the same verb that in 1:20 spoke of God's mighty work in raising Christ from the dead. One could say this means that Satan has a controlling interest in the lives of unbelievers. His supernatural work in their lives gives him power over them and results in their disobedience to the things of God. The phrase is "sons of disobedience," a Jewish idiom that means their lives are characterized by disobeying God. Rather than living life God's way, they prefer to reject God's will and live a life of sin.

In verse 3 Paul includes himself and his coworkers by saying "all of us."[1] In the first two verses the emphasis is on the external factors of the age and the demonic forces, as these two enticed unbelievers into sin. Now Paul switches to the internal power of the flesh. The lifestyle they all embraced when they lived among the non-Christians he now describes in three ways:

(1) They were "gratifying the cravings of the flesh." This identifies the internal force that had enslaved them in sin. Externally they were tempted by the satanic powers, and internally by the human proclivity to sin. "The cravings of the flesh" are those self-centered impulses that define the pleasure principle—seeking out pleasure and avoiding pain at all costs. The "flesh," according to Paul, is that part of the "old

---

1. For the "you-we" distinction, see the discussion at 1:11.

self" (see 4:22) that constitutes the human tendency to sin. For Christians, while the old self is nullified at conversion, the sinful impulses remain. Sin is no longer an internal force controlling us but an external force trying to invade us and appealing to our fleshly tendencies. Unbelievers are internally controlled by these cravings, and Christians are externally tempted by them.

(2) The unbelievers are also "following its desires and thoughts." Not only are they living in sin, but they are allowing it to dominate their minds. No wonder it controls their actions! When it controls their thought life it will naturally guide their deeds as well. The whole person—the mind and the conduct—is enslaved to these narcissistic impulses. The Jewish people spoke of battle between the two impulses: the *yetzer hatob*, the "impulse to good," and the *yetzer hara'*, the "impulse to evil." For the unbeliever the latter usually wins. But, it may be asked, what about the unbeliever who is basically a moral person and is "good" by most people's standards? Do they fit this category? Yes, because the so-called "smaller" sins—like greed, lust, rampant consumerism, giving in to anger, and so on—are still "following the desires" of the world. They are still worldly.

(3) As a result, like all the unsaved they are "by nature deserving of wrath." When Paul says "by nature," he is speaking of the doctrine of the imputation of sin. He describes this doctrine more fully in Romans 5:12, where he says that in Adam "sin entered the world," and then he adds, "because all sinned." This refers to the fact that all human beings were in Adam and therefore inherit from him the proclivity to sin, participating in that sin by their own willful choices. Human nature is controlled by depravity. Since every person is dominated by sin, all are "deserving of wrath." Our sin separates us from God and makes us his enemies. Therefore, all sinful human beings will of necessity face the wrath of God. We must realize that God is above all a holy God, and that the two interdependent aspects of his holiness are his justice and his love. His justice demands that he destroy sin, but his love led him to give his Son as the

atoning sacrifice for those sins. Those who reject the loving gift of his Son are destined to face his wrath, which is his just condemnation of all that is not holy.

## MERCY LEADS TO BEING MADE
## ALIVE WITH CHRIST (2:4–7)

In verse 3 Paul highlighted the justice of God, but here he turns to God's mercy and love. There is no hope for fallen humanity, for there is no way any of us can remove our depravity or pay for our sins. Since our very nature is depraved, there is no payment we can make that would be sufficient to atone for our fleshly desires, as verses 1–3 have made clear.

### God's Love Leads Him to Give Us Life (2:4–5)

This is where the merciful God intervenes and pays that price for us. In the Old Testament Yahweh is "a compassionate and gracious God," who "abounds in love and faithfulness" (Exod 34:6; Pss 86:15; 103:8). His mercy is undeserved, the result of his ḥesed, his steadfast love. This mercy is based upon "his great love for us." Every detail of this letter is the outgrowth of God's incredible love. Even creation stems from this. When God decided to create this world, he did so because his love sought an object upon whom he could pour out his affection. In this very decision God was aware that human sin would mar his loving act and make it necessary for him to send his Son to become the atoning sacrifice that would redeem us and make us objects fit for his love. The love of God in Christ is a central theme in this letter (1:6; 3:17–19; 5:1–2, 25), and our love for one another is based on our experience of the love of the Godhead for us.

The result of God's mercy and love is that he has "made us alive with Christ" (2:5). This is the first of three verbs in verses 5–6 beginning with the Greek prefix *syn*- ("together with")— made alive *with* him, raised *with* him, seated *with* him. These wondrous results could never take place apart from our union with Christ. We who were dead in our sins (vv. 1–3) have found

life in Christ. Christ died to redeem us and forgive our sins
(v. 7) so that we could have new life in him. When we believed
and turned to him, his power saved us and raised us from the
dead (vv. 13, 15, 19). In Ephesians 1:18-21 Paul wrote that the
power of God raised Christ from the dead and seated him at his
right hand. Now that same incredible power has allowed us to
become one with him and thereby to participate in Christ's resurrection and exaltation. United with Christ, we too have died
to sin and been raised to eternal life. This begins at our conversion, not just at Christ's return.

To make certain the Ephesian Christians truly understand
the significance of their new life in Christ, Paul makes the
basis of all this explicit by adding, "it is by grace you have been
saved." The means of this redemptive event is the grace of God.
Salvation cannot be achieved by human effort; there is no way
sinful human beings can ever earn or produce salvation. God's
mercy and his grace are very close in meaning. Mercy is that
divine attribute that leads to grace, that undeserved favor that
leads God to save us. Paul's presentation of salvation could be
labeled a "gospel of grace." It is centered on the free gift of salvation that is not based on any human merit or worth but is
entirely the result of God's love and mercy.

The verb is in the perfect tense—"have been saved"—
emphasizing that our salvation is based upon the past act of the
death of Christ. The present result of that act is the salvation of
our souls. Salvation means that we have been delivered from
the wrath of God and brought into his family as his adopted
children (Rom 8:14-17). The verb "saved" sums up the other
three verbs—"made alive," "raised," and "seated" with him.
Christ has taken upon himself our sin and guilt and died in
our place so that God could declare us innocent and right with
him (Rom 3:21-26). We have been spared the wrath of God that
will destroy sin and sinners and have been given power over
those evil forces that seek to defeat and destroy us (Mark 3:15;
Eph 6:10-12).

## God's Love Leads Him to Seat Us with Christ in the Heavenlies (2:6–7)

In Romans 6:4 Paul uses baptism as a salvific metaphor, saying that we have been "buried with him ... into death in order that, just as Christ was raised from the dead ... we too may live a new life." This new life is the result of our union with Christ. As we share in his death and die to sin, we share in his resurrection and are raised to life. Yet that is not all, for we also share in his exaltation and are "seated with him [God] in the heavenlies in Christ Jesus." This was stated in 1:20, where we learned that Christ was "seated at his right hand in the heavenlies." It is taken from Psalm 110:1, the most often quoted Old Testament passage in the New Testament.[2]

Astonishingly, this is the only verse in the New Testament where that concept is applied to the saints. It means that we participate in Christ's enthronement at the right hand of God the Father; we are seated with him and share his victory. Yet we must qualify this carefully. This is not the future physical resurrection at the second coming but a present foretaste on the spiritual plane. We are exalted with Christ spiritually, and while eternal life is a present possession we will not enter eternity until we die. Paul has said that we are citizens of heaven right now, in expectation of the full realization of that status later on (Phil 3:20–21), and the sister passage in Colossians 3:1–2 shows that though we live on earth we can seek and think "the things above" right now. Our final glory has already begun, but is not yet fully realized. The demonic powers no longer reign, and their ruler has been deposed in the lives of these victorious saints who are already seated in the place of power with God in Christ.

The purpose of this (2:7) is "in order that in the coming ages he might show the incomparable riches of his grace." God has

---

2. See comments on 1:20.

exercised his love and mercy to make a public demonstration of his wondrous grace. All creation is meant to stand in awe of his grace, but especially those of us who are its recipients. This has been an emphasis throughout the letter so far; the blessings of 1:3-14 are intended for "the praise of his glorious grace" (1:6, 12, 14). Thus all of us who have been raised out of death to life in Christ are a show-and-tell to all around of God's gracious mercy.

Paul's description of this as "incomparable riches" recalls 1:19, where the same adjective was used in adverb form for the "incomparably great power" of God exercised on behalf of believers. It is emphatic, referring to the "extraordinary" or "surpassing" riches of God's grace, which as in 1:7-8 have been "poured out" on his people. In his loving grace God has poured out on us not only salvation but eternal life. He has not only raised us but exalted us in Christ and turned our afflictions and suffering into glory.

Moreover, this has all been "expressed in his kindness to us in Christ Jesus." This is another aspect of his *ḥesed* or "lovingkindness" (see 1:4). To understand the depth of God's tender love and mercy we must remember that "while we were still sinners, Christ died for us" (Rom 5:8). This lovingkindness was shown not to those who deserved favor but to those who deserved destruction. Titus 3:4-5 tells us that God's kindness and love led him to save us, "not because of righteous things we had done, but because of his mercy." God's grace is not only extraordinary but also unfathomable.

This outpouring of grace is not a temporary phenomenon but will take place "in the coming ages," referring not just to the near future but to the eternal future. Jewish thought divided time into "this age" and "the age to come," but Paul here goes beyond that to describe all the ages, both in this world and the next, piling up one upon another. God's grace is unceasing. It will last not just through this age but through all the ages of time and eternity.

## PAUL PRESENTS A SUMMARY: THE
## FREE GIFT OF GRACE (2:8–10)

### The Gospel Message is "Saved by Grace through Faith" (2:8–9)

There are few passages better known than this one. God's grace has been the spearhead of Paul's narrative thus far (1:2, 6, 7; 2:5, 7); now these two verses act as a summary, telling us grace is the means of our salvation. In a sense God's grace encompasses his mercy and love. The very act of creation stemmed from his grace, for he knew that his creation would turn against him and embrace self-centeredness and sin. Yet he created us, knowing that he would have to give his Son to die for our sins so that we might be able to return to him. Salvation is a free gift from God, and the basis for that gift is his grace. The "have been saved" is the same form of the verb as in verse 5, and the perfect tense once again stresses salvation as the ongoing result of the death of Christ.

While our salvation is entirely the result of God's grace, we appropriate it "through faith." Faith is a critical aspect of the salvation process, with the noun occurring seventeen times and the verb seven times in Romans 3:21–4:25. Saying that faith is critical does not imply that we save ourselves. The act of believing faith describes our decision to accept God's saving work in us, but it is God who enables us to receive his "abundant provision of grace" (Rom 5:17).

Paul especially wants his readers to understand that they do not find salvation in their own strength, nor can they work hard enough to produce it: "this is not from yourselves, it is the gift of God." While some have thought this is speaking of faith, it is actually saying that *salvation* is achieved not from ourselves but from the grace of God. The pronoun "this" is neuter, not feminine like the noun "faith," and the neuter normally encompasses the entire previous sentence; thus "by grace you have been saved." Fallen humanity cannot save itself, for it is "dead in sin" (2:1). Only God in his grace can redeem us.

Since we are "by nature deserving of wrath" (v. 3), salvation can come only from God. It is "the gift of God," meaning that it is not something earned by our own efforts but is freely received (Rom 5:15-17; 6:23). God is the giver, we the recipient, of the free gift of salvation. Paul states this another way in 2:9: "not by works, so that no one can boast." The identical truth is stated in two ways for emphasis.

If we could perform enough good deeds to earn salvation for ourselves, we would be on the throne of our lives and God would be relegated to the margins. We could then boast of our eternal achievements. But the fact is that any sin at all makes us guilty of all of them (Jas 2:10), and we can never produce enough goodness to warrant forgiveness and salvation. Paul says clearly elsewhere that "the works of the law" can never save (Rom 3:20; Gal 2:16; 3:10-14; Titus 3:5). Human pride is ruled out because the only things we can earn through human effort are condemnation and judgment. After his discussion of justification by faith in Romans 3:21-26, Paul summarizes in 3:27, "Where then is boasting? It is excluded ... because of the law that requires faith."

## THE NEW CREATION MAKES GOOD WORKS POSSIBLE (2:10)

The theme of new creation is very important in the New Testament. In John 1:3-5 we are told that Christ was the instrument of creation ("through him all things were made," v. 3) and also that he has provided a new spiritual creation: "In him was life, and that life was the light of all mankind" (v. 5). Then in 2 Corinthians 5:17 (also Gal 6:15) Paul states, "Therefore, if anyone is in Christ, the new creation has come. The old is gone, the new is here." This theme continues here, where Paul declares that "we are God's workmanship," a term used in the **Septuagint** for God's creation of the world (Ps 91:4; 142:5), as well as in Romans 1:20. The emphasis is on the perfection of God's work in creating humanity and on Christ's work in re-creating and returning humanity to its place as the image of God.

"Created" is a divine passive, meaning that God has accomplished this re-creation "in Christ Jesus." We have become God's new creation through our salvation and union with Christ. Christ is both the agent (through him) and the sphere (in him) of our new life as part of God's family. This new life has begun and is in the process of developing as we grow spiritually in him. It will be consummated at the return of Christ and the beginning of eternity. The resurrection life is not a future event but is already taking place as part of this new creation (Rom 6:1–3; Col 3:1–2). As Paul said in 2:6, "God raised us up with Christ and seated us with him in the heavenly realms." As later in 4:24, the "new self" we receive at conversion is "created to be like God in true righteousness and holiness." The image of God in us has come full circle, and in Christ we return to the goal of the original creation: to be like him.

While works cannot produce salvation ("not by works," 2:9), they are the true byproduct of salvation. We are saved entirely by God's grace through the sacrificial death of Christ. Yet an absence of works resulting from our conversion will constitute proof that conversion has never taken place. In fact, the language here shows purpose: God recreates us in Christ's image *so that* we can perform good works. This is a frequent emphasis in Paul's writings.[3] These good works, coupled with living a godly lifestyle and the fruit of the Spirit in Galatians 5:22–23, encompass acts of service to God and others.

This God-centered activity was "prepared in advance for us to do." The Greek says literally that God prepared a path "so that we could walk in it." What has been called "the Christian walk," the path of good works, was made ready for us even before creation took place. This was the path Adam and Eve were supposed to walk in the garden, but that path was marred when they ate the forbidden fruit. Christ has now cleared it, and we can once again travel on the Godward road. God chose us "before

---

3. Rom 2:7–13; Gal 6:10; 1 Tim 2:10; 6:18; 2 Tim 2:21; 3:17; Titus 2:7; 3:8.

the creation of the world" (Eph 1:4), and in the same eternity past he marked out the way he wanted us to go with our lives. In Ephesians 2:1–3 Paul pointed out that, while in the past we had "followed the ways of this world" and walked the path of darkness, now the light of Christ has enabled us to find the way of God-centered living, the way God originally intended for us.

This passage is a wonderful summary of the biblical doctrine of sin and salvation. Because we have inherited a sin nature and have willfully chosen to live in sin, we can never save ourselves. It was God's love that led him to create us in the first place. That love led to his mercy and grace, with the result that he sent his Son to die for us so that we could find salvation through our faith response to his gracious gift. The result is our union with Christ in his death, resurrection, and exaltation. We are made alive in him and both raised from the dead and seated with God in him. Therefore, we now have power over the demonic forces and are enabled to live a life of victory and of good works in him.

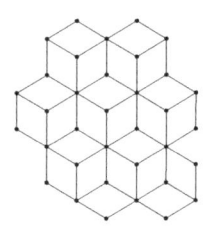

# THE NEW UNITED PEOPLE OF GOD: JEWS AND GENTILES

## (2:11-22)

Paul has been moving toward this point throughout the letter, talking about "you," the Ephesian believers (mostly Gentile) and then introducing "we" at several points (Paul and his Jewish and Gentile coworkers). Part of the new creation that Christ has effected is the unity of all—Jew and Gentile—in sin and salvation. A "new humanity" (2:15) has been created, and this concept involves a new unity of Jew and Gentile in Christ. This is a new era in what is known as salvation history, which describes God's presence in this world and its events. It seems as though history is random and ever changing, but God is actually in control. Salvation history narrates God's change from the old covenant centrality of the law to the new covenant reality of Christ. God's salvation and God's final kingdom have entered this world through Jesus Christ, and a new reality has taken over. This change involves the reconciliation of all peoples of the world and results in a new peace and unity between former enemies. In this a new community has been forged—the church, a new Israel, a new people of God no longer based on ethnicity but based solely on relationship with Christ. The old barriers and hostility between the groups have been eradicated in the cross, and both peace and unity are the result.

## PAUL DISCUSSES THE PAST AND PRESENT STATE OF THE GENTILES (2:11–13)

This introductory section presents the sad state of the pagan Gentiles and prepares for the wondrous act of God as he overcomes their depravity through his Son. In the past they were characterized by alienation and condemnation, but in the present they have been brought near by God's gracious act of reconciliation through the blood of Christ. This parallels Ephesians 2:1–3 (past sin) and 2:4–9 (present grace). Here the Jew-Gentile situation comes to the fore, but it is not social tensions that are uppermost. Rather, the emphasis is on the inclusion of Gentiles in God's plan of salvation.

### The Former State: Uncircumcised and Excluded (2:11–12)

On the basis of the truths stated in 2:1–10 ("therefore"), Paul wants his readers once again to remember their former state. Remembering here means more than just bringing something to mind; it entails careful reflection and acting on the memories. In Ephesians 2:1–3 Paul asked the Ephesians to recall their state as sinners who have been cut off from God; here he wants them to recall their plight as Gentiles, estranged not only from God but also from God's covenant people. The focus has shifted, but the progression is the same—from estrangement to reconciliation and acceptance. "Remember" also alludes to Deuteronomy, where Israel is urged to bring to mind how God rescued them from slavery in Egypt (Deut 5:15) and redeemed them as his covenant people (8:18). Now these Ephesian believers are to recall that God has included them in his covenant people. By recalling their past emptiness they realize afresh their present blessings in Christ.

Paul's readers were at one time Gentiles "in the flesh." This alludes to the fact that they were outsiders to the covenant people, with no relationship to the God of the Jews. This led, of course, to the Jews calling them "the uncircumcised." To the Greeks and Romans circumcision was a disgusting, barbaric practice, and many Gentiles who otherwise followed Jewish beliefs refused to be circumcised and thus remained "God-fearers" (Acts 10:2; 13:16) rather than fully converting. To the Jewish people this distinction constituted a major difference between the two peoples, for circumcision was the covenant rite that separated them as God's chosen people.[1]

Paul often referred to circumcision when discussing the Jew-Gentile distinction (Rom 4:9–12; Col 2:11, 13). In his earlier life as a Jew he had been an ardent proponent of "circumcision on the eighth day" (Phil 3:5). But now this was unimportant, for Christ had fulfilled the law (Matt 5:17–20) and was its culmination (Rom 10:4). It is true that Paul was willing to circumcise Timothy, but only so Timothy could minister to the Jews (Acts 16:3). When a group of Judaizers demanded that Gentile converts undergo circumcision when they became Christians—that is, when they linked circumcision with salvation—Paul viewed this stance as anathema or heresy (Gal 5:2–6; 6:12–13). Paul stresses this here by adding that circumcision is "done in the body by human hands." In other words, it is now merely a human physical rite. In Christ Jew and Gentile are equally part of the body, the church.

In addition to recalling their former state, Paul wants the Ephesian Christians to remember their former alienation from Christ and the covenant people (2:12). There are five aspects of this:

(1) They were "apart from Christ," meaning that they knew nothing of Jesus (or of the Jewish Messiah more generally) and were completely cut off from him. Some may have been God-fearers (see above) or even converts to Judaism, but most would have known nothing of Judaism or Christianity. Not only were they cut off from the Messiah; unlike the Jews they were removed from any understanding of a messiah, a royal

---

1. Circumcision, then as now, involves the cutting off of the foreskin of the penis. God instructed Abraham to circumcise his descendants to signify God's covenant with his people (Gen 17:10–14).

deliverer who would redeem them. For these Gentiles coming to know Jesus as Messiah was a double blessing.

(2) They were also "excluded from citizenship in Israel." This speaks of alienation from another people group. There had always been animosity between Israel and the nations that surrounded it, but here it is more than just a social estrangement; there is a religious dimension as well. Citizenship was very important, indicating not just belonging and membership in a community but also protection and privileges. The Ephesians were cut off from the covenant, having no access to the blessings of being the chosen people. Those who are minority groups in a culture that looks down on them, like African Americans in the United States, can understand this feeling of religious and social estrangement.

(3) They were "foreigners to the covenants of the promise." Paul is piling on the language of alienation. Note the contrast between Yahweh and the pagan gods. The Roman gods did not care about their people; there was no sense of covenant love. Only Yahweh had established that deep relationship, a sense of family in which his people were the recipients of the divine largesse. The term "covenant" implies a solemn divine-human treaty involving both promises and obligations, and the three main covenants in the Old Testament were the Abrahamic (Gen 12:1–4), the Mosaic (Exod 24:1–8), and the Davidic (2 Sam 7:12–17). The Gentiles had missed out on all this. They were foreigners not just to Israel but to God himself. It is true that the Abrahamic covenant had intended that the Jews bless "all peoples on earth" (Gen 12:3; 18:18; 22:18; 26:4), but that did not take place until the Gentile mission launched by Christ (Matt 28:18; Acts 3:25). Until Christ, these people (with a few exceptions like Ruth) were given no share in these promises.

(4) They were "without hope," meaning that without God they had no future and no part in the eternal promises. The Greco-Roman "hope" of an afterlife involved crossing the River Styx, paying the boatman Charon with a coin one "hoped" relatives or friends would place in the dead person's mouth when they

died, and walking the Elysian fields for eternity. But there was virtually no certainty that this would come to pass. By contrast, 1 Peter 1:3 speaks of a "living hope," a dynamic expectation that the future is guaranteed in Christ. For the pagan the future was uncertain, but for the Christian, Christ is indeed going to return, and we will inherit both an eternal glorified body and a heavenly existence.

(5) Worst of all, they were "without God in the world." Here Paul uses the Greek word *atheoi* ("godless"), from which "atheist" is derived. In fact, they had countless gods, but they were atheists in the sense that these deities were not actual beings. In ancient religions the gods represented natural forces or facets of human behavior, but according to the Bible there is only one God, who has created the world. This means that their religion simply individualized different aspects of God's creation. From that standpoint they were "godless"—they worshipped nonbeings and were "without [the one true] God in the world."

This is true of all nonbelievers, even today. It is so important in evangelism to help people understand the true reality of life apart from Christ. All who are outside of Christ are completely devoid of hope and have no true God to help them through life or give them meaning for the future. Every secularist holds on to a false brand of hope, perhaps that the right person will be elected president or that the economy will pick up. Such hope is false because its fulfillment can never be anything but possible; there is never any assurance that it will indeed come to pass. We do not know, for example, whether there will be a United States for our grandchildren (and many would say that things at the moment are looking bleak).

## The Present State: Brought Near by Jesus' Blood (2:13)

Christ Jesus came not just for the Jews but for all humanity. The estrangement of the Gentiles from God and his people has ended in him. Paul's language of "you who once were far away have been brought near" alludes to Isaiah 57:19 ("Peace, peace, to those far and near"). In Isaiah "you who were once far away" referred at least in one sense to exiles returning to their homeland and joining those who had remained in a land that had finally found peace. At the same time several scholars believe that Isaiah is describing the result of the national sin that has driven the nation far from God. Both interpretations are likely correct, and this two-pronged explanation would fit the context in Ephesians. By the time of the early church this language was being used of Gentiles who had converted to Judaism. Paul is taking another step, using it of all Gentiles who would come to Christ and embrace the free gift of salvation.

This takes place not by following the Torah but "by the blood of Christ." All peoples find union with God and one another when they discover the peace offered to them through the atoning sacrifice of Christ. Their estrangement from God and from one another is over, and peace at both the religious and the social levels is finally theirs. Converts to Judaism had to meet a series of conditions, while God-fearers, one step below converts, believed completely in Judaism but could not be converts until they had been circumcised. In reality, the only condition for becoming a Christian convert is faith in the blood of Christ, and conversion is open to all Gentiles who by faith become full members of the body of Christ, the church.

## PAUL DISCUSSES THE NEW PEACE AND UNITY ACHIEVED IN CHRIST (2:14-18)

### ACHIEVED BY THE REMOVAL OF THE DIVIDING WALL (2:14-15A)

Paul has told the Ephesians in verse 13 that Christ has brought them near. Now he tells them how Christ and his death for them have achieved this incredible effect. The influence of Isaiah 57:19 in the last verse continues here, as Isaiah's "peace" (Hebrew, *shalōm*) is now attained in Christ. Peace is the central topic in this paragraph, with the word occurring four times, in 2:14, 15, 17. Biblical peace is more than a personal sense of tranquility and well-being. It carries the idea of harmony, first with God and then with those around us. It includes the idea of order and wholeness, of disparate areas of life and people groups coming together with a cessation of conflict and a sense of security.

We can see Isaiah's messianic promises coming together in this, as, for instance, in such passages as Isaiah 9:6, where the coming child is called "Prince of peace," and 52:7, declaring the beauty of "the feet of those who ... proclaim peace." In Christ this messianic promise of peace has been fulfilled. Note that Paul does not say "Christ brings peace to us" but that "he himself *is* our peace." This is connected to the "in Christ" theme seen throughout the letter thus far. The blood of Christ has not only saved us; it has united us with him. He has not only *brought* peace *to* us; he has *become* peace *in* us. Christ's peace is an internal reality in our lives. The peace that is Christ is now a critical aspect of who we are.

Paul tells us three ways in which Christ has become our peace and produced peace in us: (1) he "has made two groups one"; that is, he has overcome the hostility between Jew and Gentile. One of the defining characteristics of peace is unity forged between former enemies. Christ did not simply make them neighbors or friends but re-created them as one new entity, the church, as we will see in verse 15b. This is not "world peace," the absence of conflict that so many long for. This peace comes only in Christ and takes place because both groups have become the children of God and siblings of one another.

(2) In forging this new peace and unity he "destroyed the barrier, the dividing wall of hostility." This may picture the barrier between Jew and Gentile as the wall of a city or building that functions as a partition between insiders and outsiders. Christ on the cross laid siege to this rampart and tore it down. The barrier, in this view, is the enmity that exists between the two groups.

It is also possible to see this more specifically as the inner wall or balustrade of the temple, a four-and-a-half-foot-thick wall between the court of the Gentiles and the inner court, which contained the court of Israel and the sanctuary. In this view the barrier is what kept Gentiles separate from Jews, referring either to the temple itself or to the law. The Jewish people even pictured their oral tradition of laws as "building a fence around the law." In other words, their legal tradition both protected the Jews and kept the pagan Gentiles outside the covenant people. This second option makes the best sense of the imagery and leads naturally to the next point.

(3) In making and becoming our peace Christ has abolished or set aside "in his flesh the law with its commands and ordinances." The verb "set aside" (*katargeō*) can be translated "render ineffective" or "nullify." Christ, by becoming our sacrifice ("in his flesh" = "by his death"), has nullified the need for the law and therefore set aside the enmity it had created between Jew and Gentile. By being made right with God both groups are also made right with each other. The "commands and ordinances" are the specific injunctions of the law. When the law is set aside, the hostility it produces disappears as well.

As Christ pointed out in Matthew 5:17-20, he has not destroyed the law but has fulfilled it. He has brought it to completion. Thus Paul can say in Romans 10:4, "Christ is the culmination of the law." This means that the law is still intact in Christ but that the specific commands are no longer in effect. Some have tried to limit this to the ceremonial rather than the moral aspects of the law, but neither Jesus nor Paul makes this distinction. In Matthew 5:21-48 moral commands are specifically said to be fulfilled by Christ. The moral aspects of the law continue not because there is a distinction between ceremonial and moral but because they are taught by Christ.

Several years ago I took part in a Promise Keepers study group dedicated to writing a position paper on racial and denominational reconciliation. The study consisted of three members each from African American, Native American, Asian, Hispanic, and Caucasian groups. As we discussed racial reconciliation, the Lord led us to this passage. We were excited about the message here, showing that racial divides are nullified in Christ. Unity is the God-intended goal for his people, and we must solve our differences and find oneness in him.

## A NEW, UNITED HUMANITY, RECONCILED
## THROUGH CHRIST (2:15B-16)

There are two parts to this section—the new creation in verse 15b and the reconciliation of this new, united people to God in verse 16. Peace is still the primary theme, but now it is linked with the new creation in Christ. A critical element of this is the creation of "one new humanity out of the two." This does not refer just to a new corporate community. Rather, it is a new humanity that is no longer divided into various socioreligious groups but has been forged into a new, united humanity in Christ. The racial and ethnic divides are gone, replaced by "one new man" (hena kainon anthrōpan) and thus forged by Christ into "one body" (heni sōmati). In Ephesians 4:22, 24 the "old man"/"new man" distinction relates to the individual believer (also Rom 6:6; Col 3:9-10), seen corporately as part of the new creation, but here the "new man" stresses the corporate entity itself—a "new humanity." Christ in Romans 5:12-21 is the New Adam, and in Christ believers also constitute a New Adam, a new order of humanity in which the religious and social barriers that separated people have been abolished by the cross, so that true peace and unity can be found.

This new corporate entity or society is created by Christ and exists only in Christ. It is entirely a new creation (see 2:10, above), for this unity had not existed since Adam and Eve had brought sin into this world. Of course, sin still disrupts and complicates the experience of unity in the pure form God intends, but hostility has evaporated whenever Christ and the life-giving Spirit (2 Cor 3:6) are given control. "If anyone is in Christ, the new creation has come" (2 Cor 5:17), and the old distinctions have been nullified.

Through this creation of a new, unified humanity Christ "makes peace." You could say this constitutes a reversal of Babel (Gen 11), where God confused the languages and forced division on humanity because of its hubris. Now he has removed those divisions and re-created a united people.

The second part of this section (Eph 2:16) flows out of the first. This new creation of a united humanity has taken place because both groups have first been reconciled to God. They could not become one group until they had first been brought into the family of God. Since Jew and Gentile have been made one with Christ, they can also be made one with each other. God in Christ has set aside the dividing wall, the effects of the law, enabling the new creation to take place. In him we are meant to solve and remove the tensions between "red and yellow, black and white" (in the old gospel song).

The basis of all this is that they we have been reconciled "to God through the cross." Reconciliation is the social side of the salvation process, describing how two estranged parties could be brought together and peace between them achieved. Paul stresses often that the act of God in Christ has made this possible.[2] The generating force is God, who brought us to himself by sending his Son to die on the cross in our stead, redeeming us so that our sins could be forgiven. The primary barrier to reconciliation is not social but religious, as sin has estranged both Jew and Gentile from God. While 2:1-3 describes the sin of the Gentiles, the Jewish people were equally separated from God: They had rejected their Messiah, and their sins were if anything more egregious (see Rom 2:1-3:8). The death of Christ as an atoning sacrifice made reconciliation equally possible for the two groups.

Here Paul extends this image to the reconciliation of all groups with one another. Since they are reconciled to God, Jews and Gentiles are reconciled to each other "in one body"— another way of saying that Christ has created "in himself one new humanity"(2:15b). The unity between enemy people groups has been accomplished only in Christ and by Christ, who has "put to death their hostility" toward one another. By being killed Christ has killed the differences between us. His blood sacrifice

---

2. Rom 5:10-11; 11:15; 1 Cor 7:11; 2 Cor 5:18-20; Col 1:20-22.

has removed the terrible product of sin: human hatred. All barriers, both religious and social, have been set aside, and peace can finally come, first between ourselves and God and then among ourselves. This hardly means that all Christians are immune from racial hostility. We have all seen too much of it in the church, as well as in society. However, it does mean that God especially intends for us to become models of racial and ethnic harmony, and that Christ and the Spirit are at work in God's people to achieve just that.

## Peace Proclaimed to Both Jew and Gentile (2:17)

In verse 14 Paul told the Ephesians that Christ "is our peace" (echoing Isa 9:6), and now Christ "preaches peace" (Isa 52:7). Also in the background is Isaiah 57:19, part of a section depicting God comforting the righteous remnant and stating, "Peace, peace, to those who are far and near. ... I will heal them." The verb "preach" (*euangelizō*) connotes the proclamation of the gospel, so some translate this "preaches the gospel of peace." It is difficult to know whether "when he came" refers to Christ's incarnation, his earthly ministry, or the effects of the cross and resurrection. Perhaps the best option is to understand this as the exalted Christ proclaiming peace through the church as his followers are led by the Spirit. The preaching is done in Christ by the Spirit. This also means that Paul intends racial harmony to be an important part of the gospel message; it is not peripheral but essential to the gospel!

The language of "near and far" reminds us of 2:13: "you who once were far away have been brought near." There it was used of the sin that kept us far from God. Here the terms are used in a covenant sense of Jews (near to the covenant) and Gentiles (far from the covenant). In Isaiah this would be part of the procession of the nations to Zion (Isa 49:6; 60:11; 61:6; 62:10). Both Jews and Gentiles will find peace with God and thus be enabled to have peace between themselves.

CONCLUSION: BOTH HAVE ACCESS TO GOD BY THE SPIRIT (2:18)

This proclamation of peace takes place because of ("for") the work of Christ and the Spirit. As I have been saying, the unity of former enemies is possible only because both have become part of the family of God the Father. Since they have the same Father and are now siblings, they can become one with each other. This can be accomplished only "through him," that is, through the blood sacrifice of the cross, which has paid for the sins of both groups and has enabled "access to the Father" because of his forgiveness. As stated in 2:1-3, the sins of Jew and Gentile created an insuperable barrier between them and God, but the shed blood of Christ has removed that barrier, bringing reconciliation (v. 16) and making possible access to God.

Moreover, as a "new humanity" and "one body," people no longer come into the presence of God as Jews or Gentiles. They approach God as one, as part of the new people of God. As citizens of heaven they sit with God in Christ in the heavenly realms (vv. 6-7) and come into his presence through prayer whenever they wish. In the Old Testament they came to the temple to be in God's presence, but Gentiles had to stay outside while the Jews could get closer to God in the court of Israel (but no closer). Priests, usually once in their lifetimes, were privileged to serve in the holy place, but only the high priest once a year could come into the very presence of God in the most holy place, and that only because he represented the nation.[3] But now in Christ, Jew and Gentile alike can bask in the presence of God and experience the **Shekinah** glory (from Hebrew *shakan*, "to dwell," referring to the glory of God dwelling with them) at all times of the day or night!

---

3. Some think the metaphor of "access to God" comes from the secular sphere, whereby access to the king was highly restricted and available to very few. While I prefer as explanation the religious background, above, the point remains the same. We can come into the throne room of God whenever we wish because of the work of Christ and the Spirit.

This access to God comes not only through Christ but also "by one Spirit," as in 1 Corinthians 12:13: "We were all baptized by one Spirit so as to form one body." There is a trinitarian emphasis here: Christ provides access to the Father via the Spirit. There are two ideas: first, the Spirit is both the sphere (*en*, in the sense of "in" the Spirit) and the instrument (*en*, as in "by" the Spirit) that make this access possible. It is in the Spirit that the presence of God dwells, and at the same time the Spirit is the means by which we enter into that presence. Second, the "one Spirit" is the uniting force in the church; it is through him that oneness is achieved (see also Eph 4:3-4).

## PAUL DISCUSSES THE NEW CITIZENSHIP AND BUILDING WE HAVE IN CHRIST (2:19-22)

### THE GENTILES: NO LONGER FOREIGNERS BUT CITIZENS (2:19)

Paul now switches his metaphor from family to citizenship, echoing verse 12, which speaks of the Gentiles as "excluded from citizenship in Israel and foreigners." His opening "consequently" or "so then" means that here he is developing the implications of what he has said in verses 14-18. He recapitulates what he has stated in verses 11-13 of the Gentiles, who were formerly "foreigners and strangers" (see Heb 11:13; 1 Pet 2:11), echoing Old Testament language about those Gentiles living among the Jews (Exod 12:45; Lev 22:10). That alienation from the covenant people has ended in Christ, so the Gentiles are no longer separate from God or his people.

Believing Gentiles are now "fellow citizens with the saints." Philippians 3:20 states that "our citizenship is in heaven," and since Gentile and Jew are both citizens of heaven they are fellow citizens with one another. Note that Paul does not say "with the Jews" but "with the saints," stressing that in the new Israel (the church) there is no longer Jew or Gentile (ethnic or national identity) but "one new humanity" (Eph 2:15). For us this means that we are no longer American or British citizens, for our true home is not Chicago or London but "the Jerusalem that is above" (Gal 4:26). Therefore, we are no longer alienated from each other but are "foreigners and exiles" to the people of this world (1 Pet 2:11). We belong not to any one nation but to the people of heaven and to each other.

We have a new home and a new citizenship, but we also have a new family—we are "members of the household of God." We are no longer a part of this world but are part of the eternal family of the Triune Godhead. We are children of the heavenly Father (Eph 3:14-15) and joint-heirs with Christ (Rom 8:17). The theme of the church as the household of God is developed further in 1-2 Timothy (1 Tim 3:15; 2 Tim 2:20, 21). The imagery of the church as consisting of fathers, young men, and children is developed in 1 John 2:12-14.

## God's New Building: A Temple (2:20-22)

### The apostles the foundation and Christ the cornerstone (2:20)

Mixed metaphors are Paul's trademark. The new citizenship and household in verse 19 are spoken about here as a building. This makes sense, for the building will be seen as God's temple, often pictured in the Old Testament as God's house. First Peter 2:5 pictures believers as living stones built upon the living stone (Christ) to become God's building. That is the imagery here. Putting this together with verse 14, Christ has torn down the dividing wall in order to erect his new building, which constitutes the final temple, the church.

The foundation for this new building/temple is the apostles and prophets. In 1 Corinthians 3:10-15 the foundation is Christ himself, with Paul and the other leaders being the construction team who have built upon that foundation. Here the leaders of the church are the foundation, and Paul links them together as foundations of God's church.

The term "apostles" refers to the Twelve and to others (like Paul, Barnabas, and Apollos) whom God called and gifted to lead the early church. Their teaching anchored the church's views (Acts 2:42), and theirs was the foundational gift for all other spiritual gifts (1 Cor 12:28). Some have understood "prophets" here to refer to Old Testament prophets, but if that were the case we would have expected the order to be "prophets and apostles." New Testament prophets will be listed in Ephesians 4:11 as representing a valid office in the church. Prophets are listed second, both there and in 1 Corinthians 12:28, and they were central figures in building up the church (1 Cor 14:4–5). Like Old Testament prophets their primary function was edification, and prophesying future events was secondary. The one thing apostles and prophets in the early church had in common was teaching, and Paul is probably saying that the kingdom truths of Christ and the creedal truths of the church erected the foundation of God's new building.

The "chief cornerstone" of this new building is Christ Jesus, meaning that the entire edifice rests upon him. There is some debate as to whether the image is of the foundation stone at the corner of the building or the capstone at the top of the arch. If the latter, the emphasis is on Christ's prominence and splendor in the most conspicuous part of the building. If the former, the imagery centers upon his strength and importance, with the stones of the structure resting on him. While the idea of a capstone would make sense, the evidence for this image is slightly later than the New Testament period, and the imagery in the New Testament favors the cornerstone option.

Three relevant Old Testament stone passages are cited in the New Testament: Psalm 118:22 ("The stone the builders rejected has become the cornerstone"); Isaiah 8:14 ("a stone that causes people to stumble and a rock that makes them fall"); and Isaiah 28:16 ("I lay a stone in Zion, a tested stone, a precious cornerstone for a sure foundation"). The Isaiah passages definitely favor the cornerstone option, and the third passage is the one behind the imagery here. The cornerstone was chosen not only for its size and strength but also for its beauty, and inscriptions were often placed on it identifying the structure and its purpose. This fits Paul's message. While the apostles are the foundation, Christ is the stone upon which the others rest and the basis for the purpose of the building. Indeed, he is the foundation stone on which the apostles themselves rest (see 1 Cor 3:10–15; 1 Pet 2:4–6).

The imagery and message are striking. We are pictured as stones that have become the façade of God's temple, the church. Some massive stones of Herod's temple have been discovered, one of them 55 feet by 14 feet by 11 feet in size. These were known for their magnificence, as pointed out by the disciples in Mark 13:1: "Look, Teacher! What massive stones! What magnificent buildings!" That is what we are. As "living stones" built upon the Living Stone, we are united with Christ as "chosen and precious" (1 Pet 2:4–7a).

### The building erected as God's temple (2:21–22)

These verses draw together the whole unit of verses 11–22 and culminate its message. As the "whole building" (stressing the church as an organic unit) is being erected—"joined together and rises"— its essence and purpose are gradually revealed, and it becomes apparent that it is growing into "a holy temple in the Lord." Herod's temple was never truly finished (John 2:20, "It has taken forty-six years [so far] to build this temple"), and it was still being completed when it was destroyed by the Romans. The church as God's temple is also unfinished and continues to develop over the centuries as more and more "stones" are added to it.

This is also true at the local level, as each church continues to evolve and grow through ministry and conversions. Each stone is a person, and each ministry is a room as God's construction project continues. The togetherness of the church involves more than just stone with stone, though that is one aspect of the image in light of the emphasis, above, on the unity of Jew and Gentile (see also 4:15–16). This also indicates the union of the church together with its cornerstone, Christ. The union that is to typify the church is made possible entirely by the union of each part of the church with Christ.

Joined together, the church becomes "a holy temple in the Lord." Paul sees the church as God's temple because God dwells in it via his Spirit (1 Cor 3:16–17; 2 Cor 6:16). Elsewhere Peter says that we as living stones are built up to be both the "spiritual house" and the "holy priesthood" that inhabits it (1 Pet 2:5). The point is that the Triune Godhead dwells in us, so that we are his temple. This can be possible only in Christ, for it is our union with him that draws us together to constitute his holy temple. Holiness is a key theme in the letter,[4] seen in the frequent use of the term "saints," which can also be translated "holy people."[5] We are set apart to belong to him and to constitute the new Israel, the church that unites all races and ethnic groups into one temple in the Lord. We are also called to live holy lives, to live wholly (pun intended) for him as we become his temple in this world. In other words, we as the church are a sacred people in this world.

The points of verse 21 are explained further in verse 22. We are "joined together" in verse 21 and "built together" in verse 22, both pictures of the Master Builder fitting together the stones and constructing his new temple, the church. In verse 21 the church is "a holy temple in the Lord," and in verse 22 it is "a dwelling in which God lives by his Spirit." In verse 21 the means is the Lord. Here it is the Spirit, as in 1 Corinthians 3:16: "you yourselves are God's temple and … God's Spirit dwells in your midst." The temple was holy because God's **Shekinah** glory (from the Hebrew *shakan*, to dwell) dwelt in it in the most holy place. The church is a temple because the Spirit is God's Shekinah dwelling in it.

It is difficult to overstate the importance of this section of the letter. While Ephesians 2:1–10 summarizes the doctrine of sin and salvation, this summarizes the doctrine of the church. Sin estranged us not only from God but from each other, as religious, racial, and socioeconomic divides dominated and made us enemies of one another. In Christ all these barriers

---

4. See 1:4; 2:21; 3:5; 5:26, 27.
5. See 1:15, 18; 2:19; 3:8, 18; 4:12; 5:3; 6:18.

have been rendered null and void, and it is God's will that among his people all divisions among people groups disappear. The church is first of all a new humanity in which we all cherish and respect one another. In Christ there are no longer color differences, and ethnic divides no longer exist. This doesn't mean that we cease to be African or Asian or Caucasian but that we are all completely equal and brothers and sisters of each other. We cherish one another, and our differences are family differences. Moreover, the church constitutes God's building, a new, heaven-centered temple that celebrates God's presence with his people. Here there can be no place for alienation within God's new people group (never again "groups"), but only unity and togetherness.

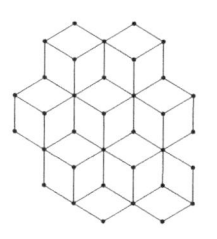

# PAUL'S STEWARDSHIP
# OF GOD'S MYSTERY
## (3:1–13)

Chapter 3 is often called the "Pauline parousia" (the Greek word for "coming, presence") because Paul is meditating on his ministry in general (3:1–13) and his particular ministry to the Ephesians (vv. 14–19). He begins the section with what he intends to be a prayer for the Ephesians but breaks it off and does not get back to his prayer until verse 14. The intervening material (vv. 2–13) constitutes a lengthy digression on the meaning of Paul's ministry of God's grace to the Gentiles, conceived as an "administration" or stewardship of God's mystery: the inclusion of the Gentiles in the people of God.

The organization of this section is determined by grammar. An opening and a closing (vv. 1, 13, respectively) frame two lengthy sentences (vv. 2–7, 8–12), and the two parts of this material are verses 1–7 and 8–13. These two parts describe the *what* (the mystery of God revealed, vv. 1–7) and the *how* (proclaiming and illuminating the mystery, vv. 8–12) of Paul's ministry. There is a close connection here with Ephesians' sister letter, Colossians 1:23–28, with "I Paul" (v. 1 = Col 1:23), stewardship (v. 2 = Col 1:25), the mystery and Christ (v. 4 = Col 1:27), revealed to God's people (v. 5 = Col 1:27), became a servant (v. 7 = Col 1:23), hiddenness (v. 9 = Col 1:26), and Paul's suffering (v. 13 = Col 1:24).

## GOD REVEALS THE MYSTERY (3:1–7)

### THE INTRODUCTION OF AN INTERCESSORY PRAYER (3:1)

Paul begins this section with an introduction to a prayer for the Ephesian Christians. Verses 14–19 likely provide the prayer introduced in verse 1, so Paul is reminding his readers of his current predicament in prison as a prelude to praying for their own spiritual strength through the indwelling presence of Christ and the Holy Spirit. "For this reason" points back to 2:11–22 and the fact that Gentile and Jew have been molded together into a new humanity in Christ. Together they have become God's temple, the church.

Paul reminds his readers of his current situation as "the prisoner of Christ Jesus" (cf. 2 Tim 1:8; Phlm 1:9). This could emphasize that he is imprisoned "because of" Christ but more likely means that he is Christ's prisoner, under the control not of Caesar but of Christ. While Rome will decide whether he lives or dies, Christ is the true sovereign. Paul states well his attitude toward imprisonment in Philippians 1:21: "to live is Christ and to die is gain." In spite of his dire circumstances God and Christ are controlling the situation. If that could be true for Paul in his trying times, how much more can it be true for the Ephesians (and for us)!

The point is the same as that of Jesus' teaching in Matthew 10:26, 28: "So do not be afraid of them, for there is nothing ... hidden that will not be made known. ... Do not be afraid of those who kill the body but cannot kill the soul." As Jesus suffered for humanity, Paul suffers "for you Gentiles"—so that the Gentiles can come to Christ and be included among God's people. In Romans 9:3 Paul states that he is willing to be accursed by God if that might bring his people, the Jews, to Christ. Here he adds the Gentiles to that ministry goal. The idea of Paul suffering for the Ephesians occurs again in verse 13 and frames this section.

## PAUL'S STEWARDSHIP OF THE MYSTERY
## OF GOD'S GRACE (3:2–3)

The thought of Paul's sacrifices for his readers leads him to reflect upon the meaning and purpose of his mission. His mind is going at warp speed, and he keeps interrupting himself. First he interrupts his prayer to digress on his mission, and then he interrupts his conditional sentence ("If [NIV 'surely'] you have heard…"—the "then" clause doesn't come until verse 13) to discourse on the meaning of God's mystery. There is so much he wants to say that it leads to another extremely lengthy sentence (vv. 2–7), with one minor clause after another.

The way Paul expresses the verb phrase ("you have heard" rather than "you know") shows that many of the readers had not met Paul and knew little about him. It had been several years since Paul had been in Ephesus, and the letter was intended for all the churches in the province of Asia, so there would have been many who knew little about him.[1] He wanted all the believers to understand the basis of his ministry and God's purpose for the gospel spreading throughout the world.

To describe his ministry Paul chooses the same term he has used in 1:10 for the "administration" (*oikonomia*; NIV "put into effect") of the fullness of times. In Paul's writings this speaks of both God and Paul administering their work in the world, using the metaphor of a steward overseeing a household. In Ephesians 1:10 it is God; here it is Paul. God has created a new, united household in which Jew and Gentile live as an integrated family. He has chosen Paul to oversee that household and bring it together. Note how the images for the church coalesce in chapters 2 and 3: The church is a community in which disparate people groups have been reconciled, and as such they are brought together as a united family. As one, they constitute a household and also the building in which that family lives (echoing 1 Pet 2:5). Finally, that building has become

---

1. See "Recipients" in the introduction.

God's temple, the house in which the Godhead dwells with God's people. The images just keep piling up on one another! The next time you go to church, picture yourself and the others in the service as God's family sitting in the most holy place celebrating his living presence!

Moreover, Paul has become a steward "of the grace of God," overseeing God's work as his grace brings more and more converts into God's family. Grace (*charis*) in Ephesians is always connected to Paul's gift of salvation by the blood of Christ.[2] The extension of God's salvation to all the peoples of the earth is entirely the result of God's grace and mercy, as is the gift of life to undeserving sinners. Moreover, God gave this grace-gift to Paul, to become "apostle to the Gentiles" and to be used by God to bring many into the kingdom. Paul does all of this "for you"— that is, the goal of his ministry is not self-aggrandizement but the salvation of the lost. He has no interest in what he might get out of it, only in what God can do through him for the benefit of the Gentiles. Ministry is not a job or a career; it is a joy and a privilege, a high calling and sign of divine grace for all who are gifted to be a part of it.

This grace-gift entails administering God's mystery (3:3). As I stated in 1:10, the term "mystery" describes the content of the hidden secrets God has kept from his people until now. This is the "fullness of time" (Gal 4:4), and God is now revealing these end-time truths concerning salvation for the Gentiles that he first revealed to Paul in the Damascus road vision (Acts 26:13–18; Gal 1:12, 16). There God "made known" to him that Christ died not only for the Jews but for all humanity. As a zealous, ultra-conservative Jew, Paul needed some time to come to grips with the place of Gentiles in God's plan, so God anchored Paul's call to be a missionary to the Gentiles first in Ananias (Acts 9:15) and later in the temple vision (Acts 22:21).

---

2. 1:2, 6, 7; 2:6, 7, 8 thus far.

Paul points out to his readers that he has already "written briefly" about this call. He is either referring to his discussion of this issue in Colossians 1:25–27 or to points he has made earlier in this letter.[3] It is impossible to know for certain whether these readers had access to the Colossian letter, but that is certainly possible. We must leave it there.

## THE NEED TO UNDERSTAND THE MYSTERY NOW REVEALED (3:4–5)

Verse 4 begins with the preposition *pros*. This could show the purpose for the revelation of the mystery in verse 3, but in this context it more likely means "according to which" and states the basis for that revelation. In other words, on the basis of God making known his mystery to Paul on the Damascus road, the readers can now share Paul's insight and understand more deeply God's redemptive plan.

Their "reading" about this plan is undoubtedly tied to what Paul has just said (v. 3, "as I have already written briefly"), so it could refer to the readers going back to the Colossian letter or returning to the earlier part of this one. However, neither option is likely. In the first century there were very few scrolls available, since they had to be hand-copied by scribes and would as such have been quite expensive. It is also unlikely that Paul could be asking them to pick up this scroll and read the earlier parts. So most agree that this refers to the public reading of the entire letter in the church service. Through that they could share in Paul's insight into the meaning of the mystery revealed to him.

A critical determination here is the meaning of "the mystery of Christ." If Paul means "the mystery *that is* Christ," the text would then parallel Colossians 1:27, "this mystery, which is Christ in you," and 2:2, "the mystery of God, namely Christ." This would lead to a two-part revelation: God reveals the mystery

---

3. See 1:9–10; 2:15–17 on the "one new humanity."

here as Christ and then reveals in verse 6 that through Christ the mystery brings about the inclusion of the Gentiles. But it is better to take this as "the mystery *about* Christ," the mystery that has come to pass in Christ. This mystery is the salvation for all the peoples of the earth that has taken place through the sacrifice of Christ on the cross. Paul wants to share his insight into the very meaning of the gospel in Christ, that now it is part of the universal mission to all the world. We take part in this when our churches become mission minded. Any church that fails to make world missions a critical aspect of its ministry is disobedient to God and to his call.

The center of the concept of "mystery" is its hiddenness, so Paul makes it clear that in previous generations God did not "make it known" (v. 5). These **apocalyptic** truths had not been revealed to either the Jews or the Gentiles of the past. God had been hiding them, intending to reveal them only to the present generation at the coming of Jesus the Messiah, as stated also in Romans 16:25–26: "the revelation of the mystery hidden for long ages past, but now revealed and made known" (also Col 1:26).

This doesn't imply that the Old Testament saints were completely ignorant. In fact, Paul says in Galatians 3:8 that "Scripture foresaw beforehand that God would justify the Gentiles by faith, and announced the gospel in advance to Abraham." In the Abrahamic covenant the Jews were chosen to bless the Gentiles.[4] But the details regarding how this would come to pass were kept hidden. The Old Testament people understood the basic contours of God's plans for the Gentiles but never quite accepted or acted upon those plans. They never realized God's full purposes regarding the union of Jew and Gentile, nor did they fully understand the coming and work of the Messiah that would bring all this to pass. In fact, even the early church failed to realize the significance of the Great Commission for world evangelism. They believed they were to stay in Jerusalem

---

4. Gen 12:3; 22:18; 26:4. See also Isa 49:6; Zech 8:20–22.

and wait for the Gentiles to come to them (the "procession of the nations to Zion" in Isaiah 60:11; 62:10). The Spirit had to take over and lead them to the nations (see below).

The time of fulfillment, Paul continues, is "now," with the coming of the messianic age. According to the Bible the coming of Christ is the midpoint in time. "Now" is the time after his coming, death, and resurrection. In this new age divine revelation has continued, and the final mysteries have been "revealed by the Spirit to God's holy apostles and prophets." The apostles and prophets were presented in 2:20 as the foundation stones of the church, and here, as there, Paul indicates New Testament prophets.

Once again the Holy Spirit is the channel for this revelation. In 1:17 Paul prayed that God would give the Ephesians "the Spirit of wisdom and revelation," and in 2:18, 22 the Spirit is the means by which we experience the indwelling presence of God. Here the Spirit mediates these new revelations and brings insight to the church regarding their significance. Paul is now the particular apostle and prophet used by the Spirit to provide this insight to the Ephesian church, but Jesus first revealed this new apocalyptic reality.[5] This was understood (with great difficulty) by Peter at the conversion of the Roman centurion Cornelius in Acts 10 and then accepted by the church when Peter returned to Jerusalem in Acts 11:1-18. Acts 7-11 details the steps to the Gentile mission by which the Spirit guided the church to understand and fulfill God's will in mission.

The apostles and prophets are called "holy" in verse 5 because they have been set apart by God for this task.[6] They have been called to live holy lives as God uses them to carry out his work in this world. In Ephesians 2:21 the church as God's

---

5. For instance, the Great Commission in Matt 28:18-20 and in Acts 1:8.
6. It would be possible on the basis of the grammar to think that only the apostles are called "holy" here, but that is unlikely because of the unity of these two offices in 2:21 and here. Both groups are holy because both serve the Lord and his church.

temple is called "holy in the Lord," and this idea is central here as well. These two offices are the foundation for God's temple, so the holiness that typifies the church also forms the essential core of these central parts of the structure.

## THE MYSTERY AS THE INCLUSION OF THE GENTILES IN THE CHURCH (3:6)

In this verse Paul connects the mystery with the gospel, which comes last (in the Greek) for emphasis. It is through the gospel that Gentiles come to Christ and enter into union with the Jews as the new Israel, the church of Christ. The gospel, of course, is the "good news" that salvation has come to this world through the atoning sacrifice of Christ. His sacrifice has paid for our sins and made us right with God (our justification); because of it we are the children of God. It is clear that the essence of the mystery is not just **christological** (in Christ) or ecclesiological (in the church as a united body) but also soteriological (centering on the salvation Christ has provided).

Three new realities regarding the Gentiles constitute the mystery here. All three employ the prefix *syn-*, stressing the union ("together with") between Jew and Gentile: (1) they are "heirs together with Israel." Here Paul uses the same joint-heirs motif as in Romans 8:17: Believers are united with Christ, and in Christ with one another, as both share that inheritance with Christ. There are several dimensions of our inheritance. In Ephesians 1:14 the Holy Spirit is given us as God's guarantee of our future inheritance in glory. This is further defined in 5:5 as a kingdom gift. The primary thrust is the final inheritance in heaven, but life in the Spirit is part of that inheritance.

(2) Jew and Gentile are also "members together of one body," a point I have already discussed in conjunction with 2:14–18. Both socioreligious groups are part of the "one new humanity" (v. 15) created in Christ Jesus, and both groups are members of the "one body" of Christ, the church (v. 16). Together they form a new, united people and a new, united body. The latter

emphasis on the church as the body of Christ is central in this letter.[7]

(3) They are also "sharers together in the promise in Christ Jesus." The term "sharers" means fellow partakers or participants in an enterprise, and the promise refers to "the promised Holy Spirit" in 1:13. Jew and Gentile in this sense are virtual business partners in the Spirit's promised new enterprise, the church. There is probably also a reflection of the Abrahamic promise that in Christ the Gentiles would be blessed (see above on 3:5). All of this takes place "in Christ Jesus," a key theme throughout Ephesians. It is only through the work of Christ and in him that all these wondrous new realities have come to pass.

As Paul stresses throughout this letter, the union of the disparate people groups in the church takes place only through their union with Christ. Union with him makes possible our union with one another. Only in this way can the wall of hostility between us be nullified (2:14). This is just as critical today as it was in Paul's, considering the racial and economic tensions that exist in our society. The church must be a beacon for unity between peoples in a world gone mad with hatred and prejudice!

## PAUL CALLED TO BE A SERVANT OF THIS MYSTERY (3:7)

The final point regarding this new mystery revealed by the Spirit is the place Paul has played in making it known to the church and in this world. In Ephesians 3:2 Paul speaks of himself as a "steward" of God's grace given to him; here he calls himself a "servant" of God's grace, again given to him. The two images are closely tied together; they bracket verses 2–7 with Paul's reflection on his role in mediating God's mystery through his mission. To him the grace of God is the central element; he is merely a servant of that great mission God has given him.

---

7. See 1:23; 2:16; 3:6; 4:4, 12, 16; 5:23, 30.

Paul here equates the gospel with the mystery of God revealed in Christ. The union of Jew and Gentile into a new humanity is a direct result of this greatest mystery, the sacrificial death of Christ and the salvation that came about through that blood sacrifice. This union is possible only because the blood of Christ has broken down the walls of hostility (2:14). This points back to the Damascus road vision of Acts 9, when Paul was converted and given his marching orders as apostle to the Gentiles. In his version of that event in Acts 26:16-18, Paul states that Christ has appointed him "as a servant and as a witness" and sent him to the Gentiles "to open their eyes and to turn them from darkness to light" so that they might have "a place among those who are sanctified by faith in [him]."

Paul is not the central figure in this mission but a mere servant of Christ, bringing in God's harvest to him. He says that his servanthood is based on (*kata*) the divine gift of grace, consisting undoubtedly of his salvation and call to ministry, with emphasis on the latter. This is seen in Ephesians 4:7, "to each of us grace is given," with the gift defined in 4:11 as the leaders given to the church and then in 4:16 as the works of service done by the members of the church. We might also think of spiritual gifts, as Paul taught in Romans 12:4-8 and in 1 Corinthians 12:12-21.

This gospel reality and the gift of ministry God gave to Paul were both achieved by means of "the working of his power." The idea behind "working" occurs in Colossians 1:29 ("the energy Christ so powerfully works in me") and 2:12 ("the working of God who raised him from the dead"). Pictured is a mighty outpouring of energy from heaven on behalf of the church. The term for "power" is the basic term for God's might, as in 1 Peter 1:5 ("kept by the power of God"). Together these verses depict God exercising his power to strengthen his chosen leaders of the church, like Paul. When the Corinthians mocked Paul for his inadequacies, he agreed and stated that he delighted in his weaknesses, for Christ's "power is made perfect in weakness" (2 Cor 12:5-10).

This invaluable paragraph has great relevance for us today. We too are stewards of the grace of God. We too demonstrate to a lost world caught up in racial prejudice and narcissistic self-involvement that Christ has not only saved us from our sins but also brought us together to become a whole, new humanity and, finally, to find oneness with each other. In Christ we belong to one another and can finally glory in what each of us can add to that one body when it truly achieves unity in Christ. This is the plan of God, and it can be achieved only in him. Paul is asking his early readers, as well as us, to become what he was: servants of the gospel of peace and unity.

## PAUL'S MINISTRY IS MAKING KNOWN THE MYSTERY (3:8-13)

### THE TWOFOLD NATURE OF HIS MISSION (3:8-9)

*Proclaiming Christ's riches to the Gentiles (3:8)*

Now Paul turns to the practical side, the ministry through which this mystery is made known to the nations. The emphasis is on the grace-gift of God, as Paul repeats "the grace given me" from verses 2 and 7. The point here is how little he deserves all that God has done on his behalf, since he is "the least of all the saints" (also 1 Cor 15:9; 1 Tim 1:15). We can see how strongly Paul feels this unworthiness by the fact that he takes a superlative adjective, "least," and adds to it a comparative form—literally, "more least" (Greek, *elachistoterō*, rendered in the NIV as "less than the least"). Paul never forgot his opposition to God's people before his conversion, as seen in Philippians 3:6 ("as for zeal, persecuting the church") and Acts 26:10 ("I put many of the Lord's people into prison, and when they were put to death, I cast my vote against them"). For Paul, God's grace is greater than anything he could have imagined in that God had saved a sinner like himself.

God not only saved Paul; he gave him the most precious of all ministries—to bring a new people group into the kingdom, to "preach to the Gentiles the boundless riches of Christ." The verb "preach" (*euangelizō*) means to proclaim the gospel or good news; it is transliterated into English as "evangelize." Paul uses the term "riches" in Ephesians and Colossians (seven times), as often as in all of his other writings put together. He wants his readers to realize the incredible provision of God for his children, the limitless outpouring of his grace he has lavished upon them (Eph 1:7–8).

Here his riches are "boundless," a term referring to unsearchable treasure, beyond our capacity to comprehend. In Romans 11:33 Paul proclaims, "Oh, the depth of the riches of the wisdom and knowledge of God! How unsearchable his judgments, and his paths beyond tracing out!" We will never be able to fathom such an endless supply of grace but can only accept the bounty God pours out on us! Paul is filled with awe as he contemplates how much God has done for him and for each one of us.

### Illuminating the hidden truths of the mystery (3:9)

Paul does not wish only to present the gospel; he wants people to realize the grace and mercy that lie behind it. The verb "make plain" (*phōtizō*) here means to shed light on or illuminate something so that the truths will become clear and plain. The "all" would be Jew and Gentile, but especially those who respond to the gospel.

What Paul wants to make clear is the "administration of the mystery"—the way God intends to carry out the mystery that "for ages past was kept hidden in God." As stated in the commentary on 1:10 and 3:2, "administration" builds on the metaphor of a steward overseeing a household. Here the emphasis is not on the *what* of the mystery but on the *how*: the way God has implemented his plan of salvation for the world. As missionary to the Gentiles Paul is part of that plan, and he wants to pass on his insights to the church so they can take their place as part of that mission. In other words, the mystery is the outworking of the gospel in the mission of the church, the proclamation of the salvation brought about through the sacrificial death of Christ and the new union of all people groups that has resulted.

This new reality was "hidden in God" in ages past, waiting for the fullness of time (Gal 4:4) when it was to come into reality and be revealed. The old covenant period was a time of preparation during which God was readying his people for the day he had foreseen and predestined. At the perfect time in God's eternal plan Christ came, and that plan was revealed to the world.

Paul adds that the God who planned and oversaw all of this is "the creator of all things." This tells us that creation itself was part of God's plan, and the coming of Christ into the world was a critical element in God's created order. When God created this world, he knew of the fall of Adam and Eve and that Christ would need to come as a man and die. Revelation 13:8 speaks of "the Lamb who was slain from the creation of the world," telling us that the cross was an essential part of God's plan from the very beginning. Without the cross creation could never have occurred, for sin had to be remedied in order to realize the very purpose of creation.

## REVEALING THE CHURCH'S MISSION TO THE COSMIC POWERS (3:10–12)

### God's wisdom made known to the cosmic powers (3:10)

Because of the centrality of magic in the Roman province of Asia (the result of the temple of Artemis and its influence), Paul places great emphasis in Colossians and Ephesians on the defeat of the cosmic powers.[8] The language of "making known" here does not mean that the church is to evangelize the demonic forces. They have made an eternal decision to oppose God (Rev 12:4, 7–9) and are beyond redemption. Rather, the church reiterates Christ's preaching to the spirits in prison (1 Pet 3:19) and tells the cosmic powers they have lost. It does so through its victorious ministry in the world. Though they have rejected God, the fallen angels are supremely aware of his wisdom, for

---

8. See "Recipients" in the introduction.

they know the Scriptures and see God's wisdom worked out every day in the lives of his victorious people.

In this context the wisdom of God is especially the proclamation of the gospel and the inclusion of the Gentiles in the church. This demonstrates the boundless riches of God that are absolute proof of his wisdom. Moreover, it also proves that his wisdom is "manifold"—multifaceted or composed of diverse aspects. Here Paul has created a compound word composed of "many" and "diverse, various." It could also be translated "many-sided," and it demonstrates the great complexity and diversity of the work of God in the world.

All of this communicates in ever-new ways to the forces of evil that they have lost, that their days are numbered. In a very real sense all of Ephesians thus far has evidenced the diverse abundance of God's wisdom—predestination, redemption, revelation, grace and mercy, and the unity of all peoples of the world in the church. God is the source of all of this, and Paul and the church are the means by which the mission is acted out and the gospel proclaimed both to the world and to the demonic forces.

Many believe that the "rulers and authorities" are composed of both good and bad angels, but Paul is interested here only in the forces of evil, who are focused on doing harm to the cause of God and Christ in this world. When Satan entered Judas and led Christ to the cross, he may have thought this was a great victory (though he undoubtedly knew Isaiah 52-53 as well as we do), but Colossians 2:15 tells us that at the very moment of his death Christ disarmed the evil powers and led them in his victory procession. The church participates in that victory every day through its mission to the world and by believers living holy lives.

*The dimensions of the mission made known in the church (3:11-12)*

Verse 11 begins with *kata* ("according to"), indicating that what follows presents the basis of the revelation of the mystery to the world, the church, and the demonic forces in verses 8-10.

Behind the hiddenness of the mystery, its revelation in Christ, and its unfolding through the mission of the church is "the eternal purpose that he accomplished in Christ Jesus our Lord." The critical point is that at every level it was God who conceived it, executed it, and guided its outworking in salvation history.

Note the development of Paul's thought in verses 10-11. The church through its triumphant mission makes known God's wisdom to the cosmic powers, and the unfolding wisdom of God is completely in accordance with his eternal purpose in creating this world and producing his salvation in it. The term for "purpose" (*prothesis*) is the same as in 1:11, where it was used of the divine plan that is the basis of our predestination. This could be translated as God's "planned purpose" that lay behind the coming of Christ, as well as the salvation that has resulted from it. That purpose is eternal; every part of God's plan—from creation to the new creation in Christ to the final creation of the new heavens and new earth—is encompassed in it.

As throughout the letter, this has all taken place "in Christ"— in his incarnation, death, and resurrection. All of this was achieved through the central event of history, the advent and actions of Christ. Paul uses our Lord's full title, "Christ Jesus our Lord," and both parts are emphasized. *Tō Christō*, including the definite article *tō* ("the"), stressing Jesus' messianic office, is placed first for emphasis. It is King Jesus, the royal Messiah, who has taken sovereign control of salvation history and redeemed sinful humanity from certain death. At the same time his lordship is stressed, as it often is in Ephesians (twenty-six times). The two titles work together to bring out Christ's absolute victory over death and the hostile powers as he brings God's salvation into reality.

When the people of God experience the victory and power of the sovereign Christ, we have direct access to God (3:12). There are two ways this access is mediated to us. We experience it first "in him," as we have seen throughout this letter. Our union with Christ produces everything we have of eternal value. Second, this access comes to us "through faith in him." Some have taken this as subjective, meaning "through his [Jesus'] faithfulness," referring to Jesus' faithfulness in carrying out God's plan. While possible, it is more likely, in light of the influence of 2:8-9 (saved by grace through faith), that our faith in him makes possible our access to God.

Christ's salvific actions and our faith result in an approach to God characterized by a freedom and confidence that would otherwise be impossible. The Greek, literally, is "freedom and access with confidence" (NIV "approach" = "have access"). In 2:18 we are told that "through him we both have access to the Father by one Spirit." That trinitarian thrust is implicit here. The first two terms form a hendiadys (two words that, taken together, convey a single meaning, like "nice and warm"). Together they mean "free access," and through this combined freedom, access, and confidence we now have boldness or confidence to enter freely into the presence of God. Believers can approach God confidently and at any time they wish in worship and prayer. Since our sins are forgiven and we have been made right with God through Christ, nothing prevents our access. That original saving faith (2:8-9) has now become an ongoing trust that we are indeed the children of God, with full access to our Father.

## CONCLUSION: AN ADMONITION NOT TO BE DISCOURAGED (3:13)

The mention of Paul's suffering here brackets this section, along with verse 1, where he calls himself "the prisoner of Christ." Paul's own suffering prompts him to think of what the Christians in the province of Asia are going through for Christ. There was indeed intense persecution, as seen in 1 Peter and, reflecting the situation thirty years later, in Revelation; both these letters were written to churches in the area. Paul's point throughout this section is that his and their suffering is more than worthwhile, since through them the gospel is being proclaimed and the mystery of Christ being worked out in the growth of the church. All of this takes place in the midst of, and partly because of, all they are going through. Paul has never minded afflictions as long as they are serving the cause of Christ (see Rom 8:31–39; 2 Cor 12:21–29).

The theme of 1 Peter can be summed up as "Suffering is the path to glory."[9] That is the theme of this verse as well. Paul had by this time been suffering imprisonment for about four years. He had been arrested in Jerusalem (Acts 21:27–36), was taken to Caesarea after the Jews threatened his life (Acts 23:23–35), and was incarcerated there for two years (Acts 24:27) before being sent to Rome. There he stayed in a rented home for which he himself paid, though he was chained to Roman guards (Acts 28:20, 30). He had freedom and space in his apartment to entertain visitors (Acts 28:17, 23) but was on trial for his life before Nero. Even two years into his imprisonment he did not know whether he would live or die, though he expected that God would spare him for his ministry's sake (Phil 1:19–26). Still, Paul rejoiced because God was using his imprisonment to advance the gospel (Phil 1:12–14). Could we handle all of this— four plus years on trial for our life, with an entire nation ostensibly seeking our death? From this perspective our own difficulties suddenly don't seem so arduous!

Therefore, Paul admonishes the Ephesians not to be discouraged at all the suffering he is enduring. There were certainly grounds for despair after four years, with about another year to go—Ephesians was probably written a year or so into the Roman imprisonment.[10] Most of them likely saw his problems as emblematic of their own, with the Roman world turning progressively against them.

In this light Paul wanted to encourage the Ephesians. He writes that his sufferings are "for you" and will be "your glory." Every step of Paul's sufferings came about as a result of his bold ministry. His work with Gentiles, such as those addressed in this letter, was especially despised by the Jews,

---

9. 1 Pet 1:11; 4:14; 5:1, 4, 10.
10. See "Date" in the introduction.

as seen in Acts 22:21-22. There Paul defended himself, retelling on the steps of the temple the story of his conversion and call to ministry. His Jewish audience listened quietly—until he related how God had called him to minister to the Gentiles, after which they erupted, "Rid the earth of him! He isn't fit to live!" His imprisonments in Caesarea and Rome were the result of that animosity.

There is another idea in the background that sheds light on Paul's connection between his present sufferings and future glory: the doctrine of the "messianic woes." This is the view, found in a few New Testament passages, that God has established a certain amount of suffering for his messianic community to endure. When that quota has been reached, Christ will return, and the end of this world will arrive. Two other passages help us understand this. In Revelation 6:9-11 the martyrs are calling out to God for vindication, and God asks them to "wait a little longer, until the full number of … their brothers and sisters [have been] killed." This seems to suggest that God has preordained the number of martyrs he will allow. In Colossians 1:24 Paul defines his suffering as filling "up in my flesh what is still lacking in regard to Christ's afflictions"—that amount of suffering with Christ that God has allotted. So Paul is saying here that his suffering for the Ephesians will end in the glory that he and they will share at the return of Christ, and that it is in fact hastening that glorious end (2 Cor 4:17; 2 Tim 1:10).

This awesome description of the way God has revealed his mystery through the ministry of Paul and the church has important ramifications for us today. As we continue to live out the wondrous riches of God's mysterious plan for a new, united people of God, we also experience his power and grace through a renewed sense of Paul's universal mission to the world. A church that is concerned only for its "Jerusalem" and not for the "uttermost parts of the earth" (Acts 1:8) is missing out on the full blessings and purpose God has for it. The truth of Ephesians 3:10 is so important: when we are part of the great mission of God to the world, we demonstrate his wisdom to the demonic powers and show them that they are doomed. Our victory in Christ is a victory over the satanic hordes, and this encompasses both our salvation and our mission to the lost. It is seen in the new life we have and the new unity the worldwide church can find in Christ. There can be no greater witness in this world than in the "one new humanity" (2:15) of the church, where every race and ethnic group achieves love, peace, and togetherness!

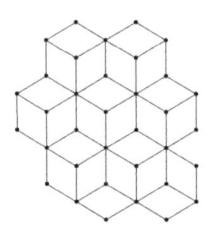

# A PRAYER REQUEST FOR POWER AND LOVE

## (3:14–21)

Paul began a prayer in verse 1 but got caught up in his desire to explain the place of God's mystery to his readers. He returns to that prayer now. This ends the doctrinal portion of this letter (1:3–3:21), which he frames with two prayers for insight and spiritual strength, in 1:15–19 and 3:14–21. Chapters 1–3 centered on the unity of Jew and Gentile in the church as a "new humanity." Chapters 4–6 center on the new life of the church in all its unity and diversity.

The prayer in chapter 1 centered on Paul's request that God would give the Ephesians wisdom to understand his great power and find the hope that realization will bring. Here Paul prays that God will pour his strength into them so they might experience the indwelling presence of Christ and be rooted in him. The prayer provides a fitting conclusion to the first half of the book and leads into the rest of the material, for that influx of divine power is what they will need to live for God in a sin-filled world.

## PAUL SOLEMNLY ADDRESSES THE FATHER (3:14–15)

Paul repeats the opening of 3:1, where he had originally intended to begin his prayer. "For this reason" now looks back especially to 3:2–13 and his explanation of the church's role in the divine mystery that has been revealed: the reality of Jew and Gentile in a united, new covenant people, the church. This remarkable reality has been made possible by the reconciling work of Christ on the cross (2:1–10). This reality was also the theme of 2:11–22, so this passage is a prayer for the church to find God's strength to complete the mission to the world described in chapters 1–3.

To provide the strength necessary for such a high calling, Paul calls on the Father of all creation. He begins with "I kneel" or "I bow the knee," showing his humility and complete dependence upon the high and holy God. The Jewish people in prayer sometimes stood with hands outstretched, sometimes knelt, and sometimes prostrated themselves before God. Kneeling demonstrated total submission to God and reverence before him.[1] Paul here addresses God as Father, likely with an emphasis on God as Abba (Aramaic term for "father"; Mark 14:36; Rom 8:15; Gal 4:6), reflecting his intimate love and care for his children.

This becomes a solemn invocation when Paul addresses the Father as the One "from whom every family in heaven and earth derives its name" (3:15). There is a play on words between "father" (patēr) and "family" (patria); in the same way fathers have authority over their family, the heavenly Father has sovereignty and power over every aspect of creation. Adam's naming the animals in the garden of Eden (Gen 2:19–20) signified his authority over the animal world and his responsibility to take care of them. God as Creator has supremacy over his creation. The God who answers prayer is not only the compassionate Father but also the Creator God:

> Lift up your eyes and look to the heavens:
>     Who created all these?
> He who brings out the starry host one by one
>     and calls forth each of them by name.

---

1. See Ps 95:6; Isa 45:23; Luke 22:41; Acts 9:40; Phil 2:10.

Because of his great power and mighty strength,
   not one of them is missing. (Isa 40:26)

What are the "families in heaven" to whom Paul refers? There is
general agreement that these are the orders of angels. The Bible
doesn't tell us a great deal about the hierarchy and classifica-
tions of angels. Archangels seem to be the highest order, but we
don't know much about the cherubim that guarded the garden
in Genesis 3:24 and held up the throne of God above the ark in
Exodus 25:18–22 or about the seraphim above the throne of God
in Isaiah 6:2, 6. These terms seem to signify powerful kinds of
angels that are attendants of the heavenly court. There also
seems to be a heavenly council of angels who have some judicial
functions (Job 1–2; Rev 4:4). At any rate, the point here is that God
has named all creatures and remains sovereign over his creation.

## PAUL PRAYS FOR THE EPHESIAN CHRISTIANS (3:16–19)

This builds on the prayer of 1:17–19, in which Paul asked God
to give the Ephesians wisdom to understand his great power.
Now Paul asks God to strengthen them by pouring his power
into them. Both the knowledge and the power would come to
them through the Spirit (1:17; 3:16). This strength comes from
"his glorious riches," or perhaps better "the riches of his glory."
God's glory is a primary aspect of his being, referring to his
heavenly splendor, his omnipotence, and the riches of heaven
he has at his disposal. As Almighty God, he provides for his
people incredible resources, keeping them "by the power of
God" (1 Pet 1:5). God lavishes his riches on them (Eph 1:7–8). This
prayer is similar to that of Colossians 1:11, where Paul asks that
his readers be "strengthened with all power according to his
glorious might."

### PRAYER FOR STRENGTH AND THE INDWELLING
### PRESENCE OF CHRIST (3:16–17)

The prayer asks that God would "strengthen you with power,"
using two terms that signify God's might poured into the Ephe-

sian believers. This influx of power will afford them strength and courage to face their increasing problems, as throughout Scripture (for example, Ps 105:4; 1 Cor 16:13; Eph 6:10). This gift of strength comes to them "through his Spirit," who is the channel of the power that fills believers. In the New Testament the Spirit is the agent of power both to us (Acts 1:8) and to Jesus in his exaltation (Rom 1:4). This infusion of strength leads to powerful preaching (1 Cor 2:4), proclamation of the gospel (1 Thess 1:5), deeper knowledge (Eph 1:17–19), and miracles (Rom 15:19). Here it grants us power to live the Christian life.

The sphere in which this power operates is the "inner being," the inner workings of the mind and heart. This internal reality determines the course of our lives and our actions. It needs constant renewal and strength from the Spirit, as in 1:17, where Paul asks for wisdom "to know him better," and in 1:18, where he asks for inner enlightenment to understand the hope that guides us. In 2 Corinthians 4:16 Paul contrasts the aging of our outward bodies with this inward renewal of our hearts (see also Col 3:10; Eph 4:24). On an outward level we move inexorably toward decay and death, but inwardly in the Spirit we become, as it were, younger and younger, stronger and stronger.

There are two different understandings of 3:17a. Some versions make this a part of the prayer itself ("that you may be strengthened ... and that Christ may dwell in your hearts," as in NRSV, KJV). However, since infinitives (literally, "Christ to dwell") ordinarily indicate purpose, such an interpretation is better here. The purpose (v. 17a) is "that Christ may dwell in your hearts through faith." The Spirit strengthens us spiritually "so that" we may experience the indwelling presence of Christ. "In your hearts" means the same as "in your inner being" at the end of verse 16. Both refer to the inner spiritual life of the believer.

At first glance Paul's asking Christ to dwell in the hearts of the Ephesians may seem strange, since Christ comes into the heart of every believer at conversion. Paul's request here is similar to "be filled with the Spirit" in 5:18. How can Christ take up residence and the Spirit fill Christians when they are already "in Christ" and in the Spirit? The key is that Paul is referring not to the initial indwelling but to the continuing Christian life. Paul has in mind the process of spiritual growth, so his prayer here is that each of the readers might experience more and more of Christ's indwelling presence and the increased power this produces. When our thought life is continually strengthened with the presence of Christ and the Spirit, spiritual growth will be the natural result.

This growth can take place only "through faith." Faith as surrender to the triune God and a growing dependence upon him are the results of the saving faith of 2:8-9, as we saw above in 3:12 ("through faith in him we may approach God"). It is our ongoing trust in him that produces the stronger Christian life. An increased faith in God and Christ leads to greater and greater internal power, and this allows us to be continually renewed and to grow day by day in the Spirit.

The syntax of the next clause, "rooted and established in love," is difficult. It comes before the *hina* ("that") translated in the NIV as "I pray that," so it is separate from the second prayer passage. Some translations (NIV, KJV, NASB, NET) take it as part of this second prayer statement; others as a separate prayer ("that Christ will live in your hearts ... that your life will be strong," NCV); others as part of the first prayer-wish ("that Christ may dwell ... as you are being rooted," NRSV); and still others as a separate, independent statement ("That Christ will make his home. ... Your roots will grow," NLT).

The problem with the more common first interpretation is that subordinate clauses in Paul's writings hardly ever come before the "I pray that." It is probably better to take this as part of the first prayer (the third option), specifying the result of Christ's indwelling. The import of verse 17 would then be: "so that Christ may dwell in your hearts through faith, with the result that you are rooted and grounded in love."

Some wonder whether Paul may be thinking specifically of God or of Christ as the One whose love roots and establishes us.

That is a false dichotomy. The Triune Godhead is likely in Paul's mind; all three members of the Trinity are performing the action here. The perfect tense of the verbs emphasizes that our rooting and grounding are the result of our being established in the Godhead. Paul here combines agricultural (rooted) and architectural (grounded) metaphors to stress the same idea.

This provides an overall image that makes this passage memorable: the church consists of a family (the people of God) living in a sacred structure (the church as a house and a temple) where Christ dwells in and with us. At our home we have a landscaped yard (rooted) and a firmly anchored house (grounded). The love that roots and grounds us is the love of the Godhead more than it is the love of church members for each other. It is divine love that anchors us in the church. All of this calls to mind Christ's brief yet wonderful parable about the wise man who built his house "with its foundation on the rock" (Matt 7:24–27).

### Prayer for a Deeper Grasp of God's Power and Love (3:18–19a)

In the first part of his prayer Paul asked God to strengthen the Ephesians through the Spirit and the indwelling Christ. In this second part he specifies the purpose of that divine strength— so that they will "grasp how wide and long and high and deep is the love of Christ." The request of verses 16–17 dealt with the power to act; now Paul turns to the power to comprehend truth. He asks that God empower his readers to understand spiritual realities, specifically the incredible depth of the love of Christ.

The verb "grasp" (*katalambanō*) is a military term used for attaining and capturing a goal. It refers to the complex process of overcoming obstacles to reach an objective and achieve victory. There is a four-dimensional objective Paul wants the Ephesians to grasp. The four dimensions function together to describe a single attribute of God that is quite ambiguous. They could refer to: (1) the incredible power of God, which would be in keeping with 1:18–20, as well as this context; (2) the multifaceted wisdom of God (3:10), so strongly emphasized in Ephesians and Colossians[2] and the source of the revelation of the mysteries; (3) the love of Christ (and of God), as in Romans 8:39 ("neither height nor depth ... will be able to separate us from the love of God that is in Christ"); and/or (4) the mystery as God's plan of salvation, which would fit the emphasis in 3:2, 9 on Paul's stewardship of the mystery of God's plan.[3]

All of these explanations are viable, but none is ultimately verifiable. The text does mention divine love, as in option three, but Paul actually separates the four dimensions from love as two separate points. In the Greek there are two concepts to grasp, not one (as in the NIV). This verse literally says "to grasp what is the width and length and height and depth, and to know the love of Christ."

Perhaps it is best to see all four of these dimensions as summing up this chapter. If this is the case they may be said to refer to a combination of the last three possibilities—the revealing of the mystery as a result of the love and wisdom of God. Paul is then asking for the multidimensional plan of God to work itself out in the church and the world, manifesting God's wisdom and Christ's love as one person after another is converted to Christ.

Through the outworking of this plan believers come to "know the love of Christ" as it manifests itself in the victorious work of the church. Paul's point is that believers need to attain a deeper and fuller recognition of all that the Triune Godhead has done for us. This knowledge produces a God-awareness that results in a renewed dedication to a deeper walk with Christ. Knowing the love of Christ means that we become increasingly aware of its wondrous depths, acknowledging and appreciating it as the love that led him to become incarnate and die on the

---

2. Eph 1:8, 17; 3:10; Col 1:9, 28; 2:3, 23; 3:16; 4:5.

3. Other interpretations have been suggested from time to time; these include the multidimensional temple, the church (Eph 2:19–22), or the new Jerusalem as a heavenly inheritance (described as a cube in Rev 21:15–17). These have failed to gain much support in recent times.

cross so that our sins could be forgiven and we could become the children of God and joint-heirs with him. That level of multidimensional love is more than we can ever comprehend— we will spend our lifetime probing those depths! Paul adds that these believers should explore the recesses of that boundless love "together with all the saints." Paul wants these Christians in the Roman province of Asia to realize that they are part of the universal church. These truths are difficult to understand, and Paul wants us to realize the communal nature of all of this— our need to discuss with each other the meaning of these profound truths and to remind one another of their importance.

This leads Paul to add another nuance: "to know this love that surpasses knowledge" (3:19a). This apparent contradiction doesn't imply that we cannot know Christ's love, but only that we can never *fully* grasp it. As soon as we begin to contemplate the love of Christ, we discover that it is far too deep for our human minds to wrap themselves around. Divine love (1:4; 2:4; 5:2, 25; 6:23) is too great, too "wide and long and high and deep" for our finite knowledge to begin to appreciate. Paul's point is that we must continue to expand our understanding and our experience (true knowledge includes experience) so that we may more deeply live out that love every day of our earthly existence. The love of the Godhead will never leave us (Rom 8:35–39), and this allows us to probe it ever more fully as we grow in him. Its infinite depth will always elude us, but we will never stop growing as we explore it more and more deeply!

## Prayer That We Might be Filled With the Fullness of God (3:19b)

This third request, "that you may be filled to the measure of all the fullness of God," summarizes the others in this prayer, for the fullness of God includes the infusion both of divine power and of divine love. This request actually encompasses all of chapter 3, including God's plan and the revelation of the mystery. Paul explored this fullness in Colossians 1:19; 2:9 (all God's fullness dwelling in Christ); there it refers to the "allness" of

God in his trinitarian splendor and richness—to everything that God is, Christ is, and the Spirit is. God's fullness was made visible in Christ. Moses could not look upon the face of God and live, but the disciples gazed into the countenance of God in Christ and basked in his glory.

In a very real sense being filled with God's fullness is a reference to our being indwelt by the Holy Spirit, who is the presence of God living with us and within us (John 14:17). Moreover, since we experience this fullness "in Christ" (Col 2:10), this prayer-wish is mediated to us by the Triune Godhead. The fullness of God fills us both through the Spirit taking up residence within us and by Christ himself indwelling us (John 14:23; Eph 3:17). This is the meaning of spiritual growth—it is a process by which the fullness of the Godhead burrows deeper and deeper into our lives as we yield ourselves ever more fully to his presence and power.

## PAUL CONCLUDES THIS PRAYER
## WITH A DOXOLOGY (3:20–21)

Paul concludes not just his prayer but the first half of the letter with this magnificent doxology. It culminates chapters 1–3, celebrating the God who has loved us enough to send his Son as the sacrifice for sin so that sins can be forgiven and sinners saved. He has not only brought redemption but has also united a fractured humanity. He has broken down the walls of hostility between Jew and Gentile and created a new humanity in Christ (2:14, 15). This is proof positive that we worship a God who "is able to do immeasurably more than all we ask or imagine."

### PRAISING THE GOD WHO DOES MORE THAN
### WE CAN IMAGINE (3:20)

This doxology also culminates 3:14–19, as it centers on God's power to accomplish miraculous things. The verb rendered "is able" is *dynamai*, which often means simply "can do" something but here carries the sense of "has the power to" and celebrates

God's mighty work in our lives (as in vv. 16, 18). The addition of "his power that is at work" later in this verse shows this to be the key theme of the doxology. The meaning is not "He can do whatever, if he wishes" but rather, "Our omnipotent God has the power to do amazing things for us." There is no limit to what Almighty God can accomplish. Paul can't find the words to describe all that God is doing for his people and can only add "more than all we ask or imagine." It is impossible for the human mind to think deeply enough to encompass the reality of all that God can do.

I have often said the following in discussions about heaven: "Take all the biblical portraits, use your imagination to think about the greatest situation you can possibly imagine, then multiply it a million times; and that is still inadequate to describe how wonderful it will be." That is what Paul is saying here. Human thought cannot comprehend the extent of God's power—the same mighty power that keeps us (1 Pet 1:5).

The term behind "immeasurably more" (*hyperekperissou*) is a rare compound with two prepositional prefixes (*hyper,* "above," and *ek,* "out of"). These prepositions have perfective force, meaning a superlative emphasis ("the most possible"). This force gives this word the sense of "exceedingly beyond the greatest abundance," or, as several have translated, "infinitely more than, beyond all measure." There is no task too great for God, yet we regularly underestimate what he can accomplish in our lives. The title of J. B. Phillips's classic work is true of all of us: *Your God Is Too Small.*

The basis of God's omnipotent action is "his power that is at work within us." There are two terms for God's strength here, and together they could be translated "his power that works powerfully." The verb is *energeō,* and the English equivalent is apt: "the God who is the true 'energizer.'" This mighty work was displayed in his raising Jesus from the dead (1:19–20), empowering the church's mission to the world, proclaiming the reconciling work of Jesus (2:16), and uniting hostile peoples so as to produce a new humanity never before thought possible

(vv. 13–15). This same world-changing power is now at work within us.

## Praising the God Who Deserves Eternal Glory (3:21)

The God who exercises his omnipotent strength to empower us in our spirit and life deserves all the praise we can give him. Meditating on this is the heart of worship, so we can see verse 21 as the natural response to verse 20. God's people have been given lavish gifts from God (1:3, 8), and it is natural in return for us to give God glory. In other New Testament doxologies it is Christ who glorifies the Father (Rom 16:27; 1 Pet 4:11), but since the church has been central in Ephesians 2 and 3 it is fitting that the church be added here as an instrument for glorifying God. God is to be glorified "in the church and in Christ Jesus." "Glory" here refers to the recognition of God's majesty, splendor, and worthiness to be worshipped by the saints. It is not that God needs us to glorify him; it is that we desperately need to acknowledge and celebrate his glory. We are the bride of Christ, and there can be no true marriage without our regularly telling our spouse that we love them.

This is not simply saying that the church and Christ are separately praising God. Rather, the people of God are enabled to glorify God through being "in Christ Jesus." There are two spheres from within which this praise emanates: the united church in Christ proclaims God's "manifold wisdom" to the cosmic powers (3:10) and throughout the world (v. 8), and the church, which is a "new creation" of Christ, gives glory to God (2:15-16). This takes place both in the proclamation of the gospel and in individual and corporate worship, all of it in a church that is incorporated into Christ, using the spiritual blessings it has received "in Christ" (1:3) "for the praise of his glory" (v. 12). This worship will be eternal, "throughout all generations, forever and ever." We could take this as meaning "for the rest of human history and throughout our eternal future in heaven." "Forever and ever" is the most extensive descriptor of eternity in the New Testament—Paul is emphatic about the magnitude and duration of this praise. Praise is both a defining character-istic of our own future life with God and the aspect of our eter-nal destiny most frequently discussed in the New Testament. It is natural for the bride of God (Israel) and of Christ (the church) to be filled with joy and gratitude and to return to him some measure of the love that he has shown us. The "Amen" that closes this doxology is both a prayer-wish and a solemn state-ment of agreement ("May it be so"), used to close major sections or books of psalms[4] and to conclude worship.[5] So too here, as all the readers are asked to join in the "Amen" that concludes this prayer and the first half of the letter.

In this section of Ephesians we have been at the heart of what it means to be a Christian. Prayer and worship are at the apex of the life of every believer. Moreover, that for which Paul is praying in verses 17–19—strength and the fullness of God through the indwelling presence of Christ—should summa-rize all of our hopes and desires as we seek to serve the Triune Godhead. We cannot live the Christian life in an evil world in our own strength. However, as the doxology reminds us, we have an omnipotent God who works tirelessly and with greater power than we can ever know to fill us with the strength to live victoriously in this sinful world. We do not have to go it alone; all we need to do is surrender and rely entirely on him, and he will infuse us with a strength beyond anything we could ever imagine.

---

4. Pss 41:13; 72:19; 89:52; 106:48; 150:6.
5. 1 Chr 16:36; Neh 8:6; 2 Cor 1:20; Rev 7:12.

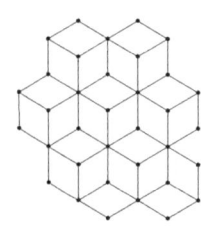

# UNITY AND DIVERSITY
# IN THE CHURCH
(4:1-6)

Now Paul turns to the ethical exhortation of his letter. This section comprises chapters 4–6 and includes a series of challenges for his readers to live the Christian life God's way. This opening section is brilliantly conceived, stressing first that the unity of the church reflects the unity of the Godhead (4:1-6) and then that this unity must be lived out in diversity, with every member of the body taking their place and working together to enable the church to grow (vv. 7–16). As stated in Ephesians 2:11–18, the conflict among cultures in the church is insufficient to fracture it, for as each believer is united with Christ they are also united with each other. Christ's reconciliation via the cross has broken down racial and ethnic divisions, and all the diverse peoples form a new humanity in Christ.

## THE BASIS OF THE CHALLENGE IS A
## LIFE WORTHY OF THE CALL (4:1)

Paul begins this second half of the letter with *oun* ("then" or "therefore"), looking back to the first half. On the basis of the great Christian truths regarding sin and salvation, as well as the mystery of the unity of Jew and Gentile in the church, Paul is now drawing conclusions regarding the kind of life God wants his new people to live. Chapter 4 begins with language similar to what Paul used in 3:1, in effect saying "I, a prisoner in the Lord, exhort you." In the earlier passage Paul called himself "the prisoner *of* Christ Jesus," while here he is "a prisoner *for* (in some translations *in*) the Lord," stressing his unity with Christ. We could almost define Ephesians as being the "in Christ" letter, since the phrase appears so often. As in 3:1 the basic message is that while Paul may be incarcerated by Rome, he has actually been captured by the Lord. Christ, not Rome, is truly in charge, and Paul belongs to him and has been incorporated into him. He is also stressing the cost of discipleship, using his own trials (pun intended) as the model.

The verb in this verse defines this section, which consists of a series of ethical and spiritual exhortations. Several versions render it as "urge" or "appeal," but Paul is not pleading with his readers. Rather, he is exhorting them to a deeper Christian walk. In general Paul tends to use the language of exhortation rather than of command. His purpose is to instruct and build up his readers rather than to demand blind obedience (2 Cor 10:8).

Paul here admonishes the Ephesians "to live a life worthy of the calling you have received." Christian belief comes before Christian living. The mindset must be changed before one's conduct can follow suit. Many of Paul's letters have a similar format, with right belief (Rom 1–11; Col 1–2; Eph 1–3) producing right living (Rom 12–16; Col 3–4; Eph 4–6). "Live a life worthy" is literally "walk worthily," which sums up every aspect of Christian behavior. "Walk" is used throughout the Old and New Testaments to describe the conduct of God's people, and it is virtually the title for this entire section (4:1–5:20). New Testament ethics centers on living a worthy life before God.

In Revelation 4:11 and 5:12 God and Christ are said to be worthy of worship (as opposed to Caesar, who is not). Here Paul enjoins us to imitate the Godhead and live a life deserving not only of God and Christ, whose children we are, but of the very calling we have received from them. The Greek reads "the calling to which you were called," stressing the critical nature of our call. In Paul's letters the call is to salvation; Paul borrows the concept of predestination and choosing emphasized in Ephesians 1:4-6, 11. The call comes from the "hound of heaven" depicted in Francis Thompson's famous poem—the One who has "called you out of darkness into his wonderful light" (1 Pet 2:9). As a result we have been adopted into God's family and been made citizens of heaven. In light of this incredible new reality we must live lives appropriate to our new calling.

## FOUR SETS OF QUALITIES PRODUCE UNITY (4:2-3)

These two verses expand on verse 1, telling us how to live a life worthy of God's calling. The emphasis is on those Christian attributes that aid community. Ephesians is the premiere New Testament document dealing with ecclesiology (the doctrine of the church), so it is fitting that the qualities in these verses are corporate in nature—dealing with relationships within the church. There is little place in the Bible for the individualism that so often marks American culture. Every believer is a member of the body, the church, and we are meant to live in community as a family.[1] The first three qualities Paul lists (humble, gentle, and patient) appear in the same order in Colossians 3:12, where they serve the same purpose of enhancing the corporate life of the church. Paul wants four sets of qualities to define community life in the church:

(1) Humility and gentleness. There is no place among Christ's followers for pride. Christ exemplified servant leadership, demanding the same of his followers (Mark 9:35; 10:41-45). Paul emphasizes the importance of this calling by stating that the Ephesians should live with "*all* humility and gentleness," making this a supreme mandate and connecting the two words into a single idea. This went against Greco-Roman practices of the day, which exemplified the belief that "meekness is weakness"

---

1. See Eph 1:23; 2:16; 4:12, 16; 5:23.

and that the highest qualities are proven by self-serving success (much as in "the American way"). Jesus completely reversed this pagan practice, making humility one of the most important of the virtues in the eyes of God. To be honest, I have witnessed a lack of humility in all too many Christian leaders. We must come to realize that pride is one of the truly deadly sins in the eyes of God; it is only when we acknowledge this that we can be honest with ourselves regarding the true level of our humility.

The Bible regularly castigates arrogance and self-centeredness.[2] Perhaps the clearest expression of this is Philippians 2:3-4: "Do nothing out of selfish ambition or vain conceit. Rather, in humility value others above yourselves, not looking to your own interests but each of you to the interests of the others." Humility demands a life directed toward others rather than toward self-aggrandizement. The other word Paul uses, "gentleness," describes the way in which a life of humility treats others: with kindness and concern. This quality too is highly prized in Scripture.[3] The Greek word *praütēs* here is often translated "humble" or even "the poor" (who had to throw themselves under God's care). And gentleness, a "fruit of the Spirit" (Gal 5:22-23), is certainly a prime attitude we need to adopt when admonishing another person (Gal 6:1; 2 Tim 2:25).

(2) Patience. The Greek term (*makrothymia*) literally means "a long time before one gets angry." Connoting a person with a long fuse, it is often translated "long-suffering" and describes the manner in which God puts up with sinful humanity. Indeed, he is described as being "slow to anger" (Exod 34:6; Neh 9:17; Ps 145:8; Joel 2:13; Jas 1:19) and "patient" (Rom 2:4; 2 Pet 3:9). In the New Testament the need for patience in church relationships is frequently discussed as a key virtue (2 Cor 6:6; Col 3:12). Paul tells the Thessalonians to "be patient with everyone"

---

2. Prov 11:2; 16:18; 18:12; Isa 2:9, 11; 66:2; Luke 1:51-53; Phil 2:9-11.
3. Pss 37:11; 147:6; 149:4; Isa 11:4; 29:19; Matt 5:5; 11:29; 1 Pet 3:4.

(1 Thess 5:14) and defines this quality as a core aspect of love (1 Cor 13:4).

(3) Bearing with one another in love. In one sense this further defines patience, describing how patience works itself out in our social interactions within the church. In another sense it defines how we are to "walk worthily" before God by extending and combining all of the attributes discussed thus far and thereby becoming a separate category. God's people exercise humility, gentleness, and patience by putting up with each other. The concept is related to endurance—specifically to how we are to tolerate each other's foibles and peccadilloes. For instance, Jesus, in his frustration at the disciples' inability to cast out a demon, exclaimed, "How long shall I put up with you?" (Mark 9:19). And Barnabas in Acts 15:37-39 not only put up with Mark's (likely) youthful rebellion but split up with Paul in order to take Mark back home to Cyprus and disciple him so that he might become the great Christian leader he would later prove to be.

Implicit in this forbearance is forgiveness, as in 4:32: "Be kind and compassionate to one another, forgiving each other, just as in Christ God forgave you." We as human beings will always face conflict in relationships. This will require us to stretch our minds to respect and even welcome the differences between ourselves and others. That will often mean overlooking those differences, while at other times it will demand that we forgive slights that have been directed against us (see Col 3:13). We are to do this "in love." Our experience of divine love provides the basis and model, and the result is our love for one another. Peter identifies love as a defining purpose of our very salvation. We must exercise it deeply, with all the energy we possess (1 Pet 1:22). Paul echoes love's importance—there can be no rapport or peace in a church without mutual, reciprocal love.

(4) Keeping the unity of the Spirit through the bond of peace. We now arrive at the heart of the matter, providing the connecting idea between the emphasis on the unity of Jew and Gentile in Christ from 2:11-22 and that on unity and diversity

within the church in 4:1–16. Paul begins with a strong admonition: "make every effort," meaning that the Ephesian believers need to work very hard, exercising diligence to accomplish the task. This is so important that it will require everything they've got.

The idea of "keeping" something implies guarding and preserving it. Paul's readers must maintain unity and peace in their churches at all costs. Through the phrase "unity of the Spirit" Paul is identifying the Spirit as the creative source; it is he who has produced this unity. In 2:18 Paul stated that Christ made access to God possible "by one Spirit," and here he picks up that thread. Unity is a trinitarian gift to God's people. The unity of the saints is critical to God's plan and exists as a primary result of Christ's reconciling work on the cross (Eph 2:11–22). When each of us is reconciled to God through Christ, we are of necessity also reconciled to one another. Paul's point here is that we have to work that out in our daily relationships and through a cooperative spirit within the church.

We can achieve this unity "through the bond of peace." Perhaps better than "through" here would be "in," with peace the sphere more than it is the means for achieving unity. Peace provides the matrix for achieving oneness in the church. It was central to 2:14–15, where Christ, "who is our peace," created "one new humanity ... thus making peace." The sequence begins in peace with God; only when that is in effect can we find peace within Christ's body. The new humanity, the new Israel, is a new community in which peace has replaced conflict and fractured relationships. The word "bond" (*syndesmos*) is reminiscent of Paul's description of himself as a "prisoner" (*desmios*) in 4:1. In the Spirit the saints are bound to each other with chains of love and peace.

## THE GOAL IS THE ONENESS OF THE CHURCH (4:4–6)

This section is trinitarian in that it contains three triads, each featuring a different member of the Trinity. The third and last triad begins with the seventh instance in verses 4–6 of "one," this time referring to God (seven in the Bible is the perfect number, here reflecting God's perfect plan). This order shows the importance of unity within the church. We do not achieve such accord easily, but neither do we work at it alone. The Triune Godhead enables us to find the strength to produce peace amongst ourselves. While not a formal creedal confession, this section does have the style of a creed, and it follows a poetic rhythm. These verses build on verse 3 ("keep the unity of the Spirit"), conveying that the church is meant to reflect the perfect unity of the Father, Son, and Spirit.

### THE SPIRIT: ONE BODY, ONE SPIRIT, ONE HOPE (4:4)

The first item focuses on the church as a whole. The "one body" refers to the unity of the church, the body of Christ, certainly one of the major emphases of this letter (along with Paul's exalted **Christology**).[4] The church as a local entity is actually part of "one new humanity" that is further identified as "one body" (2:15–16). The church's newness is defined via its oneness, in a sense a reversal of Babel in Christ's new creation. Each believer as a member of the body must use all her gifts in the service of the body, as we will see in 4:15–16, below.

This unity takes place because of the work of the "one Spirit." In Ephesians 2:18 we are told that access to the Father has been accomplished "by one Spirit," and there I noted Paul's background declaration in 1 Corinthians 12:13: "We were all baptized by one Spirit so as to form one body." Both in Corinthians and here the one Spirit is identified as the basis and foundation for the unity of the one church. As the Triune Godhead is One, so the church must be characterized by oneness.

Paul culminates the first triad with "just as you were called to one hope when you were called." Hope is the byproduct of the Spirit's enabling power as he brings unity to the church. As the Spirit is the basis of our unity, so our calling to Christ

---

4. Eph 1:23; 2:16; 4:15–16; 5:29–30. See also Rom 12:4–5; 1 Cor 12:12–20; Col 3:15.

is the basis of our hope. Frequently in Ephesians (for example, 1:4-5, 11; 4:1), Paul has stressed our chosen nature and calling. We did not choose God; he chose us and made us his children, giving us the Holy Spirit as the guarantee of our future inheritance (1:13-14) and the basis of our living hope (1 Pet 1:3-4). The Greek refers to "the one hope of your calling," meaning that our hope is the result of God calling us to himself (see also Eph 1:18). It is "one hope" because we all share the same hope and are meant to celebrate it together in unity. Our future hope in a final inheritance in heaven is anchored in the present reality of our calling and inclusion in the one body of Christ.

### THE LORD: ONE LORD, ONE FAITH, ONE BAPTISM (4:5)

Paul strongly stresses in Ephesians the lordship of Christ (mentioning it more than twenty times), and this touches on every issue of the letter. The emphasis on "one Lord" reminds us of the Shema (Hebrew for "hear") in Deuteronomy 6:4: "Hear, O Israel, the LORD our God, the LORD is one." Throughout the Old Testament "LORD" (often rendered in the English with small caps) is the title that translates God's covenant name, Yahweh. In the New Testament Jesus is Lord or "I AM" (see Exod 3:14; John 8:58). So this is first of all a statement of his exalted nature as Lord of the universe; it is also an implicit acknowledgment of his deity. In Ephesians the Lord is the source of all blessings (1:3), the object of our faith (v. 15), the basis of our unity and worship (2:21; 5:19-20), the content of God's eternal plan (3:11), the essence of God's will (5:10, 17), and the basis of all our relationships (vv. 21, 22; 6:1, 4, 8).

While a few interpreters think that "one faith" is subjective, referring to our personal trust in God and Christ, it is much better to go with the majority and see this as objective, referring to the Christian faith as a confessed set of beliefs and doctrines (see also Eph 4:13; Col 1:23; Gal 1:23; 1 Tim 3:9). Since the early church often had to deal with false teachers, the development of creedal traditions and a body of true doctrines was essential; otherwise the believers would have fallen prey to all kinds

of lies. This is vitally important in our day; there are far more
heresies rampant in our world than first-century Christians
could ever have dreamed of. The early church was united by
its common core of doctrines, and still today, though there are
many different denominations and groups, often separated by
differing theologies, those with a core of cardinal doctrines
like the Trinity, the deity of Christ, substitutionary atonement,
and others find a higher degree of unity in Christ. They can dif-
fer on the secondary issues (for example, predestination, charismatic gifts, the rapture, and the mode of baptism) yet remain
one on the central tenets of the faith.

"One baptism" most likely refers to water baptism, though
it could include Paul's idea of being "baptized into Christ" in
Galatians 3:27–28. Though both are included here, the emphasis is not so much on the rite of baptism as it is on its theological significance as symbolizing union with Christ in his death
and resurrection (Rom 6:1–3) and the unifying reality of being
"baptized by one Spirit so as to form one body" (1 Cor 12:13).
All the saints are united by their common experience of baptism and the incorporation into the body of Christ that it sig-
nifies. They have been made one with Christ and, through him,
with one another.

## THE FATHER: OF ALL, OVER ALL, THROUGH ALL (4:6)

Verse 6 sounds very much like a formal creed, beginning,
beginning as it does with "one God and Father of all." It is commonly thought that this verse, along with 1 Corinthians 8:6,[5]
represents a new Christian Shema modeled after Deuteronomy
6:4 (see above). It is likely, in fact, that Paul was thinking of the
Shema when he penned this verse in Ephesians. The greeting
in 1:2 comes "from God our Father," and the fatherhood of God

---

5. "Yet for us there is but one God, the Father, from whom all things came
and for whom we live; and there is but one Lord, Jesus Christ, through
whom all things came and for whom we live."

is mentioned eight times in this letter. Seeing God as Father emphasizes his loving care but also his sovereign authority.

The central term is "all," occurring four times in this verse alone. It is debated whether the word is masculine, referring to God's authority and compassion for all believers, or neuter, referring to his cosmic lordship over all of creation. Some ancient manuscripts have even added "us" or "you" to make it explicitly masculine (reflected in KJV, NKJV). There is general agreement of late, however, that it should be taken as neuter, referring to cosmic rule, as well as to concern for God's people. The emphasis in Ephesians on the "unity of all things" (1:10), Christ's headship over all things (vv. 22, 23), and God having creating all things (3:9) supports this view.

The three prepositional phrases here are similar to the doxology in Romans 11:36: "For from him and through him and for him are all things." There God is seen as the source, instrument, and goal of all creation. This verse is similar, looking to God the Father as the supreme Lord, the instrument, and the sphere within which his entire created order exists. He is the Creator who has named and is totally sovereign over "every family in heaven and on earth" (Eph 3:15); this affirms his transcendence ("over all"), his omnipotence ("through all"), and his omnipresence ("in all") in both heaven and earth.

The first six verses of chapter 4 make up a critical paragraph that serves as a transition between the two parts of this letter. They sum up the theme of unity from chapters 2–3 and at the same time provide the perspective for the issue of corporate care within the body of Christ in the chapters that follow. The unity of the church here is an outgrowth of the unity of the Godhead (much as in John 17:20–23). If the Father, Son, and Spirit are one, the church as Christ's body must project oneness as well. While the impetus is vertical, coming from the united Godhead, it must be worked out horizontally in the life of the church. This outworking demands lives of humility and patience.

This is an incredibly important point for our day. The church today is divided along denominational, ethnic, and even worship style lines. We are disobedient to God and a detriment to the evangelization of the world due to our disunity, and we must do all we can to break down these unbiblical barriers and learn to both cherish our differences and forge a deeper unity so we can fulfill our purpose in this world. The simple truth is that we need each other and individually have so much to offer with which to enrich one another. May we find that unity of which Paul is speaking here.

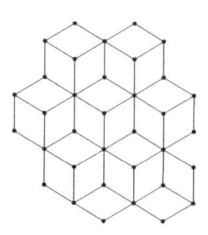

# UNITY THROUGH DIVERSITY
(4:7-16)

All of Paul's passages dealing with spiritual gifts and the body of Christ (for example, Rom 12:4-8; 1 Cor 12:12-31) emphasize the diversity of the church in the midst of its unity as one body. The body consists of many members, all of whom must function together in order for the body to grow. Each member discovers her role in the body by taking the grace-gifts Christ has given her and using them for the benefit of the body. The gifts bestowed in 4:7-8 enable the body to grow (vv. 15-16). Interestingly, the gifts referred to in 4:8 are not Christian ministries, as in 1 Corinthians 12, but Christian leaders (v. 11) who guide the church and help it to mature.

## THE GRACE OF CHRIST IS GIVEN
## TO EVERY MEMBER (4:7-10)

### CHRIST'S GRACE-GIFT GROUNDED IN PSALM 68:18 (4:7-8)

An important truth implicit in verse 7 is that God does not give gifts on the basis of race or social status. They are distributed equally to "each one of us," and the basis is "as Christ apportioned it" (literally, "the measure of the gift of Christ"). In other words diversity is grounded in unity, for the entire body is involved. In 1 Corinthians 12:11 it is the Spirit "who distributes them to each one, just as he determines," while here it is

Christ who is in sovereign control of the gifts. Paul describes them as grace-gifts; the very term for spiritual gift is *charisma* (Rom 12:6; 1 Cor 12:4), meaning "grace given" to a person.

The emphasis here is on the source of these graces: Christ. There is no haphazard, random distribution of gifts. Every gift is carefully chosen and apportioned according to the sovereign will of God. In our narcissistic world we too often are dissatisfied with what Christ has given us and want more. That is to deny God's grace and will for the sake of self. God gives us exactly what he wants us to have and what is best for us. It is our privilege to unquestioningly accept and use his gracious gifts. The joint ministry we have in the church is the result of the particular gifts each of us has received.

The emphasis on "each one" is important, for this means that no one is exempt from contributing to the church. Since in the average church only one third to half of the members are truly involved, this means that a majority are disobedient to the Lord. This is partly the fault of all of us who are leaders, for we too often fail to challenge our members enough and are willing to carry too much of the load ourselves. Delegation of ministry is essential to a growing church.

The doctrine of spiritual gifts is critical for the church today. As the body of Christ it is composed of many diverse members, and the Triune Godhead (God in Rom 12:3, the Spirit in 1 Cor 12:11, and Christ here) has sovereignly given each member appropriate spiritual gifts. Every believer must accept and be satisfied with their particular grace-gifts, develop them, and use them to enhance the church and build up those around them. We are to use our grace-gifts to serve, not to be served (Mark 10:45) or to enhance our status in the church and society. We are all called to service, and the church grows when all its members are using their God-given gifts for the glory of God, the ministry of the church, and the well-being of one another.

Paul now anchors this promise of grace-gifts (4:8) in a quote from Psalm 68:18. Old Testament quotes in the New Testament often include the context of the Old Testament passage, and that is certainly the case here. Psalm 68 pictures Yahweh as a Divine Warrior descending from Mount Sinai, striding across the earth winning victory after victory for his people, and then ascending Mount Zion surrounded by an entourage of the heavenly host in order to establish his throne room (temple) there. It is the prayer of the psalm that this power of God be exercised once again to deliver his people.

The first line of Psalm 68:18 pictures the Divine Warrior ascending the heights of Mount Zion. He has won the victory and now ascends to his newly established throne on Zion to receive the accolades of his grateful people. The second line summarizes the triumphs of the Divine Warrior over the enemies of Israel (Ps 68:1-2, 6, 12-14, 23, 30-31) when he "took many captives" from the opposing armies. These captured armies are pictured bound and marching behind the victory chariot of Yahweh as it proceeds up Mount Zion. The third line depicts the conquering Lord "receiving gifts" from a grateful Israel. In this psalm David provides a panoramic view of the entire history of Israel from the exodus to the establishment of the temple on Mount Zion. God the Divine Warrior is the Savior and redeemer of his people, the only One worthy of worship.

All these themes in the original psalm are part of Paul's message here in Ephesians 4:8, with Christ the Divine Warrior winning the victory and returning to his grateful people, the new Israel, to establish his throne among them. The first line pictures Christ ascending on high after winning his great battle on the cross to take his place at the right hand of God (Ps 110:1 in Eph 1:20-21) on his heavenly throne. The second line depicts Christ's great victory over death and the evil powers and alludes to Colossians 2:15: "having disarmed the powers and authorities, he made a public spectacle of them, triumphing over them by the cross." That picture fits closely the image here, as Christ "took many captives" (the demonic forces) in his train. This "binding of Satan" (see Mark 3:27) visualizes the evil powers bound and marching in defeat behind the victory chariot of Christ at his ascension.

But the picture of Psalm 68:18 has been changed here to that of Christ "giving gifts to his people." Why has Paul altered the psalm's portrayal, and what is his message? Several scholars believe that he is following a Jewish Targumic tradition. The Targums were Jewish paraphrases of the Old Testament in Aramaic, the language of the common people, so they could understand the Hebrew Old Testament. Targums on Psalm 68:18 read this as Moses ascending from Sinai to heaven to receive the Torah. What Moses took captive was the Torah, and then he returned to earth to give it to the Jewish people. According to this understanding Paul would now be seeing Christ as the greater Moses giving gifts to the new Israel, both in terms of the Holy Spirit at Pentecost and of the spiritual gifts here. The difficulty with this interpretation is that the Targums were written later than this (fourth century AD). Even if that tradition did go back to the time of Paul, it is an Aramaic tradition with little evidence of having been known in the **Hellenistic** Jewish world. So, while interesting, this is not the likely explanation here.

It is more likely that Paul himself made the wording change from "received gifts" to "gave gifts." This fits the movement in his thinking from "grace has been given" in verse 7 to "Christ himself gave" in verse 11. In Psalm 68 it is Yahweh who ascends to his newly established throne on Mount Zion to receive gifts from his people and their defeated enemies. Here it is Christ the Divine Warrior who ascends into heaven after defeating the cosmic enemies and then distributes his gifts to his delivered followers. The defeat of the hostile powers is central to Ephesians (1:20-22; 3:10; 6:10-20) and part of the imagery here. The switch to "gave gifts" is not a casual change. Paul is reading Psalm 68:18 in light of the whole of the psalm, which details the victories God gave Israel. Using Jewish exegesis, Paul is taking the gifts of Yahweh to the people of Israel in the psalm and applying it to the gifts of the ascended Christ to the people of the new Israel.

### CHRIST'S GRACE-GIFT GROUNDED IN HIS EXALTATION AS LORD OF ALL (4:9–10)

Paul now provides commentary on the meaning of Christ "ascending on high" in the psalm quote, looking at the chronology of events that led to Christ's exaltation. He begins with "What does 'he ascended' mean except that he also descended to the lower, earthly regions?" (NIV). The last part of the verse literally reads, "descended into the lower parts of the earth." This has led to a number of interpretations:

(1) The lower parts are the underworld, and this describes *descensus ad inferos*, or Jesus' "descent into Hades" at his death. This is paralleled by similar interpretations of Romans 10:6–7 ("descend into the deep") and 1 Peter 3:19 (Christ preaching to the spirits in prison) and has long been a popular view; it goes back to Tertullian and Jerome and is found in the Apostles' Creed. This view is indeed viable, for these Gentile Christians would have grown up with stories about the underworld. If we understand Hades to be the grave, it would refer in a poignant way to Christ's death. Yet it seems to be a strange way to speak of the death and burial of Jesus.

(2) This refers to Jesus' incarnation, seen as the descent into this world of the preexistent God-man. The "lower parts" then refer to the lower part of God's cosmos, the earth. This would fit Psalm 68, where Yahweh descended from Sinai to deliver his people and then ascended to Zion to rule over the redeemed nation. John 3:31 provides a close parallel: "No one has ascended into heaven ... except the one who descended from heaven." This then would be a reference to the glorified Christ as the One who descended to earth at his incarnation and later ascended to heaven at his resurrection. This is similar to the picture in Revelation 12:4–5, where the woman gives birth to the "male child" (incarnation), who is then snatched up to heaven (exaltation), thereby defeating the dragon. But like the first option, "lower parts" seems like a strange way to speak of the earth.

(3) This refers to Jesus after his death returning to earth via the Holy Spirit at Pentecost, which would fit the giving of gifts to the church. This would parallel the Targumic understanding of Psalm 68 noted above: Moses ascended to heaven, received the law, and then descended to earth to give it to Israel. Christ's actions were comparable in terms of his receiving and distribution of grace-gifts. However, this option is further from the imagery of the text than the previous two, for the Spirit and Pentecost are nowhere to be found in the context. While an interesting possibility, this interpretation is not as likely.

Deciding between the first two is difficult, for both make sense of the passage and stem from a viable use of Jewish background. When all is said and done, the incarnation view (option two) makes best sense of the passage. The descent to the "lower parts, namely the earth" is perfectly appropriate **apocalyptic** language conveying the important truth that the Christ, the preexistent Divine Warrior, descended to earth in his incarnation and then ascended to heaven, first defeating the cosmic powers and then distributing the tribute of his triumph, God's grace-gifts, to the church.

Regardless of how "lower parts" is understood, however, the emphasis in these verses is on Christ's ascent or exaltation. He ascended "higher than all the heavens," referring to the Jewish picture of three—or at times of seven—heavens (2 Cor 12:2). Christ is supreme over all creation, having "the name above every name" (Phil 2:9). With all the fullness of God dwelling in him, all things have been reconciled to him (Col 1:19-20), and he has been seated "far above all rule and authority" (Eph 1:21). All creation, including the demonic powers, is subject to his rule.

The purpose of Christ's exaltation is that he might "fill the whole universe"—building on 1:23, where the church is called "the fullness of him who fills everything in every way." This is not immanence, Christ filling the world with his presence, but transcendence, Christ exercising his rule and might over all things. In this age the rule of Christ is extended through the proclamation of the gospel and the conversion of the nations. At the **eschaton** (the end) he will be openly recognized as head over every aspect of his creation as he reigns forever and ever.

## GOD GIVES THE CHURCH LEADERS WHO HELP IT GROW (4:11-16)

Verse 7 discusses the doctrine of spiritual gifts in general. Here Paul narrows this down to one particular grace-gift: God supplying leaders who will enable the church to grow. This and 1 Corinthians 12:28 are the only places in the New Testament where *charisma* designates people rather than spiritual qualities or ministries (Corinthians uses both), and it provides an important perspective for our day. Gifted leaders are not just hired or appointed but are sovereignly bestowed, and the church should consider its staff and volunteer leaders to be gifts from God. Their purpose is not just to do the work of the Lord but to train and involve every member in that work. In other words, gifted leaders help all members to develop and use their gifts.

After he ascends to the highest heaven and defeats the cosmic powers, the Divine Warrior showers his redeemed people with gifts, distributing to them gifted leaders who can train them properly in spiritual warfare. There are five categories (as I will argue)—apostles, prophets, evangelists, pastors, and teachers. The list is not comprehensive, for deacons, coworkers, and perhaps elders/overseers (often synonymous with pastors) are not mentioned. Possibly these particular leaders receive mention here because they are all connected to the proclamation of the Word and the training of Christians for service.

### THE GIFTS GIVEN: THE LEADERS OF THE CHURCH (4:11)

The first two categories of leaders, apostles and prophets, are part of the list of gifts in 1 Corinthians 12:28 and designate the two primary offices of the first century church. In Ephesians 1:1 Paul called himself "an apostle of Christ Jesus," and in 2:20 apostles and (New Testament) prophets were labeled the "foundation" of the church—those who had led the church from the beginning. In Ephesians 3:5 apostles and prophets are presented as channels through whom the "mystery" had been revealed to the church. They were still functioning that way in the fourth decade (the 60s) of the church age. It is possible that the category of "apostles" here goes beyond the nucleus of the Twelve, along with Paul, Barnabas, and Apollos, to designate other gifted church leaders whom Christ had "sent" (the meaning of "apostle") to lead the church. The prophets were those like Agabus (Acts 11:27–28; 21:10) and others (Acts 13:1; 15:32; 21:9) who had been called to be vessels for particular critical messages from God for his people. Prophecy deals not just with future predictions but also with (perhaps more important) messages to or directives for the church. Paul was both an apostle and a prophet.

It has often been argued that these two offices ceased in the first century and have since been replaced by the others in this list. There is no evidence for the cessation of these offices in the New Testament. Some have interpreted 1 Corinthians 13:10 ("when the perfect is come, that which is in part will cease") this way, but that is a misinterpretation. The "perfect" there is the final age after Christ returns, not the completion of the canon or the apostolic age. There is ample evidence that prophecy and miracles have continued down through the church age to our present day, as evidenced, for example, by the miraculous events that took place in the early centuries in the missionary spread of the gospel (as in the times of Irenaeus and Tertullian and Joachim of Fiore). While the apostolic office as held by the Twelve and Paul did not continue, "apostles" continued both in the first century and afterward, referring to those "sent" to establish churches and proclaim the gospel. In the second-century document the Didache (also called the Teaching of the Twelve Apostles), prophets were the primary church leaders, and "apostles" referred to missionaries sent out to distant lands.

"Evangelists" were those gifted specifically with an ability to spread the gospel. Philip is called "the evangelist" in Acts 21:8, and in 2 Timothy 4:5 Paul challenges Timothy to "do the work of an evangelist"—to preach the good news and win converts for Christ. It is interesting that Paul views this as a particular church office. This does not mean that only certain people were tasked with evangelism; all Christians are expected to evangelize. This may especially refer to those who oversaw that aspect of church ministry or to the wandering missionaries who, like Paul, carried the gospel to new areas. Their role was distinct from that of apostles, though they worked together.

There is considerable debate regarding to the final two designations. Paul says literally, "And he gave some apostles, some prophets, some evangelists, and *some pastors and teachers.*" The question is whether Paul was referring to a single office of "pastor-teacher" or to two offices, those of "pastor" and "teacher," respectively. It was my view for a long time that this was a single office, but many, especially recently, see here two separate categories. The grammar suggests a close relationship between pastoring and teaching, and at the least it emphasizes that pastors must also be teachers (see 1 Tim 3:2, "able to teach"). This is needed advice in our day as well as in Paul's, since too many pastors have shallow teaching ministries. Most likely this speaks of two offices, though Paul viewed them as overlapping, with pastors required to teach well and teachers playing a pastoral role in the church.

The term "pastor" stems from the metaphor of shepherd as leader, used in the Old Testament for the "shepherds of Israel" (Ps 80:1), those whom God chose to lead his flock. It is also related to Jesus as "the good shepherd" (John 10:11). Jesus used this concept later to require his disciples (through Peter) to tend and feed God's sheep (John 21:15-17). In this sense pastors continue the ministry of Jesus to his church (1 Pet 5:2). In the New Testament pastors are also called "elders" and "overseers" (Acts 20:28). They are mature believers filled with wisdom who watch over the people of God and oversee his work among them.

"Teachers" are those who explain the truths of Christ to the people and lead them into the deep things of God and his word. Their authoritative function is especially stressed in the Pastoral Letters, where they are depicted as those who transmit "sound doctrine" (1 Tim 1:10; 2 Tim 4:3) and pass on the tradition of the apostles to the church (2 Tim 2:2). There is no excuse for weak teaching in the church, as Paul pointed out to Timothy (2 Tim 1:6–7; 2:15; 4:2).

## The Purpose and Goal of the Church (4:12–13)

The threefold purpose of the leaders in verse 12 centers on the task of helping the church to grow, with reference especially to the internal spiritual growth of every member. The officers of the church are tasked with involving its members in serving one another and helping each other in the Christian way of life.

There is a significant debate as to whether the three phrases in this verse together describe the duties of the leaders from verse 11 or whether the second two describe the responsibilities of the saints after they have been trained by the leaders. The distinction is critical, for the first reading contains a strong presentation of pastoral authority, while the second stresses the role of the laity in church ministry.

The second option is likely better, since Paul changes his preposition from *pros* in the first to *eis* in the second two. While these are synonyms (both mean "for" or "in order that"), Paul is probably intentional in making the second and third subordinate to the first, leading to the following arrangement:

> For the equipping of the saints
>> For the work of ministry
>> For the building up of the body of Christ

In this scenario the pastors and teachers are responsible to train the members of the body so that they in turn can minister to one another and build up the church body. This makes the best sense of this verse in the context of 4:11–16.

The leaders of the church are primarily responsible to "equip the saints" (NIV "his people") for service. The verb means to train or prepare people. It is also a medical term for the setting

of broken bones and thus can be understood as restoring people to their God-given task in the body of Christ. The meaning
"equip" is particularly apt in light of Paul's later discussion of the
armor of God (6:10-20); it conveys the image of training God's
people in using God's armor. There is also the idea of rendering
a person fully trained and qualified for a task, as in Luke 6:40
and 2 Timothy 3:17. It is not enough for church leaders to perform their pastoral duties; they are responsible to the Lord to
get laypeople participating in that work. They do this by teaching them how to minister to one another effectively.

The fully equipped saints are then responsible to do "the
work of ministry." Every member is responsible to work at his
Christian walk, and here that productive life is defined as "ser-
vice/ministry." For the rest of the letter the responsibility of
"each one" of the members is central (see 4:7, 16, 25; 5:33; 6:8), as
is the emphasis on ministry to "one another" (4:2, 25, 32; 5:21).
No one is exempt. This is a common feature of teaching on spiritual gifts (Rom 12:4-5; 1 Cor 12:7, 11) and an essential feature of
church growth. Each child of God is given those ministry gifts
that will enable her, as God wills, to take her place in the life of
the church.

The next purpose is also the result of the leaders' training
and the members' serving. The body of Christ will be "built up,"
a construction metaphor that depicts the church as the temple
of God (2:21) arising stone by stone. This is an apt word picture
in light of the fact that Herod's temple was still in the process
of being built at the time Paul was writing. A good parallel is
1 Peter 2:5, with the saints seen as "living stones" built on the
"living stone" (Christ) and growing into "a spiritual house." Paul
amplifies this picture in 4:15-16, where he writes that the body
"grows and builds itself up in love, as each part does its work."

Paul turns from the threefold purpose of Christ's gifts in
verse 12 to the threefold goal of the church in verse 13. The goals
are defined by three eis ("to") phrases, all of which stem from
the main clause, "until we all reach" (or "attain"). The verb
means fulfilling a goal or reaching a destination, stressing the

end of a journey. In all three goals the primary idea is growing up to attain maturity, like a child reaching adulthood. The image is of all the body members growing together and enabling each other to become mature. No single believer can do this by himself; all must strengthen each other to reach the goal. In a human body, what would it mean if the arms were to grow while the legs did not? The body would be crippled. The point is that those members who fail to grow and use their gifts are hampering the church.

The first goal is a united vision of faith and knowledge. Unity was the primary theme of chapter 2 and of 4:1-6, and here faith and knowledge are the two spheres in which this unity functions. "Faith" once again (see 4:5) refers not to the spiritual aspect of trusting in Christ but to the dogmatic aspect of church doctrine. Christians are united in that all hold the same biblical truths that define the Christian faith. The teaching arm of the church (v. 11) is tasked with training the faithful in these core doctrines. The specific part of this faith stressed here is "knowledge of the Son of God." In Ephesians 1:17-18 Paul prayed that God would give the Ephesians "the Spirit of wisdom and revelation" to "know him better" and that they would be enlightened. Here he stresses specific understanding, specifically of "the Son of God." This is the only place in the Prison Letters where Paul uses that title. His is a high vision of Christ that centers on Jesus' sonship and deity. This is in keeping with his lordship, which dominates this letter. He is the exalted Son who has brought unity and peace into the world.

The second goal is maturity—literally, "a mature man" (*andra teleion*). The use of "man" is similar to that of the "new humanity" of 2:15; the term refers to the body of believers that constitutes the church. Along with "attain" earlier, this depicts the children of God growing to maturity (see Col 1:28). The noun can also mean "perfect," recalling Matthew 5:48: "Be perfect, therefore, as your heavenly Father is perfect." Mainly, though, the idea is Christian maturity in contrast to the status of the spiritual infants of verse 14.

The third goal unpacks further the idea of maturing to adulthood, "to the measure of the stature of the fullness of Christ" (my translation). This colorful depiction of Christlikeness pictures the child of God wanting to grow up and attain the stature of a big brother. When I was in the sixth grade I was terribly skinny but the tallest kid in my class (5′ 4″). I put a mark on the wall of my bedroom with the goal of attaining the stature of six feet. I missed it by a quarter of an inch. The mark on my spiritual wall is the "full stature of Christ." In Ephesians 1:23 the church is defined as "the fullness of him who fills everything in every way," and in 3:19 Paul prayed that its members might be "filled to the measure of all the fullness of God." This culminates those challenges. God's goal for us is spiritual growth—not just to spiritual maturity but to full Christlikeness. In every area of our life we must seek to be more like Christ.

### The Danger of False Teachers (4:14)

This verse provides three pictures of weak Christians and two of the deceitful ways of false teachers. These are opposite the mature, for they are "infants." Paul has in view not necessarily young Christians but those who have never grown in their faith. Church leaders have fed and cared for them, yet they have never responded, preferring to remain weak and undernourished. To make explicit the picture of helplessness Paul adds two further images: those of a small boat at the mercy of the storm-tossed sea and of a small bird at the mercy of a hurricane. Neither has the strength or maturity to enable it to cope with these insurmountable forces. The steep waves and howling winds have rendered them unstable. As in James 1:6 they are "blown and tossed by the wind." In Jesus' parable of the sower the forces that cause disarray and spiritual failure are adversity and worldly desires (Mark 4:17, 19); here they are the wayward winds of false teaching. As a result these weak Christians drift onto the rocks (Heb 2:1).

Paul graphically portrays the false teaching, mentioning the false "winds of doctrine/teaching" only here in Ephesians.

He does not describe it, but he may have had in view the false-hoods about which he writes in Colossians or the Pastoral Letters. Perhaps that heresy had not yet reached Ephesus, so Paul provides only this warning of storms to come.[1] This teaching was clearly dangerous and would destroy the church if allowed to go unchecked. He has already encouraged these believers to remain firm in the faith (4:5, 13) and now warns against the opposite: a weak faith.

To illustrate this danger Paul uses the gambling metaphor of cheating at a card game by using weighted dice (in "cunning and craftiness ... deceitful scheming"). The heretics he describes were indeed cunning and crafty, not simply misled by ignorance but deliberately twisting the truths of God into lies. They had plotted their approach carefully and turned religion into a moneymaking scheme, luring the weak into their trap and stealing their lives for personal gain. Elsewhere Paul accuses false teachers of being satanically inspired and controlled (2 Cor 11:13–15; 1 Tim 4:1), and that is likely implied here as well in light of Ephesians 3:10; 6:10–12. Still today it is rare for false teachers to simply be misled; most follow a deliberate strategy of deception inspired by demonic powers.

## THE FORMULA FOR PRODUCING MATURE CHURCHES (4:15–16)

As the heretics try to tear down the church and replace it with their own fiefdom, Paul provides an antidote. Instead of spreading lies in selfish greed for gain, the people of God will "speak the truth in love." Malicious falsehood is countered by loving truth. Several have suggested that the verb "speaking" (*alētheuontes*) connotes not just spreading truth but living it out as well (NET, "practicing the truth"). While both ideas may be present, the emphasis here is on the teaching office of the church.

---

1. In Paul's Pastoral Letters, written a few years later, these heresies are depicted as raging in full force.

In Ephesians 1:17–19 Paul prays for Spirit-inspired teaching that leads to wisdom and understanding. In Ephesians 3:3–6 his emphasis is on coming to understand the divine mysteries and in 4:13 on the church's knowledge of the truth as the basis for unity in the body. A loving church is a confessing church, and love is the atmosphere within which this confessing and teaching must take place. In fact, love frames this passage, as the truths are proclaimed "in love" (v. 15a) and the church "builds itself up in love" (v. 16c). This emphasis is critical, since many apologists for the faith are lacking in love, going for the jugular every time they see the slightest deviation from their own particular interpretation of theology. The key is to be firm on the cardinal doctrines (such as the deity of Christ, salvation by grace through faith, and so on) but tolerant on the secondary issues (such as eternal security and charismatic gifts).

When love and truth characterize the church, it will "grow into him in every respect" (my translation). Here Paul again stresses the spiritual growth of the body as a whole. This repeats the emphasis of verses 12–13, where the teaching of the church trains God's children so they may grow to maturity. As in verse 13c Paul defines that maturity as Christlikeness ("into him"), which is connected to his emphasis throughout the letter on being "in Christ." This adds to earlier material by emphasizing that the Ephesian believers are to grow "in every way"—in every part of the Christian life, especially in the areas on which he focuses in this letter: wisdom, knowledge, unity, mission to the world, good works, faith, and love.

Paul now switches from his metaphor of a child growing to maturity to another image, that of the head and the body, defining Christ once again as the head. In Ephesians 1:22–23, echoing Colossians 1:18, Paul states that Christ has been appointed by his Father to be "head over everything for the church, which is his body." In Greco-Roman medical belief the head was not only that which directed and controlled the body but also the source of nourishment, supplying the body with life-giving sustenance. The exalted Christ has sovereign control over his body, gives it life, and guides it so that it grows in him.

Paul continues his metaphor by developing the image of the body "joined and held together by every supporting ligament." The corporate body of Christ is now seen as united and brought together in him. To first-century physicians the body was held together in two ways: the life force was supplied by the head, and the joints and ligaments held the bones in place and gave them support. Paul includes both in his picture here. The Triune Godhead[2] takes the diverse members of the body and melds them together to form the church as the body of Christ.

Paul expands the metaphor to include spiritual gifts when he tells us *how* this will take place in the life of the church: "by every supporting ligament" or "joint." The head now uses the members to mold the church into a whole body. There is disagreement as to whether *aphē* here should be translated as "ligament" (NIV, NRSV, NET, HCSB) or "joint" (KJV, ESV, NASB, GNT). Ligaments would broadly indicate muscles and sinews, while joints would designate the places where the bones join together. Both renderings are viable, but since the overall emphasis is on the body parts being joined together, "joint" seems to be a slightly better alternative.

Note the emphasis once again on "every." Every single part of the body must do its part in supplying the body with those spiritual nutrients necessary for its growth. God has gifted every member in some way so as to serve the whole. As I have stated above, without active participation by all, certain parts of the body will wither and die. Those members who refuse to exercise their gifts are paralyzing the body in very specific ways, for ministering is left incomplete and believers who need help are neglected.

The positive side is seen in the concluding "as each part does its work." All parts are essential, for they distribute the

---

2. The Spirit's role is stressed in 2:18, 22.

nourishment from the head to each other as they participate in the life of the body. Two sources provide the members with that which ensures life and growth: Christ, the head, and the individual members in connection with one another. In verse 7 Christ apportions gifts of grace to each member, along with the strength to use those gifts for the good of the whole body (see also 1:19). The simple fact is that we need each other and are incomplete without the input of all of our brothers and sisters in Christ.

I have often called 4:7–16 "the perfect body-building kit." We have everything here that we need for a healthy, growing church and for the eternal benefit of each member. The exalted Christ stands at the head as ruler and Lord. But unlike earthly rulers who remain aloof, he is wholly focused on his followers who function as his body. As the head he nourishes and empowers them, giving to the members of the body gifts of grace that enable them to maintain their connectedness and thereby grow to maturity. Together they work out the unity God intends for his people, yet they do so through the diversity of gifts and ministries, as Christ has apportioned them. The leaders are gifted in a special way, but their purpose is to train and equip the saints, not to conduct all ministry functions themselves. Rather, they provide guidance for all the members of the body for mutual, reciprocal ministry to one another (2 Tim 2:2). One could say that their task is to work themselves out of a job as they pass along what God has given them so that all of the other members can function as vital components of a healthy, growing body.

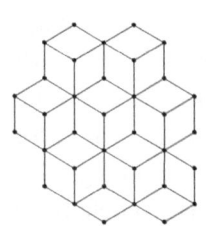

# LIVING OUT THE NEW LIFE IN CHRIST
## (4:17-24)

Paul moves here into the heart of Christian ethics, detailing how God expects us to conduct ourselves as part of the new humanity Christ has created in this new age. This entire section (4:17–5:21) is a midrashic expansion[1] of 4:1 ("live a life worthy of the calling you have received"), detailing what God expects for such a life. Living this new life means turning our back on our former life of sin (vv. 17-19, 22) and embracing the new self that has made us a part of Christ's new creation (v. 24). The ethical mandates that follow communicate the way in which we can attain this lofty goal and be worthy of all that the Triune Godhead has done for us. We are dealing with Christian conduct, the practical outworking in our daily actions of the new life God has given us .

---

1. "Midrashic" describes the way the Jewish people interpreted Scripture. This is a Jewish exposition of a text using the techniques of ancient rabbis to give a detailed analysis of the meaning and theology of the text. It looks at the nuances necessary to live a worthy life in the eyes of God.

## PAUL CRITIQUES THE PAGAN WAY OF LIFE (4:17–19)

### MANDATE TO REJECT THE FUTILE CONDUCT OF THE GENTILES (4:17)

Paul returns to the issue of the Ephesians' past sinful ways, which he first discussed in 2:1–3. Here he adds an important point about the futility and emptiness of that way of life. He begins with "therefore," building upon everything he has said in 2:1–4:16. Christ in his mercy and grace has brought redemption and forgiveness. He has made the Ephesians part of a new humanity, giving them hope and making them members of his body. With all of that newness, why return to the old, obsolete, and doomed practices of the world? Paul's language is quite strong—not just "I say" but "I tell you and insist in the Lord," turning this into a divine imperative backed by the full authority of the Lord of all. This is clearly not a mere suggestion or option for them to consider but a mandate from Christ that they must heed. This mandate is vitally important for us to hear today, when so many Christians are leading double lives, partly for Christ but mostly following the ways of the secular society around them.

There is absolutely no place for worldliness in the Christian life. The saints should "no longer live as the Gentiles do." If they are indeed saints, they have been set apart (the meaning of *hoi hagioi*, "holy [or set apart] people") from the world around them and for God. They in essence no longer belong to that world, and they should quit acting as though they do. In the past the Ephesian Christians had been Gentiles living pagan lives—but that was no longer the case and needed to remain in the past. People who have grown up in adverse circumstances never want to return to the old, sad life they have left behind, and that should be even more true of Christians who have left behind darkness for light. When one is seated with God in the heavenly realms in Christ (2:6), why go back to skulk around the old haunts?

This is even more true in light of the "futility" of the world's thinking. The term *mataiotēs* means "meaningless" or "empty," devoid of anything worthwhile and entirely the product of a vain mind. If we apply this to our own situation, we can see that the American way of narcissistic hedonism has no redeeming value whatsoever and is a complete waste. The end product is vacuity, a complete absence of any true satisfaction, and a lifestyle that can never produce anything of benefit. The only viable Christian reaction is a refusal to participate in such errant thinking and actions. Our mindset determines our actions, so if our thinking is empty our lives will be as well.

## The Terrible Lifestyle of the Pagan World (4:18–19)

Paul goes on to list eight descriptions of the dreadful condition of those who are caught up in the life of sin:

(1) They are darkened in their understanding. The first two descriptions identify their state of being, the result of their depravity. In Romans 1:21, part of Paul's famous description of the depravity of the Gentiles (Rom 1:18–32), he stated that "although they knew God [through his revelation of himself in creation] ... their foolish hearts were darkened." Paul is stressing their deliberate choice to reject God and his ways. In a sense sin has caused them to lose their minds. Their thinking process has been tainted by the dark forces of evil, called "the powers of this dark world" in Ephesians 6:12 (see also 2:2). Here the emphasis is on fleshly decisions; sinners deliberately prefer darkness to light. The rational process that should lead them to realize the truths of God is lost in the shadows of sin, and darkness prevails.

(2) They are separated from the life of God. To a holy God sin is detestable, summed up by the Old Testament word "abomination" (see, for example, Isa 66:3). Those lost in sin are forever cut off from him. When Jesus became sin for us on the cross God had to turn away, prompting Jesus to cry out in the words of Psalm 22:1, "My God, God, why have you forsaken me?" This is the worst of the seven descriptions of the horrors of sin, and

it will be the terrible reality of those who spend eternity in the lake of fire. We sometimes tell each other to "get a life"; well, there is no life apart from God. As stated in Ephesians 2:1, 12, unbelievers are dead in their sin and separated from Christ (here from God).

(3) They are ignorant. This is the result of the first description: since their understanding has been darkened, they are filled with ignorance. This is a dangerous ignorance, for it is the result not of a lack of knowledge but of a deliberate denial of the knowledge God has made available to them. In Romans 1:19–20 God has made clear his "eternal power and divine nature," but because of their darkened understanding depraved humanity has rejected that knowledge and chosen ignorance. Although the world was created by Christ, the world refused to know him (John 1:10). It is possible to acquire a PhD and be a dunce in every other area of life—an apt descriptor of so many intellectuals in our day who are controlled by political correctness (those beliefs that are demanded by the so-called intelligentsia) rather than truth. In fact, even the possibility of truth is often rejected. In this case ignorance is *not* bliss!

(4) They have hard hearts. This is the reason the world is steeped in ignorance. Once again this describes a deliberate process with a distinct cycle—the world of sin darkens the mind, leading to a calcified heart that is impervious to God's truths and producing a stubborn (the meaning of "hardness") refusal to listen and an ignorance that remains closed to God and separated from him. This further darkens their understanding, and the cycle repeats itself endlessly, leading to an ever-increasing hardness. Apart from Christ there is no hope for extricating oneself from this downward spiral.

(5) They have lost all sensitivity (4:19). Ignorance leads to hardness, which in turn leads to callousness, the inability to feel pain—here it refers to the inability to feel shame or guilt in the presence of abiding evil. Repetition anchors a practice in one's muscle memory. Great athletes have the touch because they have practiced moves thousands of times. In a similar way,

when we sin repeatedly the muscle of our mind learns to practice evil with a sense of impunity. That is the definition of a psychopath: one who feels no remorse for their terrible evils. In a sense we can become psychopathic sinners. First Peter 4:4 says it well: the world expects us to "join them in their reckless, wild living" (literally, "to plunge with them into a flood of wild sin"). This pictures us jumping into a Niagara Falls of sin with them. Such an action would be injudicious beyond all measure, but we willingly do the equivalent when we have completely lost our moral compass.

(6) They have given themselves over to sensuality. "Sensuality" (aselgeia) refers in general to a narcissistic lifestyle and specifically to a life of promiscuity. Both the general and the specific aspects are intended here. Such people live for themselves by the pleasure principle, especially in sexual perversions. In Romans 1:24, 26, 28 Paul states that because human beings have embraced sin God will "give them over" or "deliver" them to a life of debauchery. Here they do this to themselves, giving themselves over completely to the evil practices God detests. There are no restraints or limits to the excesses they pursue. Rejecting God's way, they willingly cast themselves into this pit of corruption from which it is so difficult to escape. Studies have shown that addiction to sex is as strong and difficult to overcome as addiction to heroin or crack cocaine.[2] That is Paul's thrust here.

(7) They indulge in every kind of impurity. Impurity and indulgence are apt descriptions of the prevailing American way of life in our day. It is shocking to see allusions to sex in nearly every kind of advertisement; this is getting to the point where we should label it "soft porn." Under the Old Testament

---

2. See, for example, a 2014 University of Cambridge study that found that pornography brings about brain activity in sex addicts that is "similar to that triggered by drugs in the brains of drug addicts." http://www.cam.ac.uk/research/news/brain-activity-in-sex-addiction-mirrors-that-of-drug-addiction

law "impurity" described something unclean, those things (animals such as pigs or dogs, along with objects or conditions like corpses or leprosy) that defiled people and rendered them unfit to stand before God. Here it indicates evil practices that separate the person from God (the second descriptor, above).

(8) They are full of greed. Paul is describing people who are never satisfied, who think they have to have more and more, who live by the old adage "When the going gets tough, the tough go shopping." In Colossians 3:5 Paul speaks of "greed, which is idolatry" (see also Eph 5:5), and that describes the problem perfectly. This is another key depiction of the American way. Even in the case of many Christians, their possessions rather than God are truly on the throne of their lives. They conduct themselves from day to day, always in pursuit of a more luxurious home or a bigger car, and they are insatiable in their constant demand for greater and greater indulgences. As Jesus cautioned, "Be on your guard against all kinds of greed; life does not consist in an abundance of possessions" (Luke 12:15). If only we could truly realize this!

## THE CHRISTIAN WAY IS TO REPLACE THE OLD (4:20–24)

### THE NEW TRUTH IN JESUS (4:20–21)

Paul turns from addressing the Ephesians' past, non-Christian mindset and focuses on the difference that finding Christ makes. The antidote to a life of debauchery and excess is to reject the old lies of this world's ways and to embrace the eternal truths of Christ. The answer can be only found in Christ. The Ephesians know this, for the description of verses 17–19 "is not the way of life you learned when you heard about Christ and were taught in him." Paul has described a new way based on new truths, but that way is new not in terms of time (for these are the eternal truths of God) but to those who have become accustomed to this depraved world. The old manner of conduct inherited from their pagan past can no longer suffice, for those practices together constitute the absolute antithesis of what they have learned from Christ through the apostle's teaching.

Paul notes two aspects here. They have "heard about Christ" at their conversion (2:8–9), and they "were taught in him" through the teaching office of the church (vv. 11–12). Actually, the Greek has "if indeed you heard Christ." In a real sense they have been schooled in Christ, who is the subject of their education (1 Cor 1:23; Phil 1:15; Col 2:6, 7), and have steeped themselves in his teaching. This is a challenge, for if they had truly entered the new life of Christ they would be living differently. They have indeed found Christ; now they must demonstrate this in a changed lifestyle. Christian belief includes Christian ethics, for the whole of life is summed up "in him."

Teaching is at the heart of church life, and this is a proof-text for Christian education. In the "pillars of the church" listed in Acts 2:42 (apostolic teaching, fellowship, breaking of bread, and prayer), teaching appears first because of its importance for the Christian walk. Today this is neglected in all too many churches, whose leaders seem to think that one sermon on Sunday morning is sufficient to educate their people. I see signs of improvement, for there seems to be more Bible-centered preaching. But all too many churches have done away with adult Bible study classes, and those that do offer them often draw only about 10 percent of the adults. Too many Christians are woefully and even willingly ignorant of the doctrines of the faith. No wonder secularism flourishes!

The new life is conducted "in accordance with the truth that is in Jesus" (literally, "as there is truth in Jesus"). In Ephesians 1:13 Paul reminded the Ephesians that their conversion had taken place in accordance with the message of truth about Jesus that they had heard, and in 4:15 he presents the antidote to the influence of the false teachers as speaking the truth in love. The Christian life is the only life worth living because it is the only true life. In a world where truth is sacrificed on the altar of relativity, we must realize that all truth coheres in Jesus, both beginning and ending with him. The Ephesians have found this truth; now they must live it.

## THE NEW WAY: TAKE OFF THE OLD (4:22)

In the Ephesians' new Christian environment they have received careful instruction regarding their new life in Christ. However, they cannot begin living that new life until they have taken care of their "former way of life," that lifestyle described in 2:1–3 and 4:17–19. They have been taught that they cannot be schizophrenic Christians, living in the world and in Christ at the same time. They have to make a choice to dwell in the truth. That means, Paul insists, that they are to "put off your old self" and tell it "Good riddance!" Once we recognize the emptiness and hopelessness of the old ways (as seen in vv. 17–19), we should be filled with horror at our terrible choices and throw them far away.

In Ephesians 4:22–24 Paul reminds his readers of three key ethical steps the Ephesian believers have been taught. These must take place in this order: put off the old, be made new, and put on the new. Until we have followed through on all of these we cannot pretend to be living life God's way. The first and third are based on a common ancient ethical metaphor: taking off old dirty clothes and putting on a new, clean garment. Ancient people did not have the variety of garments we do, and the poor barely had access to a change of clothing, but the image is universal. The Old Testament frequently uses the metaphor of clothing oneself with righteousness (Ps 132:9) or praise (Isa 61:3), or that of God clothed with majesty (Ps 104:1). And Paul speaks elsewhere of being clothed with Christ (Rom 13:14; Gal 3:27).

Here he further develops the imagery to describe life in the new creation Christ has brought about (see 2:10). To be part of the new humanity he has created (2:15) we first must get rid of the old life as though it were a set of filthy clothes. Clothes would rarely be thrown away unless they had become virtually unwearable, and that is the picture here. The old ways are so damaged that they can only be thrown into the trash. The phrase Paul uses is "the old self" (*ton palaion anthrōpon*— literally, "the old man"), which he also uses in Romans 6:6 and Colossians 3:9. We often think this metaphor describes the individual Christian who dies to self and begins life anew, but the consensus now is that it is a corporate image depicting humanity "in Adam," under the power of sin, living a life devoid of God.

The reason the old way of life must be jettisoned is that it "is being corrupted by its deceitful desires." In the Romans and Colossians passages the old self is pictured as having existed only in the past, but here it is still alive, corrupting and deceiving its enslaved captives. We may be followers of Christ and still be burdened by the old nature. We have been redeemed and made part of the body of Christ, but the process is not yet complete. The old has been nullified and rendered powerless— has been "crucified with Christ" (Rom 6:6)—but while it is no longer an internal force controlling us it is still an external force tempting and deceiving us. It operates through the flesh, the sin nature that is still a part of us. It has been defeated but not destroyed, cast out of our new being but still operative as a threatening outside force. The battle still rages, and our victory must begin with a studied repudiation of the old nature and its ways.

Corruption is a process, a rotting of the senses that occurs in stages when sin goes unchecked. Sin is a gangrenous disease that atrophies and then eats away the limbs, and it can be stopped only by cutting away the offending flesh. It cannot be toyed with or tolerated but must be removed and disposed of. The process of temptation takes place through our "deceitful desires," those self-centered impulses that seem so good in the beginning but are in reality a pack of lies that would destroy us. This runs the whole gamut from greedy accumulation of possessions to sexual cravings to a desire for power and status over others. None of these will ever truly satisfy, but they tempt us because they all seem so right, so desirable, so fraught with pleasure.

### Replace the Old with New Clothes (4:23-24)

After the Ephesian believers have rid themselves of the power of the "old self," their mindset must be "made new." The Greek literally reads "renewed in the spirit of your mind," and there is debate over whether the phrase should read "in the spirit" (the human spirit or attitude, so NRSV, NASB, NIV, NET) or "by the Spirit" (the Holy Spirit, so NLT). While it is true that *pneuma* in Ephesians and Colossians is regularly used of the Holy Spirit, the difficulty is the added "of your mind," which would be a strange way to speak of the work of the Spirit. Most likely it describes the inner being. Still, since it is God who transforms the mindset, the Spirit's activity is implicit.

Our decisions are made mentally, and the battle to control those decisions is a mental one. Thus our thinking processes must be made new by God. Until this happens we cannot truly embrace the "new self" of verse 24. Of course, this process can never come to completion in this life. Throughout our lives we will struggle with the flesh and with sin. However, as in the imagery of growing to maturity in 4:13, 15, we can day by day gain more control over our thought life. Romans 12:2 speaks of being "transformed by the renewing of your mind," which clearly intimates that the transforming power is the Holy Spirit, who changes us into a harbinger of the new being that will be ours for all eternity. This is a lifelong process in which the Spirit enables us to gain control of our thoughts and proclivities, allowing us to take incremental steps in the direction of curbing our desire to seek earthly pleasures and turning more and more to God. It is in the mind that spiritual growth occurs, and we must embrace the Christlike mindset.

After the old, filthy garments have been discarded, it is time for us to be clothed with the "new self" (4:24), when we take our place in the new humanity made possible by Christ's new creation (2:10, 15). When the old nature has been crucified with Christ and our minds have been renewed, we become a new creature (2 Cor 5:17), a miracle accomplished by God alone, through Christ. As the old self is in Adam, the new self is in

Christ (see Rom 5:12–21 for the "old Adam"/"new Adam" theme). We have a new identity, but more than that we have a new nature. Our physical bodies remain, but God has created a new person within (see the "inner being" in Rom 7:22; 2 Cor 4:16). As with the old self, this is primarily a corporate dimension: as the old self was in Adam, part of sinful humanity, so now the new self is "in Christ," part of regenerate humanity.

This new self is "created to be like God." This is reminiscent of Romans 8:29, where Paul says that God predestined us "to be conformed to the image of his Son," and of Ephesians 4:13, where we are said to grow to "the measure of the stature of the fullness of Christ." God-likeness and Christlikeness are the true goals of spiritual growth, and therefore of the new self. This God-likeness will be visible in the related areas of "righteousness and true holiness." The New Testament identifies three stages of righteousness. God has declared us to be right with him on the basis of the atoning sacrifice of Christ on the cross (the justification of Rom 3:24), after which he has made us right (the process of sanctification as the result of the new self). As a result we live righteously according to his will. This third step is the emphasis here. Holiness is the defining characteristic of God and thus of us as well, as in the **Holiness Code** of Leviticus: "You must be holy, for I am holy" (Lev 11:44–45; 19:2; 20:7, 26). This is why we are called "saints"/"holy ones." Holiness is also the meaning of sanctification, the process of being made righteous by the Spirit.

This passage summarizes the complete doctrine of sin and salvation. As unbelievers we were under the power of sin and death, enslaved by our senses and doomed for eternity. There was no hope for us. Then God intervened and sent his Son to die on the cross to bring redemption and forgiveness. We enter that blessed state of redemption through the three stages Paul lists here. We first get rid of our old nature by turning and embracing Christ, then Christ makes us part of his new creation and gives us a new mindset, and finally we clothe ourselves with that new reality and live a life of growing in righteous behavior and holiness. The WWJD bracelets that were popular in the 1990s said it well: "What would Jesus do?" God created us to be his children, and the children of good parents want to be like them.

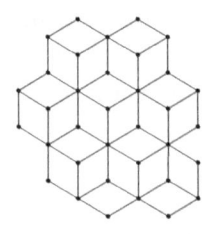

# VICES AND VIRTUES IN THE NEW COMMUNITY
## (4:25-5:2)

Paul has just established the way in which the new, corporate body of Christ becomes part of Christ's new creation, continuing the challenge he gave the Ephesians in 4:1 to walk worthily of their calling. Now he presents specific ethical advice on how they are to move from the "old Adam"/"old self" to the "new Adam"/"new self." This is Christian behavior in its essentials, presenting concrete vices to avoid and virtues to emulate. This list is obviously not exhaustive but representative of the ways in which we forge proper relationships within the new community, both with God and with our fellow saints. The pattern of verses 25-30 is paraenetic (ethical exhortation) at the core, providing three aspects of each vice: the prohibition against the dangerous practice (lies, anger, stealing, filthy talk) followed by a corresponding virtue that will negate the vice and a motivation clause that tells us why we should follow this exhortation. This passage continues with lists of five vices to avoid and three virtues to follow (4:31-32) before concluding with a discussion of the primary virtue—love—through which we imitate God, with Christ as the model (5:1-2).

## PAUL PROVIDES PRACTICAL EXHORTATIONS
## REGARDING THE OLD AND THE NEW (4:25-30)

The issues of truth and falsehood were central in 4:14-15 with respect to the danger posed by the false teachers, and now Paul presents the issue generally for all Christians, exhorting us to speak truthfully at all times. The opening "therefore" shows that Paul is consciously building on his previous teaching about unity within the new community, the body of Christ. The four sins he enumerates splinter the unity God has built in to the church. To walk in Christ as part of his new creation, to conduct ourselves as part of his new humanity, demands honesty and forthrightness rather than deceit and hypocrisy.

### Stop Lying and Tell the Truth (4:25)

The first prohibition centers on falsehood or lying, using the same command found often in the New Testament with regard to sins: "get rid of" or "put off" (Rom 13:12; Col 3:8; Jas 1:21). This terminology is used in 4:22 for removing the old self. Romans 1:25 states that sinful humanity has "exchanged the truth about God for a lie"; certainly the most central falsehood of all is to pretend we do not need God. Paul here addresses the result of that core lie, a pattern of falsehood that defines our life. I once listened to an interview with an author who had written a book about lying, and he claimed that the average human being tells as many as a thousand lies per day. These range from minor untruths, like saying "I'm doing great" when we really aren't, to deceitful business practices or cheating on our spouse. Satan is "the father of lies" (John 8:44), and to fall into such patterns is to become a child of the devil.

The positive counterpart is "speak truthfully to your neighbor." The terminology comes from Zechariah 8:16—"Speak the truth to each other"—where it is presented as one of the changes the people of God must make to avoid divine judgment on their nation. There God was promising a restored Jerusalem for the righteous remnant, and Paul is probably picking up that thought as well. The church is the new Jerusalem, restored by Christ to become the community of God (Rev 21:2), and the "neighbors" are fellow believers. As the new community the people of God must relate to each other with honesty and truth.

The motivation is in keeping with this emphasis on the new creation community, "for we are all members of one body." The responsibility for this truthful relationship falls not just on the church as a whole but on each and every member. The "one body" (4:4) theme goes back to the spiritual gifts theology of 4:15–16, detailing the involvement of every member with all others and the necessity of "speaking the truth in love." Such intimate relationships demand forthrightness, and the very life of the body depends on it.

## STOP BEING ANGRY AND GAIN CONTROL (4:26–27)

Paul realizes that in a fallen world there will always be anger. There are times when anger is necessary; the wrath of God against sin is a constant theme throughout Scripture, and Jesus felt anger at the stubborn hearts of the leaders (Mark 3:5). There is a need for righteous indignation on our part as well when we experience human depravity, but we must gain control of it and use it redemptively in situations that call for it. Handling anger well is so critical that Paul will revisit the issue in verse 31, below. There it is one of the six sins (with the others related to it) of which we must rid our lives if we are to follow the Lord. Here he introduces the topic by quoting from Psalm 4:4. The next verse of the psalm goes on to speak about the "sacrifices of the righteous," describing how God's servants are to act when they trust Yahweh. The meaning is clear: anger must not be allowed to linger and fester, for it can turn into resentment and then bitterness.

The Greek has two imperatives—"be angry" and "don't sin"—but Paul is not commanding anger. In Greek the first of two such imperatives often carries conditional force: "*if/when* you are angry." That is the case here. Anger itself is not sin when there is a valid reason for it, such as when we see another person mistreated or a loved one engaged in wrong and self-destructive behavior. But unchecked anger is dangerous and can seriously disrupt the peace and harmony of both family and church.

The key to not letting anger lead to sin is refusing to allow it to gain control of us. That is Paul's next mandate: "Don't let the sun go down while you are still angry." Sunset was an ancient metaphor indicating that a sufficient amount of time had passed. Dusk was the time when wages were paid out or when reconciliation was to be effected. Paul's point is that our anger must be controlled, and also that it is to be temporary rather than ongoing. Even in our anger we must work for peace and harmony.

The motivation for controlling anger is "not [to] give the devil a foothold" (4:27). Satan will use anger in a community to destroy its unity. When anger turns into bitterness we are giving Satan an opportunity to defeat us spiritually and to decimate our family or our church. The term *topos* ("foothold") means "place," and the picture is of letting the devil into our house and allowing him to inhabit a room. A similar term is used in Romans 7:8 for sin as an invading army that seizes the opportunity (*aphormē*) to gain a foothold in our lives. *Aphormē* is a military term for a bridgehead from which forays may be sent out to attack the enemy. This metaphor has much the same force. We do not want to permit Satan the opportunity to use our anger to gain control over us. Rather, we must gain control over our tempers.

This is closely connected to the spiritual warfare of Ephesians 6:10–18. We are engaged in a war against cosmic powers, and we dare not relax our guard lest we be overwhelmed. Unchecked anger is a major weapon the demonic powers will use against us, so we must at all times "put on the full armor of God" and refuse to allow it to gain power over us. I tell my students in seminary that if they are grappling with anger issues they should not go into ministry until they are settled.

## STOP STEALING AND WORK HARD TO HELP OTHERS (4:28)

Paul's prohibition against stealing reiterates the eighth commandment, "You shall not steal" (Exod 20:15). Thieves were strongly castigated throughout the Old Testament because stealing was such a threat to the overall economy of the time (Lev 19:11; Jer 7:9; Hos 4:2). The poor could be tempted to make ends meet by stealing, and someone else stealing from them might be enough to tip them over the edge. In 1 Corinthians 6:10 we are told that thieves, along with the greedy and slanderers, "will not inherit the kingdom of God." Today it seems as though every other week we hear of a Ponzi scheme or some such fraud that has targeted the weak or gullible and taken millions from them. If anything, theft is more widespread now than it has ever been.

The solution is to "work, doing something useful." Paul stresses the benefit for the community, as "useful" implies working for the glory of God and the benefit of the church. The term Paul uses for "work" (*kopiaō*) is a strong one, indicating strenuous labor to the point of exhaustion. Paul may have had in mind the idlers of 2 Thessalonians 3:11–13, who, believing that the Lord was to return immediately, had stopped working and were expecting their "less spiritual" friends in the church to take care of them. In contrast, Paul pointed out, "We were not idle when we were with you ... [but] worked day and night, laboring and toiling so that we would not be a burden to any of you" (2 Thess 3:7–8). These idlers were in effect stealing by making others care for them when they should have been working to take care of themselves. We have to apply this principle carefully in our time. Those families today who cannot find work should be helped; Paul's words are applicable only to those *few* who prefer not to work and to live off others.

The motivation for working is completely oriented toward community life, "that we may have something to share with those who have need." In effect, this defines the content of the "good works" for which we were created (Eph 2:10; see also 2 Cor 9:8; Gal 6:10; Col 1:10). There are two reasons for working hard. The first, which goes without saying, is to take care of oneself and one's family. Paul is stressing the second purpose: to be able to help the less fortunate. The church's obedience to this command has defined it from the beginning. In Acts 2:44-45 the principle that governed the community was to "hold everything in common" to the extent that believers sold their own property "to give to anyone who had need." This is further explicated in Acts 4:32-34: "they shared everything they had," with the intended goal "that there [would be] no needy persons among them." When that level of sharing occurs the entire church is galvanized, and we tell the world, based on our actions, that Christians truly are a different breed and have discovered what life is all about!

## STOP FOUL TALK AND BUILD UP OTHERS (4:29-30)

James 3 centers on the sins of the tongue, the danger of using the power of our words to hurt others rather than to encourage and comfort them. Here, "unwholesome talk" is signified by the word *sapros*, indicating something filthy or rotten; the term is used three times in Matthew for bad or rotten fruit (7:33-34; 12:33) or fish (13:48). Many translate it "foul talk," but the category is broader than dirty jokes. It does include that dimension, but Paul has in mind primarily slander and backbiting, using our tongue to abuse and put down others. Paul is picturing nasty people, and there are plenty of those in our time as well.

The answer is for us to instead utter "what is helpful for building others up." Paul is using the same term as in 4:12, where the purpose of ministry is "that the body of Christ may be built up," calling for spiritual edification at the heart of the church. "Helpful" here is actually "good" (*agathos*); the picture is that of exercising all our gifts, including the gift of speech, for the good of the church and its people.

When I think of this verse I often think of parents who too easily put down their children rather than lifting them up. Many of us have inferiority complexes, all too often the result of parents who expressed their displeasure more than they expressed their love. Both in the family and in the church we need people who encourage and strengthen each other, as in Colossians 4:6: "Let your conversation always be full of grace, seasoned with salt."

The goal of all of this is to "benefit those who listen"—literally, "to give grace to those who hear." Gracious speech will always center on the well-being of those to whom or of whom we are speaking. This does not mean that we will never confront people, but only that when we do so it is to help them, not to hurt them, as in Hebrews 3:13: "admonish one another daily … so that none of you may be hardened by sin's deceitfulness." The grace of God led to our salvation (Eph 2:8–9), and we are to emulate God's grace in our gracious concern for others. Everything said about spiritual gifts applies to the gift of the tongue. We must use our speech for the benefit and growth of those around us. We are to think of our tongue as a channel for God's grace to uplift others.

### Conclusion: Grieving the Holy Spirit (4:30)

All of these are sins and are detestable to God, so Paul concludes his list of sinful impulses of the flesh by warning that those who surrender to them will experience the displeasure of God. It is common to interpret "grieve" here as hurting the Spirit or bringing sorrow to him. That picture is true, as the term *lypeō* at its core connotes sorrow, pain, and grief. But Paul's point goes much deeper than that. The justice and wrath of God are indicated as well.

The reason for this is that when Paul speaks of grieving the Spirit he is alluding to Isaiah 63:9–10, which speaks of God redeeming and lifting up his people (recalling the exodus), only to watch them rebel against his loving care. God was distressed, and their rebellion "grieved his Holy Spirit." What follows is important: "So he turned and became their enemy, and he himself fought against them." The context of the Old Testament text is intrinsic to Paul's meaning here. God's redemptive work in the exodus was reenacted and deepened by the redeeming work of Christ on the cross. Yet his people today still tend to rebel and fail him, causing the Spirit to grieve over these sins and bringing down the wrath of God upon their heads.

Divine sorrow is the beginning point of divine wrath. The sins of Israel brought pain to Yahweh, and this precipitated his anger. This is even more strongly the case here, because God's saving work has intensified in Christ, and we are even more responsible than God's Old Testament people to live for him. The holiness of God will not tolerate sin. The divine justice is first of all terribly hurt and then filled with wrath, which leads to divine judgment. The four sins Paul has listed (and others) will not only cause the Spirit to grieve but will bring down divine retribution on the unrepentant.

Paul strongly states the motivating clause: "with whom you were sealed for the day of redemption." This goes back to 1:13–14, where he told the Ephesians, "When you believed, you were marked with a seal, the promised Holy Spirit." Then in 1:18 Paul identified the Spirit as the means of access to God, and in 2:22 he explained that God dwells within us "by his Spirit." The Spirit of God in our hearts provides a guarantee of our present and future salvation. Here the emphasis is on future salvation, as the day of redemption points to our final redemption when we reach heaven. The Spirit is a present deposit in our lives, anchoring the promise of that moment of final salvation and entrance into eternal life. Yet there is double meaning here as well, for the day of redemption also indicates the day of judgment, when every person—and that includes the saints (2 Tim 2:15; Heb 13:17; Rev 22:12)—will give an account to God. Paul is warning those who have fallen into the sins he describes here that they will have to answer to God for what they have done.

## PAUL PROVIDES A CATALOGUE OF
## VICES AND VIRTUES (4:31–32)

### THE NEGATIVE: FIVE VICES INVOLVING ANGER (4:31)

Paul here lists five vices that stem from anger and need to be removed from the life of God's people. He follows the same

pattern he used in the previous four—a negative admonition
(v. 31) followed by its positive counterpart (v. 32a) and then a
motivation clause (v. 32b). Apparently Paul believed that anger,
the subject of his admonition in verse 26, was a particularly
dangerous problem in the community, so here he elaborates
on the issue. He states that it must be "gotten rid of," that is,
eliminated from the community. Easier said than done! I have
observed the destructive power of rage in families, as well as
in churches. Unchecked bitterness has fractured relationships
and destroyed churches, and the problem is rarely handled well.
The conflict between Euodia and Syntyche in Philippians 4:2-3
provides a case in point. Their mutual animosity was a cancer
in their church, and Paul had to beg the leaders to get involved.
We don't know whether reconciliation ever occurred.

The order of these five vices increases in intensity, from bitterness to rage to fighting to slander, all of them fueled by malice. The descent into the maelstrom of hatred begins with "bitterness," a term that denotes growing resentment as our hurt
hardens into a settled animosity directed against the other person. This is followed by "rage and anger," two terms (*thymos kai
orgē*) that are usually synonymous in both the Old and New
Testaments. Their presence together here emphasizes the deep
rage that results when we give vent to our hurt and allow it to
fester. This is why Paul counseled in verse 26, "Don't let the sun
set on your anger."

Bitterness and rage (internal attitudes) give way to "fighting"
or "brawling" (external behaviors); the latter term suggests
yelling and screaming over someone or something that has
triggered an eruption of our temper. In the midst of this conflict between ourselves and the people we have grown to dis-
like, our screaming issues in "slander" (literally, "blasphemy").
We broadcast our anger, often reverting to unfounded and
malicious rumors, in order to turn others against the objects
of our wrath. Undergirding all of these actions is "every form
of malice." Each of the five forms of wrath has resulted from
a studied malice that cares nothing about the truth of the

situation but just wants to get even. The desire to hurt the other has removed from our consideration all reason or logic. There is no desire for reconciliation but only for vengeance.

### THE POSITIVE: THREE VIRTUES STEMMING FROM LOVE (4:32)

As the set of vices in verse 31 centers on anger, the three virtues here depict the opposite, the outworking of love within the community. There is a progression here as well, as a kind heart leads to compassion and then to forgiveness. A similar list is found in Colossians 3:12–13; it consists of five virtues— compassion, kindness, humility, gentleness, and patience. Both lists are intended to produce harmony in the church. A kind or tender heart cannot give in to anger, for it is always thinking of the good in others and, when hurt, will seek reconciliation rather than vengeance. Throughout Scripture this outpouring of love reflects an attribute of God, who out of his kindness forgives sin, motivates repentance (Jer 33:11; Rom 2:4), and shows mercy to those who come to him (Rom 11:22). We are to emulate this in our relationships within the church.

Next, compassion proceeds from a tender heart. Paul defines humility as "not looking to your own interests but each of you to the interests of others" (Phil 2:4). That is a good definition of compassion as well; rather than nursing a self-centered fixation on how others are treating us, we are to be wholly concerned about how we are treating them. As God and Christ have treated us with incredible and undeserved compassion (Matt 14:14; Luke 10:33), we are to do the same with others.

When kindness and compassion reign, forgiveness rather than resentment will result. It is important to note that the only part of the Lord's Prayer upon which Jesus elaborated was the forgiveness section: if we forgive others, God will forgive us. If we fail to do so God will not forgive us either (Matt 6:14–15). Jesus instructed Peter to forgive not just once but seventy-seven times (Matt 18:22), an idiom for "as often as necessary."

The motivation clause is in keeping with "just as in Christ God forgave you." We will never have to forgive as often or as much as God has. We forgive one sin at a time, but God forgives our lifetimes of sin. When we have experienced the unbelievable mercy and grace of God and realize that Jesus took our place on the cross to forgive our sins, it should be easy for us to forgive others. They can never hurt us as much as we have hurt God.

## PAUL PRESENTS THE SUPREME VIRTUE: LOVE (5:1-2)

### IMITATING OUR LOVING GOD (5:1)

In the previous verse Paul stressed God in Christ as the model for love and forgiveness; he now concludes the section with "be imitators of God" (NIV "follow God's example"). The indescribable love of God is the basis for everything Paul says in this letter. We can love one another in spite of our own finite and undeserving natures only because we have experienced genuine love from God and Christ. In our relationships we show love by imitating God's love. We can be kind and forgiving by emulating the kindness and forgiveness God has shown us.

In Paul's writings imitation is at the heart of discipleship. In Philippians 3:17 he asks his readers to imitate him just as he imitates Christ (also 1 Thess 1:6; 2 Thess 3:7-9). When we follow through on this injunction, we become concrete models of Christlikeness and show other people how to emulate him. Imitation especially occurs as small children copy their parents, and we model ourselves after God as his beloved children. As God's adopted children (Rom 8:14-17) we are the objects of the deep love of our Father, so it is completely natural for us to want to be like him.

### CHRIST AS THE MODEL (5:2)

All of the exhortations of this section are summed up in "walk in the way of love." Unbelievers walk in sin (4:17), but saints walk in love and obedience. This is the road to Zion, the Christward path, and it is defined by the love of God and Christ lived out in all our relationships. To "walk worthily" (4:1) is to walk in love.

The blueprint that defines what this means is "as Christ loved us and gave himself for us" (compare Gal 2:20). This is sacrificial love, and it is "for us," showing that we were the focus of his sacrificial act. This is seen also in Mark 10:45—Christ came "not to be served but to serve and to give his life as a ransom for many." Romans 5:8 says that "while we were still sinners, Christ died for us." That is the epitome of love: a sacrifice not for friends or loved ones but for those who have rejected him their whole lives.

This sacrifice is further described as "a fragrant offering and sacrifice to God." The idea of a fragrant aroma (KJV "sweet-smelling savor") stresses the acceptability of a sacrifice to God, stemming from the Old Testament idea of the temple as God's house. Bringing a sacrifice was in effect offering a meal to God; the idea is of a mouth-watering aroma given off by a burnt offering (think of a juicy steak cooking). God was pleased by such offerings, and by all of his people's offerings throughout history, but he was most pleased with the atoning sacrifice of Christ. This demonstrates the extent of the pattern Christ has established for us. It is not just love but sacrificial love that is acceptable and pleasing to God.

There are two primary themes that run through Ephesians: the exalted Christ, who is Lord of all, and the unity of the church as a new creation in Christ. This section relates to the second. In it Paul tells us how to keep the harmony and unity of God's people in the living relationships within the body of Christ. Vices fracture relationships and disrupt the church, while virtues maintain peace and bring people together as the family of God. In every area we seek Christlikeness, emulating the grace and love of God and Christ in our interactions with one another.

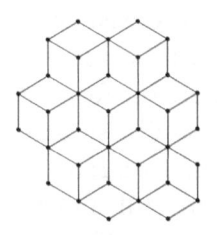

# THE MOVEMENT FROM
# DARKNESS TO LIGHT
(5:3-14)

This section continues a major theme in Ephesians, contrasting the old self with the new self (see especially 4:22-24). In Ephesians 4:25-5:2 Paul contrasted vices (characteristic of the old humanity) with virtues (characteristic of the new); now he draws an antithesis between the people of darkness and the people of light. As part of the new humanity (2:15) believers are children of light and can no longer have anything to do with darkness. Thus our lifestyle must change to reflect kingdom values. There are two main subsections here: a description of and a warning about the deeds of darkness (5:3-7) and a call to be children of light (vv. 8-14).

## PAUL WARNS ABOUT THE DEEDS
## OF DARKNESS (5:3-7)

### WARNING TO STAY AWAY FROM SHAMEFUL SINS (5:3-4)

Paul begins with two primary examples of shameful excess and the pleasure principle: sexual immorality and greed, both of which he addresses frequently in this letter (2:3; 3:19; 5:5, 12). Movies on historical themes are not always accurate, but on the decadence of Rome they are completely correct. Murals in Roman homes, such as those found in the ruins of Pompeii, often depicted pornographic scenes, and sexual profligacy was expected among Roman men. The New Testament frequently condemns immorality, which may be defined as sexual activity of any kind outside the bounds of marriage (the same Greek word, *porneia*, is used in Matt 5:32; 15:19; 1 Cor 6:18; Col 3:5).

Paul states the issue strongly here: there "must not be even a hint of sexual immorality" among believers. Such conduct is incompatible with the mandate to "walk in love" (5:2), and the Christian must have nothing to do with it. First Thessalonians 4:3–8 is a good example of how Paul deals with this issue. Pointing out that sanctification and sexual immorality cannot coexist in anyone's life, he commands the Thessalonians to gain control over their bodies, to shun "passionate lust." He goes on to warn them of divine judgment on those who live immoral rather than holy lives. This was as serious a problem in the early church as it is today. All their lives these Gentiles had assumed that loose living was not only acceptable but normative. After all, the Roman gods comported themselves in near-continuous orgies. Why shouldn't the people as well? It took new Christians from this background a while to come to grips with God's demands regarding sexual behavior. Yet the teaching of the church is clear and final: sexual sin can have no place in the Christian life.

The next two sins Paul mentions, impurity and greed, both sins of excess, are closely connected. "Impurity" relates primarily to sexual immorality, using the Old Testament image of that which is unclean or filthy in the eyes of God. Note that Paul's injunction is against "all" or "any kind of" impurity; he emphatically labels all sexual activity outside the marriage bond as wrong.

This is the second time Paul has coupled greed with impurity (see also 4:19). "Greed," often translated "covetousness," refers to the desire for that which rightly belongs to another. Many have assumed that greed in this context refers specifically to its sexual manifestation in an insatiable desire for unholy practices. That is possible but unlikely, since greed throughout

Paul's teaching (compare the sister passage in Col 3:5) refers to materialistic rather than to sexual demands. Nevertheless, when greed is condemned by the tenth commandment, the mention of "your neighbor's wife" indicates that there can be a connection between greed and sexual immorality (Exod 20:17; Deut 5:21). Then as now, wealth, status, and possessions were actually on the throne of people's lives. The true god of our time is the accumulation of goods, and we are all infected with the "affluenza" virus (affluence as a disease). Paul will come back to this in verse 5.

Paul feels so strongly about this issue that he says there should "not be even a hint" of these things among the Ephesians. The Greek says literally that these sins should "not even be named." This means more than "don't talk about it amongst yourselves"; it demands that believers have absolutely nothing to do with such practices. No one observing their lives should ever be able to levy such a charge against them, even by intimation. Paul focuses here on their actions more than their words. Such impure practices are "improper for God's holy people." Holiness means being set apart from the world, and licentious conduct is one of the primary practices that must be totally eradicated from the Christian life. Since believers are the "holy ones," they are to live apart from the evil deeds of the pagan world. Proper behavior can have nothing to do with such things.

Verse 4 explains the "any kind of impurity" Paul mentions in verse 3, noting three types of sinful sensual behavior. Building on the "no hint of" in verse 3, Paul here commands that there should be no such practices in the church. "Obscenity" refers to shameful deeds and is often translated "filthiness," as in the "filthy language" of Colossians 3:8. These are the unnatural deeds of darkness that have no place among the people of God (Rom 13:12; Eph 5:11).

Moving on a continuum from lewd conduct to lewd speech, Paul goes on to address the interconnected issues of "foolish talk" and "coarse jesting." The first is a general term, the latter specific. Foolish talk is speech that accomplishes nothing of any real value. It is empty or dull, worthless to the hearer. Coarse jesting refers to repartee that is crude or uses crass innuendo. Those who translate this "dirty jokes" or "vulgar conversation" are not far off the mark. Both terms are probably intended to describe discussions of a sexual nature.

In place of such unsuitable speech our conversation should be characterized by "thanksgiving," replacing a filthy, worldly mindset with a mind filled with gratitude to God. The self-centered thoughts of the unbeliever are to be replaced by thankfulness. We need to dwell on all that God has done for us rather than on the earth-centered pleasures in which we can indulge. In Colossians 2:7 Paul describes this as "overflowing with thankfulness." Since God has lavished his riches on us (Eph 1:7-8), we must focus on the heavenly wealth that is ours rather than on the earthly wealth and the pleasures we can accumulate.

### RESULT: LOSS OF INHERITANCE AND DIVINE WRATH (5:5-6)

Paul's warning in these verses is important for us today. We commonly think that we can give God just a part of our life, live more in the world than in the church, and still make it to heaven. After all, the thinking goes, the only thing we need to do to gain eternal life is believe in Christ, and lifestyle isn't part of this. We may lose some of our eternal reward, but we'll still make the cut. Paul responds to this kind of thinking with "Wait a minute!" We cannot truly believe and still live a worldly life. Those who are immoral and filled with greed will not simply lose reward points. They will have no inheritance at all in heaven and will face God's wrath, for they are being disobedient to God's lifestyle demands.

To get his readers' attention, Paul begins this warning with "Be sure of this!" What follows is guaranteed, certain truth. Those who fall into the practices he has listed in verse 3—immorality, impurity, and greed—are excluded from God's people and kingdom. Further, he designates the greedy as idolaters, as he did in Colossians 3:5. As the home of the temple of Artemis, one of the seven wonders of the ancient world, Ephesus was famed as a religious center, and countless idols and images were everywhere present. Paul is saying that when we are greedy we have another god in our life: wealth or possessions. Today all too many of us have a god-shelf in our homes, containing our checkbook or credit cards, along with a list of our accumulations. Millions of Americans worship the idols of wealth and possessions at temples dedicated to the purpose, whether at physical locations like the shopping mall or at the digital temples of Internet shopping. Jesus made clear that we cannot serve two masters, both God and "mammon" or money (Matt 6:24)—though many of us try to do exactly that.

Paul warns here that those who try to live in both worlds are schizophrenic Christians. They will have no place in God's kingdom, no eternal inheritance at all. First Corinthians 6:9–10 says the same thing: no immoral or greedy person "will inherit the kingdom of God"; this is another way of speaking about eternal life, and it is difficult to know how far to take Paul's statement. He can hardly be saying that anyone who falls into sin is apostate, for in that case none of us would ever make it to heaven. Nor is he interested in how much leeway God will allow us to still squeak through. This terminology is similar to that of 1 John 3:6: "No one who lives in him keeps on sinning." It is one thing to fall into sin but quite another to engage in an ongoing *pattern* of sinning.

Yet even here we must acknowledge a caveat. Most of us struggle in one way or another with "prevailing sin." A prevailing sin is one that conquers us, one we cannot seem to defeat no matter how hard we try. The key is that we not persist in the sin, give in to it, or allow it to control us. One modern-day example of a sin too many Christians have allowed to control them is Internet porn. If we are addicted to such a sin, we must seek help. Continuing to engage in such activity puts us in serious danger, and we cannot defeat such a compulsion on our own.

Most statements regarding inheritance, like the one in 1 Corinthians 6:9, are in the future tense, but this one is in the present: such a person, *right now,* "*has* no inheritance." It is a present reality that he has no part in God's kingdom. Those members of the church who take a cavalier attitude toward sin are playing games with their eternal destiny, and all merely for a moment's pleasure.

This verse represents the only New Testament instance of "the kingdom of Christ and of God," as opposed to the more typical "kingdom of God." Some have surmised that this expression stresses the unity of God and Christ and thus implicitly teaches the deity of Christ. While it is true that Paul believes in the unity of the Godhead and the deity of Christ, however, that is not his point here. Rather, this expression stresses the present (of Christ) and future (of God) aspects of the kingdom—the kingdom of Christ in this world and the kingdom of God in the next. With the coming of Christ the kingdom arrived in this world, and we are now kingdom people. At the same time that kingdom is also in process of coming into its own; it will arrive with finality at Christ's second coming. We realize our inheritance *now* in terms of the power of the Spirit and authority over the evil powers (3:10; 6:10–12), but we have not yet received our final inheritance. Paul is saying that those who live in sin are deprived of both the present and the future manifestations of the kingdom.

Then, as now, some within the Christian community sought to rationalize immorality and greed (5:6). They would listen to the unbelievers who indulged in pleasure for its own sake and believe they had the freedom to live however they chose. Paul cautions the Ephesians not to be deceived by such attempts to justify sinful behavior. The deeds of darkness will never be light, nor will God look the other way. In Colossians 2:4, 8, while this falsehood is said to be clothed in "fine-sounding arguments," it is in reality "hollow and deceptive," and its true source is demonic. Such teaching is nothing but "empty words," devoid of any truth at all. Those who fall into the trap are helpless infants, prey to cunning and crafty liars and their "deceitful scheming" (4:14).

The end game of such lies is frightening indeed. Those who give in to the blandishments of such worldly teachers will face a holy God whose "wrath comes on those who are disobedient." As Paul states in 2:3, those who "gratify the cravings of the flesh" are "deserving of wrath," and that includes Christians who fall into such fleshly pursuits. There is an "already"/"not yet" aspect to God's wrath. Sin has immediate consequences in angering God, and at the last judgment God will judge each person "according to what they have done" (Rev 20:13). The emphasis here is on the deliberate nature of these evil deeds; these people are "the children of disobedience." In the Bible "sons of" or "children of" language usually means that the characteristic is a defining quality of their life. So, as in Romans 1:18–19, they deliberately "suppress the truth" that God has made plain to them. They do not inadvertently fall into sin. They know what they are doing and choose to reject God's truth and live a lie. Their guilt is clear and their judgment certain.

### FURTHER WARNING: DON'T PARTNER WITH THEM (5:7)

To give in to the false reasoning of these raging secularists is extremely dangerous, because to follow their reasoning is to partake in their sins. "Partners with them" means sharers in all they do. There are three stages to such partnering: listening and agreeing with their false logic, participating in their sinful lifestyle, and facing the wrath of God along with them. In Ephesians 3:6 the same Greek word describes the Gentile Christians as "sharers together [with believing Jews] in the promise in Jesus Christ," connoting full participation in a joint status or enterprise. To be a complete partner in the sins of these evildoers is to participate fully in their judgment. How can any thinking individual want that? Paul is commanding these Christians to refuse to have any part in the reasoning or the actions of hedonistic fools. The dangers are too great.

## PAUL ENCOURAGES THE EPHESIANS TO
## LIVE AS CHILDREN OF LIGHT (5:8-14)

### CONDUCT YOURSELVES AS LIGHT (5:8-10)

One reason to have nothing to do with the evil practices of this world is the eternal danger they bring, but Paul has an even greater motivation in mind for such avoidance. Once we have passed from darkness to light, why would we ever wish to return to the darkness? As in Ephesians 2:1-3, 11-13, he places this in the framework of the past (once) and present (now) realities of the believers' lives. The Ephesians have entered a rich and rewarding new life and have become part of a new people and a new realm, characterized by light. To yearn to go back to the vacuous and disappointing life they once led would be insane. They should never allow themselves to be tempted by temporary pleasure, which, as they already know so well, is satisfying for a short of time but ultimately debilitating. On the surface this reversion may seem appealing, but Paul is asking his readers to think more deeply.

*Walking as light (5:8)*

Paul begins by reminding his readers of the old days and what their former situation truly meant: "you were once darkness." The old life had a pretension of light, like Las Vegas and its ubiquitous neon garishness, but this was a complete fabrication. It is only darkness—that kingdom where Satan and "the powers of this dark world" (6:12) rule. We who are light have been "rescued from the dominion of darkness" and given power over it (Col 1:13; see also Mark 3:15; 6:7). The reign of darkness is a past reality for us as saints, and there is no reason for us to have anything further to do with it.

Light versus darkness is a major motif in John's writings. His Gospel begins with the new creation; he states at the outset that Christ created a new life that constitutes "the light of all mankind. The light shines in the darkness, and the darkness cannot overcome it" (John 1:4-5). Through Christ the light of

God illuminates and convicts every person ever born (John 1:7, 9). Tragically, however, because the people of this world prefer darkness they "hate the light and will not come into the light for fear that their deeds will be exposed" (John 3:20).

With conversion the new believer enters the realm of light and becomes a new creature, part of a new humanity (Eph 2:15), so a return to the old realm of darkness should have no appeal at all. Since they are now "light in the Lord," believers are to live differently. Paul is not saying that they once *lived in* darkness and now *live in* light. He is speaking ontologically—about their very being: they *were* darkness, and now they *are* light. They are a different people, the children of the God who "is light; in him is no darkness at all" (1 John 1:5). We are a new creation, conceived as light and now inhabiting light. This takes place "in the Lord," meaning that Christ is now the sphere in which we live and the universe we inhabit.

Therefore, since we are light, we must "live as children of light." In my commentary on verse 5:6 I noted that calling people "children of" something identifies a major characteristic of the person. Here the believers not only belong to the light; they *are* light and must conduct themselves as such. Their walk must be "in the Lord" and must demonstrate the light that Christ has brought into this world. The world must see the light of God in the way Christians behave, in their daily decisions and in the manner in which they relate to those around them. The people of light recognize the despair and slow death that comes with darkness, so they should want nothing to do with dark deeds.

### The fruit of light (5:9)

Paul's discussion of vices and virtues in the previous verses has centered on the lifestyle God expects of his new community. If believers are indeed the children of God, part of his family, we must manifest the "fruit of the Spirit" (Gal 5:22-23), a term synonymous with the Christlike virtues Paul has delineated. Fruit denotes harvest, so these are the natural results of the work of the Triune Godhead in our lives. Just as light is a necessary ingredient in the growth of plants, so the light of God enables us to grow in these attributes. The presence of the Holy Spirit in our lives must produce certain fruit, the natural result of life in the Spirit. Like Jesus (John 1:7, 9), the Spirit is light, so the fruit of the Spirit is the fruit of light. This is the antithesis of the "fruitless deeds of darkness" in verse 11. Light has nothing to do with darkness, which can bear no fruit acceptable to God. This fruit produced with the light of the Spirit is "all goodness, righteousness, and truth." Note that "all" modifies each of the three. "Goodness" here reminds us of the good works for which Christ has created us (2:10). The goodness here is the mindset that naturally produces good works. Micah 6:8 defines goodness in this way: "to act justly and to love mercy and to walk humbly with your God." Good works are the theme of the central section of 1 Peter, who enjoins his readers to "live such good lives among the pagans that, though they accuse you of doing wrong, they may see your good works and glorify God on the day he visits us" (1 Pet 2:12). First Peter 3:13 reiterates the theme with a rhetorical question: "Who is going to harm you if you are eager to do good?"

"Righteousness" may be defined as doing what is right in the eyes of God. It is the natural outcome of justification, the final of the three stages of salvation: (1) we are declared right with God on the basis of Christ's atoning sacrifice (justification), (2) we are made right with him as we grow in him (sanctification), and (3) we live rightly before him (righteousness). Our holy God is defined as righteous (Ps 7:10; Isa 45:21), and since his people are to reflect his image they must also be righteous and live righteously.

"Truth" is a key quality of God and of Christ, as in John 14:6 ("I am the way, the truth, and the life") and 1 Thessalonians 1:9 ("the living and true God"). Truth must characterize his people as well, in contrast to the deception that characterizes the world and the false teachers (Eph 4:14, 22; 5:6). Hypocrisy all too often characterizes Christian relationships, and that must stop. Truth is at the heart of the gospel lived out in the Christian community, and honesty and forthrightness must be at the heart of Christian relationships (1:13; 4:21, 24–25).

### The result: pleasing the Lord (5:10)

When our lives exhibit the fruit that comes from light, we "find out what pleases the Lord"; this is similar in meaning to "understand what the Lord's will is" in 5:17. The key criterion for acceptable Old Testament sacrifices was that they please to the Lord. That concept permeates virtually every page of Scripture and is particularly critical in ethical passages like Romans 14:18, 2 Corinthians 5:9, and Philippians 4:18. Perhaps the best known such passage is Romans 12:1-2, where Paul uses sacrificial imagery to challenge believers to "offer your bodies as a living sacrifice, holy and pleasing to God." The goal is "to test and approve what God's will is—his good, pleasing, and perfect will." As I interpret Paul here, verse 1 centers on our pleasing God and verse 2 on God's will pleasing us.[1]

Just as children on the basis of love try to discover what pleases their parents and then do those things, so we as children of God seek to find out what pleases our heavenly Father. The verb "find out" indicates a studied search, and the progression Paul has in mind involves examination, reflection, and action resulting from the search. We are to study God's word and determine from it what is acceptable to God, thinking hard about how we can alter our actions to bring him pleasure.

### EXPOSE THE DEEDS OF DARKNESS (5:11–12)

Paul tells the Ephesians that they belong to and actually have *become* light (v. 8); as such, they are to have nothing to do with darkness. In order to discover how they can please the Lord (v. 10) they first have to deal with the darkness that once characterized them, as well as with the deeds of darkness that still at times infuse their lives. This is a corporate—not simply an

---

1. Many others see both as our goal to please God.

individual—responsibility. It is not enough to jettison these evil behaviors from our personal lives; we are to help others in the church defeat these sinful tendencies in their lives as well, to "admonish one another daily, while it is still called today, lest some of you be hardened by the deceitfulness of sin" (Heb 3:13).

Believers, as I have pointed out, must "have nothing to do with the fruitless deeds of darkness." This is a sweeping command, meaning that they are to shun and avoid these evil practices. The Greek says, literally, "have no fellowship with," a powerful metaphor establishing a direct contrast between fellowship with the saints/light and fellowship with sin/darkness.

This does not mean that believers are to avoid fellowship with unbelievers. Scripture is clear that we are to live among them and befriend them (Matt 5:43–47; Rom 12:14–21). Rather, it means that we are to refuse to have anything to do with their sinful deeds. According to 1 Peter 4:4 unbelievers will be baffled when "you do not join them in their reckless, wild living" (see also 2 Cor 6:14). Their works are unfruitful, the direct opposite of the "fruit of the Spirit" in verse 9. It could not be otherwise since their deeds are done in the darkness. The concept is well stated by Paul in Romans 13:12: "the night is nearly over; the day is almost here. So let us put aside the deeds of darkness and put on the armor of light." Paul links that idea here with the armor of God in 6:10–17.

Rather than participating in those dark deeds, Christians are called to "expose them," to bring them to light. Darkness hates light and hides from it (John 3:19–20). Sins are done in secret, and their perpetrators want them to remain secret, as in the adage "What happens in Vegas stays in Vegas." As in John 1:5, however, when the light shines in the darkness "the darkness cannot overcome it." Light not only exposes darkness but also forces it to recede. Some have taken this as a reference to the exposure of non-Christian practices, but Paul's context favors a setting within the Christian community. We too easily rationalize away our sins and refuse to confront them. That is why we need each other; the saints in love force one another to reexamine their deeds and be more honest with themselves. Loving admonition is not judgmental, for it confronts in order to help the individual confronted to defeat prevailing sin. The process is redemptive, to restore them rather than judge them.

When misdeeds are done in secret (5:12) they nearly always snowball. There is a progressive intensity to sin, since our increasing ability to rationalize our actions allows for worse and worse behavior. Secrecy keeps us from having to face our foolishness, and as our conscience becomes more and more inured it becomes increasingly easy for us to sin. In the end it becomes "shameful even to mention" the deeds that have resulted. They are too terrible even to talk about; we feel too sullied to bring them up.

When Paul says that such deeds are "shameful," he is not just speaking from a Christian perspective. The world considers them shameful as well. Roman writers used the same term to describe immoral acts; this language is universally recognized. Paul may have had in mind especially the sexual sins of 5:3-4, but certainly many other types of hedonistic behavior are included.

## The Illuminating Power of the Light (5:13)

This verse makes explicit what was implied in Paul's command of verse 11 to "expose" the dark deeds. When the light of God enters a situation, darkness can be seen for what it is. Since these saints *are* light and by their conduct exemplify light, the darkness around them can no longer pretend to be light. Dark deeds become "visible" in contrast. In the words of Romans 12:20 the light of Christ in us "heaps coals of burning fire" upon the heads of those in darkness. This imagery refers to conviction from the Holy Spirit, whose presence can then bring about their conversion so that they too can "glorify God on the day he visits us" (1 Pet 2:12).

The last clause of this verse is debated. If we take "becomes visible" as a verb in the middle voice, it will mean that "the

light makes everything visible" (NLT, NET, HCSB, LEB), emphasizing the convicting power of the light.[2] But if we see it as a
passive, the clause will read "everything that is illuminated
becomes [a] light" (NRSV, KJV, NIV, NASB, ESV), stressing the
power of the light to convert the lost. The first rendering is viable but redundant. The point that light makes all things visible has already been made in verses 8–13a. It would make sense
for verse 13b to show the effects of the light of the Lord in transforming darkness.

There is another debate regarding whether this transforma-
tion speaks of the conversion of unbelievers or of the restoration
of believers who have fallen into sin. I cannot help but think the
answer is a both-and rather than an either-or. The light shines
in the lives of the unsaved as well as of the saved, transforming the first into a Christian and the second into a victorious
Christian. In both cases the light of God exposes sin and transforms the person into a true child of God—that is, into light.

## CHALLENGE TO BE ALERT (5:14)

This verse culminates this section on the defeat of the darkness
by the light and applies it to the readers, saying in effect, "Wake
up! Get with the program!" A follower of Christ cannot live in
sin. Interestingly, Paul introduces this passage in the same way
he did Psalm 68:18 in Ephesians 4:8—"This is why it says" ("why
it is said" NIV). Paul's quote is not Scripture, but it is creedal,
possibly an early Christian hymn that perhaps builds on Isaiah
26:19 ("But your dead will live, LORD; their bodies will rise");
60:1 ("Arise, shine, for your light has come, and the glory of
the LORD rises upon you"); and Jonah 1:6 ("How can you sleep?
Get up and call on your god!"). Some believe this hymn was

---

2. In English there are two "voices," active and passive. Greek adds a third,
middle voice (so called because its force functions in between active and
passive). It adds that the action takes place "to or for yourself." In this case,
it slightly changes the meaning of the verb and gives it a causal thrust:
"makes everything visible."

originally part of a baptism liturgy, but it is ultimately impossible to determine whether this is the case. It is best to think of it more generally as a hymn on conversion.

The person addressed is called a "sleeper" and commanded to "wake up." Sleep in the ancient world was a euphemism for death, but the word was also used of the spiritually dead (1 Thess 4:13; 5:6–10). The vast majority of interpreters understand the term in this instance to refer to non-Christians. The imagery would then describe unbelievers asleep in the darkness of sin. The light of gospel truth shines on them, and they are called to "wake up" from their spiritually dead state and "rise from the dead" through conversion. The Ephesians were "once darkness, but now are light in the Lord" (5:8). This would make Paul's words a call for those who have not responded to turn to the Lord while there is still time.

However, I prefer to read this as describing Christians who have fallen into sin. The imagery would then parallel the words of Jesus in Gethsemane when he found the disciples asleep: "Are you asleep? ... Watch and pray so that you will not fall into temptation. The spirit is willing, but the flesh is weak" (Mark 14:37–38). Paul picks up this image in Romans 13:11 ("The hour has already come for you to wake up from your slumber, because our salvation is nearer now than when we first believed") and 1 Thessalonians 5:6 ("So then, let us not be like others who are asleep, but let us be awake and sober"). These are weak Christians (Eph 4:14) who on a spiritual level are virtually dead and need to wake up. Satan has defeated them and led them back into the darkness of sin, and they are barely clinging to their spiritual vitality. The light of Christ is on them, but their stupor is so heavy that they are unaware of it. They need to awaken and rise up; only then will it be true for them that "Christ will shine on you." Only then will they be enabled to live in the light of Christ as victorious Christians.

Light/darkness dualism is one of the primary ways in which Scripture portrays the war between good and evil. Paul uses the analogy in this section to declare that the war has effectively ended: in Christ light has conquered darkness. Yet the battles continue, and the believer must consciously and vociferously dwell in the light lest she return to the darkness that once consumed her. Those who are asleep or spiritually dead need to come to the light and turn from their dark deeds to find Christ. Those who are weak, defeated Christians need to rouse themselves and begin living in the light of Christ.

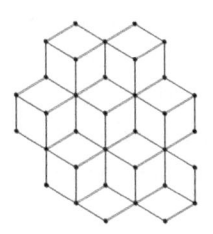

# LIVING IN THE SPIRIT
## (5:15-21)

Paul began his essay on the Christian life (4:17–5:21) by showing how the new life in Christ has nullified and replaced the old ways (4:17-24). Then he detailed the vices that must be removed from people's lives (4:25-31) and the virtues that must be emulated in the new community (4:31–5:2). Next, he deepened this understanding by using light/darkness dualism to show how the light exposes the deeds of darkness and enables the believer to walk in the fruit of light and please the Lord (5:3-14). Now he brings this ethical section to a climax by describing the "walk" of the children of light. He expresses the meaning of light in the Lord in terms of divine wisdom re-expressed in the Christian walk (vv. 15-17), as well as the life in the Spirit that makes this wisdom possible (vv. 18-21). God's wisdom and Spirit will guide the Christian, allowing the saints to walk worthily (4:1), so as to live a life pleasing to the Lord (5:10).

## THE CHRISTIAN IS NOT TO WALK
## UNWISELY AND IN IGNORANCE (5:15-17)

### Not Unwise But Wise, Using Every Opportunity (5:15-16)

Spiritual vigilance ("watch carefully" is more accurate than the NIV's "be very careful") is necessary if the saints are to overcome darkness and live as light. Many of the Ephesians had fallen asleep spiritually (v. 14) and needed to wake up and become alert. Some ancient manuscripts, followed by the KJV, change the word order here to read "See then that you walk circumspectly" (KJV, NKJV), but the better manuscripts support the reading here. "Carefully" connotes close attention, focus, and scrutiny. Every believer needs the loving and careful vigilance of those around him. This will take the form of encouragement or admonition, depending on which is needed at any given time. It is popular today to replace personal contact with online social networking, but overlooking face-to-face interaction can be dangerous. The kind of up-close observation we need cannot be accomplished through Facebook or Twitter.

Continuous watchfulness is mandatory if we want to live a life pleasing to the Lord in a world dedicated to the dark ways of sin. Any careless decision or selfish thought can seduce us into taking the wrong path and falling into spiritual defeat. Our vigilance must be corporate and not just individual. We cannot carry this burden by ourselves, for the pressures of secularity and the temptations to live by the pleasure principle are too great. We need help, both vertically, from the Spirit, and horizontally, from our brothers and sisters in Christ. Without the loving eyes of those around us, we will all too often deceive ourselves.

Paul enjoins the Ephesians to walk "not as unwise but as wise." This is true at both the personal and the corporate level. In Ephesians 1:17 Paul prayed that God would give them "the Spirit of wisdom and revelation." Believers need divine wisdom (1:8) through the Spirit to be successful in their decisions. To be unwise is to fail both to understand God's ways and to live within God's plan, which was revealed through the "wisdom and insight" (1:8-9) made known in all their variety to the cosmic powers through the church (3:10). Now it is time for us to use that wisdom to live rightly before God (Col 4:5, "walk in wisdom"). Proverbs calls the failure to do this "foolishness" (Prov 1:7; 10:14, 23; 17:21-25; 18:6-7; 23:9). The person who disregards God is indeed a fool, both empty and useless. The wise, on the other hand, are typified by an awareness of God and a desire to live out that awareness in their daily conduct.

The wise will not fritter away their lives on earthly pursuits but will make "the most of every opportunity" (5:16; literally, "redeeming the time"). The verb is a commercial metaphor used for purchasing a commodity, and it implies a period of vigorous trading while there is profit to be made. The same is true in the Christian walk. As Paul directs us in 2 Timothy 2:15, "work very hard to present yourself to God as one approved." Here the intention is that we will use our time wisely, making every opportunity count. As I write this I am 73 years old and have come to recognize how short life really is. We have only a few chances to make our lives matter, and we want to avoid squandering our limited opportunities and resources.

The reason Paul gives for paying such intense attention to the wise use of every opportunity is that "the days are evil." If the saints are not exceedingly careful to be in control of their time, evil can insert itself and take over. Most interpreters understand Paul's words here to reflect the Jewish perspective of the two ages: the present age, characterized as evil, and the age to come, when the Messiah will return and God will redeem his people. Paul may be thinking especially of Daniel's teaching about the evil forces arrayed against God's people. Since evil is in control of our world, the saints must be alert at all times and carefully work to ensure that the gospel triumphs and the church remains strong. In Ephesians 2:2 the "ways of this world" are shown to be aligned with "the ruler of the kingdom of the air," and in 6:12 with "the powers of this dark world." We as Christ's church must make certain to leave no room in the days we have been allotted for Satan and evil to take over.

## Not Ignorant but Understanding the Lord's Will (5:17)

As stated above, Proverbs calls the lack of wisdom foolishness, which may be defined as disregard for God in our lives. The true fool is the secular person who through the triumph of narcissism has become her own god. "Therefore"—literally, "because of this"—goes back to the previous clause. The implication: "because the days are evil, don't be a fool." When we freely take part in sinful activity and ignore the ways of God, we are fools. But Paul's words also build on the whole of verses 15–16 and so can be paraphrased "Because we are called to divine wisdom and to wise use of our time, we will not allow ourselves to become fools and fall into the evil practices of this age."

Rather than following the foolish paths of unbelievers, the wise follower of God will "understand what the Lord's will is." The discerning Christian seeks always to search God's word and to follow the Spirit's guidance, so as to allow the Lord to determine proper actions. Here, as in Ephesians 1:8, wisdom and understanding are linked. Once again Paul is thinking of Proverbs, which states, "The fear of the LORD is the beginning of knowledge, but fools despise wisdom and instruction" (1:7) and "How long will … fools hate knowledge?" (1:22). Psalm 11:10 puts it this way: "The fear of the LORD is the beginning of wisdom, and all who follow his precepts have good understanding" (see also Prov 9:10). Note the contrasts: the wise versus the fool and understanding and wisdom versus ignorance. It is practical understanding to discern the Lord's will in the concrete decisions of life.

"The Lord's will" here means the will of Christ, since "Lord" refers throughout Ephesians to the lordship of Christ. While there isn't a great deal of difference here—for Christ's will is certainly God's will—the section is **christological** at its core. Everything we have, including life in the heavenly realms (Eph 1:3, 20; 2:6), we have in Christ. The will of God/Christ in the New Testament refers to his guidance and demands for the Christian life. Romans 12:2 calls for us to "test and approve" God's will— to demonstrate to all around us that God's will works, that it is "good, pleasing, and perfect" for us. First Peter 4:2 challenges us to intentionally "live the rest of our lives" in accordance with God's will. Christ has brought about our salvation and has made us part of his new creation and new community. Now he wants us to live as part of his body and to follow his plan. That is his will.

## THE CHRISTIAN SHOULD WALK IN THE SPIRIT (5:18–21)

This command culminates the ethical section of the letter in 4:17–5:21, explaining how we are able to walk worthily of our calling and live as part of the new humanity. We cannot do this in our own strength or by our own effort; we must be "filled with the Spirit." It also looks ahead to the social codes that follow. It is the Spirit who transforms our relationships and our attitudes within those relationships. This does not imply that at conversion only part of the Spirit has entered the new believer and that only now will the Spirit fill her completely (see Rom 8:14–17). Rather, it means that the Spirit now fills every part of the believer. Think of yourself as the home in which the Spirit takes up residence. Previously you allowed him to inhabit an upstairs bedroom but not the whole house. Now the Spirit fills all of you.

### The Key: Filled by the Spirit (5:18)

The first command, "Do not get drunk with wine," seems out of place in verses 15–21. There have been various explanations. Some believe this relates to the pagan world of Paul's day, in which people participated in drunken orgies as part of the worship of the Greek god Dionysus. Or perhaps Paul's words reflect a problem in the eucharistic celebration similar to the one he describes in 1 Corinthians 11:20–22, or with the agape feast, similar to the discussions of 2 Peter 2:23 and Jude 12. The problem with all of these suggestions is the lack of evidence in the text for any such specific problem. It is more likely that Paul is addressing a general problem, similar to his admonitions against sexual libertinism, greed, and so on in this section. Drunkenness was as big a problem in the ancient world, as it is today, and Proverbs frequently addressed the issue (Prov 20:1; 21:17; 23:30, 31; 31:4). Moreover, getting drunk led to dropping inhibitions, which in turn often led to debauchery of all kinds and to a wasted, empty life.

Still, it would have been unusual for Paul to single out this specific problem with a prohibition like this. Certainly the issue of drunkenness within the church would have been reason enough for his concern, but I think there is more. At Pentecost some of the bystanders surmised that the seemingly excessive excitement and joy of the Spirit-filled disciples was the result of "too much wine" (Acts 2:13). Paul might in this instance be using a parable of Pentecost—saying, in effect: When you are filled with joy and singing (as in 5:19, below), may it be that it is the Spirit—and not the spirits—at work!

"Be filled with the Spirit" is a present-tense imperative, commanding a continuous infilling rather than a single, as it were, crisis experience. There is considerable difference of opinion whether the phrase *en pneumati* should be understood as content (filled *with* the Spirit) or means (filled *by* the Spirit). Both are viable, but *en* used to express content is unusual, so it is probably better to understand this as the means or sphere by which one is filled. The implied content of this filling would likely be the Triune Godhead, the "fullness" of God and Christ (Eph 1:23; 3:19; 4:13). The image is of believers being "filled to the brim" with the presence and power of the Godhead.

Our having been "sealed" with the Spirit (1:13; 4:30) results in our being filled with the Spirit. It is the Spirit who gives us the strength to say no to the temptations of the flesh (the vices of this section) and to live the Christlike life (the virtues of this section). It is the presence and power of the Godhead within us that bring us to victory in the holy war against the cosmic powers (3:10; 6:10–17).

### The Characteristics of Life in the Spirit (5:19–21)

Drunkenness leads to debauchery, but the Spirit-filled life leads to joy and worship. The basic command to be filled in the Spirit is followed by five present-tense participles that describe the ongoing practical outworking of this infilling process in the church and the lives of its members (speaking, singing, making music, giving thanks, submitting). The first three center on a new depth of worship. In John 4:21–24 Jesus told the Samaritan woman that the time was imminent for a new worship "in the Spirit and in truth," and this passage tells what that new worship looks like. In this age of the Spirit there will be a new depth of joy and singing before God.

### A new worship filled with joy (5:19)

While these participles could be seen as telling the means by which the action occurs ("filled by singing") or the manner in which it takes place ("be filled with singing"), most agree they speak of result ("be filled, resulting in singing"). When the Spirit fills us with the presence of the Godhead, joy and singing are the natural byproduct. Verse 19 breaks naturally into two clauses, with the first describing corporate worship and the second individual worship.

(1) In corporate worship God's people are "speaking to one another with psalms, hymns, and songs from the Spirit." Paul is following up on what he had also stated to the Colossian Christians, calling on them to teach and admonish each other "with all wisdom through psalms, hymns, and songs in the Spirit, singing to God with gratitude in your hearts" (Col 3:16). Hymns in the early church were used to teach theology to believers. The lyrics were chosen not for their artistic value but for their truth and depth of content. That is the emphasis here. Both preaching and worship played a teaching function in anchoring the people in the truths of God and Christ. Notice the stress on "one another." Worship is vertical and God-directed, while teaching is horizontal and directed to the worshippers. The hymns of the early church fulfilled both functions.

While many think the terms here are synonymous and together refer to singing hymns, most agree that there are nuances of difference, pointing to somewhat distinct forms of singing. The term "psalms" stems from the book of Psalms and refers to formal praise songs built upon the Old Testament psalms. "Hymns" would have been less formal, probably written more recently, and sung regularly in services. These first two designations are fairly similar, while the last category, that of "spiritual [*pneumatikais*] songs" (NIV "songs from the Spirit"), likely refers to spontaneous, charismatic singing that emanated from the Spirit's leading. Several believe that "spiritual" modifies all three terms and emphasizes that early church worship as a whole was Spirit-inspired. Regardless, Paul's purpose was not to identify the three specific kinds of early worship songs but to stress the variety and Spirit-infused power of early worship.

(2) Each of the saints personally experiences the joy of "singing and making music from your heart to the Lord." Verse 19 pictures first the powerful corporate worship dimension within the new community (v. 19a), moving on from there to depict the continued rejoicing and singing to the Lord on the part of individual worshippers going about their daily routines (v. 19b). The singing from the heart depicts a person pouring her whole self into joyous worship, holding nothing back. The focus of this joy is "the Lord"—Jesus, the Lord of all. In a sense this whole letter is an example of what Paul is speaking about here. In every section it celebrates the lordship of Christ, what he has done for the church, and how the church is to responds to his lordship. The Spirit-filled life is a life marked by praise and jubilation.

### Continuous thanksgiving (5:20)

Paul's fourth directive concerns thanksgiving. This is a major Pauline theme (twenty-four of the thirty-eight New Testament occurrences of the term appear in Paul's writings); he mentions thanksgiving twice in Ephesians (here and in 1:16) and three times in Colossians (1:3, 12; 3:17). For Paul thanksgiving was to be a regular feature of the Christian life, infusing every experience (both good and bad) and becoming a continuous focus (2 Cor 1:11; Col 3:17; Eph 5:20). The Father, through the Spirit, is sovereign over everything that takes place and guarantees that "all things work together for good" because "the Spirit intercedes for God's people in accordance with the will of God"

(Rom 8:27–28). The result: "If God is for us, who can be against us?" We represent the one group on earth who do not need to let our worries consume us, and for that we at all times should be grateful. This letter began with an enumeration of the blessings for which we are to praise God (Eph 1:3–14), and we can do no better than to prostrate ourselves in praise and gratitude for the "riches of God's grace that he lavished on us" (1:7–8).

There are four modifiers in this verse, each of which describes a critical aspect of our life of gratitude toward God:

(1) Thanksgiving should take place "always," meaning that it is to be a constant or regular facet of our prayer life. This is highlighted in the thanksgiving section at the start of many of Paul's letters (see 1 Cor 1:4; Phil 1:4; Col 1:3; 1 Thess 1:2), and he frequently commands it (Col 3:17; 1 Thess 5:16–18; see also Phil 4:4). As we pass through the painful trials of life (Heb 12:11), acknowledging that the sovereign God is superintending every part of that difficult time should result in constant gratitude for his loving care (1 Pet 5:7).

(2) We are to offer thanks to God "for everything"—for his continuing blessing through the hard times as well as the good. God's presence and power are all the more precious when we are passing through "the valley of the shadow of death" (Ps 23:4 ESV). When I am in deepest despair I can know that even at that stark moment I am not alone, for the Spirit is standing alongside interceding for me (Rom 8:26–27). Even as I am groaning in my agony of soul, the Spirit is groaning more deeply than I on my behalf, and that intercession is according to God's will! Our lives are completely secure in him, and our thanksgiving is to encompass their every aspect.

(3) We are to pour out our thanks to "God the Father" (literally, "our God and Father"). This does not mean that we are to pray to the Father alone and not to the other members of the Trinity. All prayer is primarily to the Father and yet implicitly includes the Son and the Spirit. As Jesus clarified in his farewell discourse of John 13–17, the Father is the One who receives and responds to prayer (John 15:16; 16:23, 24). The key

is the Abba theme reflected in "Father." Abba was the most intimate Aramaic term for father, and every prayer of Jesus apart from his cry of dereliction in Mark 14:34 and its parallels was addressed to his Abba. Paul is emphasizing that we have a Father who deeply loves us, enfolds us in his arms, and watches over us.

(4) We are to give thanks "in the name of our Lord Jesus Christ," who is the mediator and source of all our blessings. In John 14:13-14 Jesus says twice, "I will do whatever you ask in my name." This does not mean that Jesus' name is a magic formula that guarantees we can get anything we want. Rather, praying "in Jesus' name" means praying in union with him. All true prayer and all thanksgiving is uttered as a reflection of our oneness with Christ. I try not to end prayers "in Jesus' name" all the time so as to remind myself that this is not a formula for ending prayers but a perspective from which to pray. We give thanks because our Lord Jesus Christ has made everything possible and with his Spirit is guiding and watching over every detail of our lives.

### Mutual submission (5:21)

This final participle modifying "be filled with the Spirit" (v. 18) serves a double function: it is the final result of the Spirit-filled life, but it also serves as the title and motto of the husband-wife relationship that follows in 5:22-33. The ramifications of Paul's imperative to "be filled with the Spirit" lead naturally to changes in attitudes that affect our relationships with others. When the Spirit takes up residence in God's people, they naturally stop thinking only of themselves, and the saints together are encouraged to "submit to one another." The ethical section of this letter is framed by this theme, for at its start Paul commanded the Ephesians to "be completely humble and gentle" with one another (4:2). A church that is characterized by "the unity of the Spirit" (v. 3) must be dominated by humble Christians who defer to one another's interests and who "value others above [themselves]" (Phil 2:3-4).

The verb *hypotassomai* means to voluntarily place oneself under the authority of a person or entity (such as a government). Between Christians (like husband and wife in this section) there is to be a reciprocal arrangement whereby both are considerate and live to meet the needs of the other. There is a distinct aura here both of authority and of submission to that authority, with no implication of inferiority or subjugation. Here each member of the body of Christ of her own will accepts a subordinate role in relation to all the others. The result is a diminishing of hierarchical roles among the members of the community.

The thrust of Paul's words is debated, with several interpreters arguing that this is not actually mutual submission but rather the submission of believers to those whom God has placed in authority over them, such as wives to husbands, children to parents, or slaves to masters. They believe that the verb itself conveys submission to authority and must be understood in a hierarchical, as opposed to a reciprocal, sense. From this perspective the phrase "to one another" does not convey that everything is mutual but rather that the whole church is involved in the submission to authority. For these interpreters the unity of the church reflects the oneness of the Godhead, in which the Son is subordinate to the Father. There is for them a hierarchical order within which submission functions.

These are viable arguments, and no one doubts that there are chosen leaders who guide and watch over the church. However, the entire context of verses 18–21 (the filling of the Spirit and its results) concerns the whole church equally, implying that leaders as well as followers are intended in verse 21. In other words, the leaders, as part of the "one another," are also to submit. This position is not intended to support anarchy in the church, nor does the command to submit suggest that pastors and leaders are never to command others. Rather, they exercise authority not based on an inherent superiority but because God has placed them in this position. Moreover, they do so as servants of the congregation rather than as dictators demanding adherence (Mark 9:35; 10:41–45). There is no place in the church for "lording it over" others (Mark 10:42–43; 1 Pet 5:3). The God-ordained structure of the church, with its officers, functions within the larger edifice of Spirit-led mutual submission within the body. Servant leadership is the biblical pattern (1 Pet 5:2–4), and every Christian leader must be guided by humility and a servant stance in relation to the people to whom God has sent them.

The motive underlying interrelationships characterized by submission and servanthood is "the fear of Christ," with Christ being the object in the sense that we "fear Christ." Many versions translate this "out of reverence for Christ" (NRSV, NIV, NASB, ESV, NLT), but I believe that is too weak. Reverence is a part of the equation, but the Greek *en phobō Christou* does not convey that we are to be terrified of the judgment Christ has in store for us if we fail; rather, the implication is that we are to be afraid of failing the Lord. In a sense *phobos* is the fear engendered by the very reality of the incredible love Christ has shown us. This "fear" produces a solemn sense of responsibility: he has loved us totally, and we want to express that to the best of our ability in our own relationships. Yes, we do have a sense of awe and reverence for all that Christ has done for us, but Paul's point here goes deeper.

This section unifies and culminates the discussion of ethics in this central part of the letter (4:17–5:21). The mindset of the believer is to exhibit wisdom and perception; we are to discern the will of the Lord in the daily decisions of our life. Such a life is Spirit-filled. As elsewhere in the letter, this section is trinitarian at its core. We are enabled to discover God's will only when Christ becomes Lord of our lives and the Spirit fills us completely. The result is a new joy and attitude of worship in the Spirit, on the vertical plane, and a mutual submission on the horizontal.

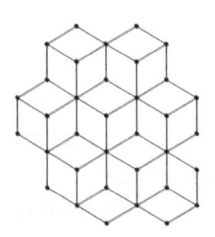

# SUBMISSION IN HOUSEHOLD
# RELATIONSHIPS, PART 1
## HUSBAND AND WIFE
### (5:21-33)

The previous section (4:17-5:21) dealt with relationships in the body of Christ as a whole, and this narrows the focus to those in the household. Here Paul is presenting what scholars have called a **Haustafeln** (English "house-table"), a social code that concerns relationships within the Christian household (for other examples in the New Testament, see Col 3:18-4:1; 1 Tim 2:8-15; 5:1-6:2; Titus 2:2-10; 1 Pet 2:18-3:7). These likely stem broadly from the **Hellenistic** background, and specifically from Hellenistic Jewish writers (Philo and Josephus have similar discussions). Jewish versions of household codes add an emphasis on the rights of those lower on the social scale (wives, children, slaves) and the importance of reciprocity (concern of each for the other) in the relationships. The early church added the single most important point: the sovereignty of God and of Christ over all relationships.

In Judaism women and wives did not have a public presence but were bound to the duties of home and family. Girls tended to wed quite young in arranged marriages; as an example, Mary was probably between twelve and fourteen years of age when she bore Jesus. They had limited educations, with training done by their mothers. There was considerable debate in Paul's day about whether girls should be allowed to learn Torah; most said no. Still, there was a general freedom of movement, especially in Galilee, where the Jewish people were less conservative than those in Judea and did not restrict women to the home. Their situation was better than that of women in pagan lands, and they enjoyed greater honor and status than did Gentile women (see Prov 31). They were permitted to worship in temple and synagogue, and there is some evidence that they were even allowed at times to read Torah, mostly in areas removed from Judea. There was even limited freedom at times to work, perhaps to sell produce or cloth or to assist in the fields. In the cities women and girls were more sequestered and kept in the homes.

Outside Judaism there was some difference between the Greek and Roman ways of treating women. The Greeks were misogynistic, and women were generally secluded. They were thought to be of low moral character, though the reality was quite the opposite. There was high infant mortality in Greek culture, partly because unwanted babies (mostly girls) were often exposed to the elements and allowed to die. There were two designated roles for women in Greek society—to bear sons or to become courtesans. Sparta was the one exception; there women were valued and even allowed to serve as warriors.

Roman women were more highly esteemed and allowed freedom, but they were still under the protection and control of men. Marriages were arranged but took place later than in Jewish communities (typically in a young woman's early twenties). The rule of thumb was that wives could have no more than three children so as not to dilute the inheritance of the family fortune and lower the family's status in society.

In first-century Roman culture at the time Paul was writing, a revolution was taking place in which upper-class women were gaining more and more freedom. Women, especially widows, were allowed to participate in the family business and even, like Lydia of Acts 16, to become quite influential, some holding government positions. The power of the matrons (wives of influential men) was impressive. Upper-class women ordinarily did not work and generally lived empty and dissolute but quite extravagant lives, although this was changing. Only about ten percent of women were upper class, and the rest were fairly poor, there being no middle class.

## PAUL PRESENTS THE KEY ATTITUDE: MUTUAL SUBMISSION (5:21)

I have already in the last chapter discussed the meaning of this verse, but we need to see its significance for this section as well. The verse does double duty, both delineating the last of the five aspects of the Spirit-filled life in 5:18–21 and serving as the lead-in to the household code here. In fact, it provides the basic parameters for the behavior of all three of the pairs— husband-wife, parent-child, and master-slave—Paul addresses in in 5:22–6:9. It was important that the authority figure in each relationship not only be aware of the needs of the one(s) under their jurisdiction but have a servant attitude as they exercised their headship. Mutual submission, demonstrated in sacrificial love, was to characterize every relationship among the members of the body of Christ. There is no verb in verse 22 (the Greek reads literally, "wives to your own husbands"). The command to submit is borrowed from verse 21, where the call to "submit to one another" shows the wife-husband relationship to be a prime example of mutual submission.

## PAUL TEACHES ABOUT THE SUBMISSION OF THE WIFE (5:22–24)

### HER DUTY TO SUBMIT AS TO THE LORD (5:22)

It is important to state at the outset that submission does not equate to absolute servitude or imply inferiority. It is the voluntary decision of an equal (the wording of 1 Pet 3:7, "joint-heirs of the grace of life," is helpful here) to place themselves under the authority of another. This is seen in the middle voice of the verb, which means, in effect, "submit yourselves."[1] While the verb is borrowed from verse 21, it still is an imperative, commanding this "decision": God expects wives to submit to their husbands. Note that the emphasis restricts this command to "your own" husbands. Paul is not speaking of male-female roles in general but only of those in marital relationships. Within marriage wives are to place themselves under the headship (see below) of their own husbands and are to both respect them and follow their leadership within the family. I will explore the implications throughout this section.

There is a difference of opinion as to whether this should be understood from an egalitarian perspective (advocating the complete equality of husband and wife) or the complementarian (each accepting their God-given role, with the husband as head of the family). Egalitarians believe that the command here to submit should be understood within the larger framework of Galatians 3:28, where "there is neither male nor female." Since Christ has removed the effects of the fall, men and women in this view are completely equal, both before God and within marriage. Some go so far as to state that Paul was reflecting ancient mores on patriarchal dominance that no longer fit the circumstances and that, already in his day, current mores on justice and equality between the sexes demanded a more tolerant understanding. This view is incorrect, as we will see.

The egalitarian view is appealing, and I am drawn to it, but my problem is that Ephesians 4:22–24 and Colossians 3:18 were written ten years after the letter to the Galatians. It is clear that Paul did not believe the submission of wife to husband was no longer mandated. Moreover, equality and unity were part of the teachings both of Christ and of Paul. I believe that the wife does indeed submit but that at the same time the husband exercises his headship via sacrificial love (more on this below). In effect, although there is a virtual egalitarian atmosphere

---

1. For more detail on the middle voice, see discussion at 5:13.

in husband-wife relationships, the husband is still the head of the wife.

The wife is to submit to her husband "as to the Lord." This means not only that she is to submit to him in the same way she does to the Lord but that her submission to her husband is *part of* her submission to the Lord. As throughout the letter, "Lord" refers here to the lordship of Christ, so a refusal to acquiesce constitutes rebellion against him. Christ not only provides the model for submission but is the one mandating it. In other words, by willingly submitting to the husband wives, are accepting the relationship assigned to them by the Lord, and when they submit they are in reality submitting to Christ. There is a reciprocal relationship of mutual submission, but within that the wife accepts her role of submission in the same way the husband accepts his role of sacrificial love. In these relational spheres each serves the other.

## THE REASON FOR HER SUBMISSION (5:23–24)

### The headship of the husband (5:23a)

Paul's stated reason for submission is that Christ has appointed the husband to be the "head of the wife." He deduces this from the Christ-church relationship, having stated earlier, in both 1:22 and 4:15, that Christ is the head of the body. All Christian relationships stem from the concept of the new creation and the new humanity Christ has instituted in this world (see 2:14–18). Yet the meaning of headship is disputed. Several have argued that the concept does not carry connotations of authority, but instead means "source," as in the headwater or source of a river. This would signify that the husband is the source of (or resource for) the wife. However, it is very rare for *kephalē* to mean "source," so before opting for that conclusion we should demand strong evidence from the context. That evidence is missing here. So while I think such an explanation a possibility, the authority of the husband makes a lot of sense and is thus in my opinion the preferred understanding. As Christ has authority over the church, so the husband has authority over the wife.

Every contemporary reader of Paul, Jew or Greek, would have understood headship in terms of authority.

But Christ's view of headship is always much broader than mere authority. In his own service as head of the body, the church, he strengthens, builds up, watches over, sustains, and in every way functions for its good. Husbands are required by Scripture to serve their wives with a heart attitude of sacrificial love, so they dare not misuse their authority. This means that the wife is not to show blind submission or indiscriminately obey just anything a capricious husband might command. This is one area in which the analogy of the headship of Christ breaks down somewhat. When a husband abuses his wife or demands from her actions that go against God's will, the wife *must not* submit. The headship of Christ is still the model for the headship of the husband, provided he consistently acts for the good of his wife.

### The model of Christ as head (5:23b–24a)

Paul defines the headship of the husband using the analogy "as Christ is the head of the church, his body." In Ephesians the stress has not been so much on Christ's sovereign control as head as it has been on his atoning sacrifice as head, in order that the members of the body might be redeemed for God. The emphasis is on service, on what Christ has done for the church rather than on what the church can do for him, as will become clear in the discussion of verses 26–27, below. The core of headship is indeed authority, but it is an authority that centers on serving rather than on using, misusing, or abusing.

The work of the ultimate Head, Christ, is defined by his status as Savior of the body. He has become Head for the express purpose of bringing salvation to humanity—it was precisely this that mandated the cross. Some have taken this to define the husband's role as that of spiritual head and protector of the family. That hardly fits this context. Paul's purpose here is to introduce the sacrificial love of Christ that will be central in verses 25–27. This love defines Christ's headship, as verified by his role in mediating God's salvation to fallen humanity and making it possible for sinners to be redeemed and to join his body, the church.

The result of Christ's saving work is that the church, as his body, "submits to Christ" (v. 24a). The present tense highlights the ongoing submission of God's people to their Savior and Lord. In every way and at every moment for the rest of their lives, believers are to follow and submit to Christ. Christ provides nourishment and growth for the body, and he keeps it intact and guides it at all times. So the church submits to its life force and source of strength. As Christ is the model and generating force for the husband's headship, so the church (the bride of Christ) is the model and generating force for the wife. When we think of the church as a family, it is clear that the nuclear family is its true core. Note, however, that the nuclear family includes single persons who are still, with their parents and siblings, a part of their family of origin. We do well to bear in mind that this imagery is used by Paul—a single person who considered himself to be a part of the nuclear family of the church. Since husband and wife are the mainstay of the church and its relationships, the husband's headship and the wife's submission form the core of all church relationships.

### Conclusion: submit in everything (5:24b)

At first glance Paul's directing wives to submit "in everything" seems to be an overstatement. I remember a couple once informing me that theirs was a biblical marriage in that the wife obeyed every command the husband gave. Yet notice that Paul instructs the wife not to "*obey* in everything" but to "*submit* in everything." A Christian marriage is not "General Husband" and "Buck Private Wife." In 1 Peter 3:7 the spouses are identified as "co-heirs" in their relation to God—as equal in his eyes. Moreover, it is as serious a sin for husbands to misuse their leadership as it is for wives to refuse to defer to godly leadership.

Paul directs the wife to "submit in everything" because he doesn't want wives to think they can pick and choose those areas in which they wish to comply. Submission is not to be occasional or partial but should be reflected in every area of the marriage. In every sphere of their life together, a wife both respects and yields to the loving leadership of her husband (see the discussion of 5:33 below). Within the overall unity of the church the pairing of husband and wife comprises the most intense and vital union of all, as the two are said to constitute "one flesh." Their union is the basis and binding twine ensuring the unity of the church as a whole. As they are, in their unification, one with Christ, they become one with each other, both in love and in mutual submission, she to his headship and he in his sacrificial love of her. For both of them the union is "in everything," not just in those areas in which they feel comfortable.

Naturally, we need to understand how this will work out on a practical level. In each marriage the husband and wife exercise hegemony in certain areas by mutual consent. The important thing to remember is that the responsibility of each is not conditional on the other appropriately fulfilling their role. A wife does not have the right to stop submitting if her husband doesn't function well, nor is the husband free to stop loving his wife if she is not sufficiently submissive. Both of them in their roles are responsible to the Lord, not simply to each other. Yet it is precisely because the primarily responsibility is to the Lord that there may be times when a wife cannot in good conscience do what her husband asks of her. As with submission to government, in light of Acts 5:29—"We must obey God rather than human beings"—wives are not to submit in situations where the husbands ask of them what is contrary to the will of God. In general, however, the wife is submissive in everything because this is a critical aspect of her walk with Christ—whether or not her husband deserves her compliance in every situation.

## PAUL TEACHES ABOUT THE SACRIFICAL LOVE OF THE HUSBAND AS HEAD (5:25-27)

### THE COMMAND TO LOVE (5:25A)

Paul devotes twice the space to the husband's obligation to love as he does to the wife's obligation to submit. This may be because it is harder for many husbands to overcome their self-centered tendencies than it is for their wives to do so. In any case, theirs is the greater obligation, and they become the focus of the rest of Paul's discussion. The imperative for them to "love" means that this loving stance is to characterize the husband at all times. The wife's submission takes place within the sphere of her husband's unconditional love, and he is to love her irrespective of how well she submits. As Paul will point out in the second half of this verse, Christ's love is in no way dependent on the believer's walk. In the same way, the husband is called to love his wife no matter what.

While the wife's submission was in keeping with the first-century cultural norm, the husband's love was out of step with the prevailing standard, which always stressed the power of the patriarch to control his wife in marriage. Nowhere in Hellenistic texts are husbands called on to love their wives. The work and central place of Christ within the marriage has completely reversed cultural patterns, and his sacrificial love transforms the husband's role.

### THE MODEL FOR LOVE: CHRIST AND THE CHURCH (5:25B-27)

#### The reality of his sacrificial love (5:25b)

The depth with which husbands are to love their wives is seen in the blueprint provided by the Lord—"as Christ loved the church and gave himself up for her." Christ did not love only when people deserved or had earned that love. Nor was the extent of his love conditioned on the quality of people's lives: "While we were still sinners, Christ died for us" (Rom 5:8). Paul repeats here his phraseology of Ephesians 5:2—also a model for our walking in love: "as Christ loved us and gave himself up for us." What husbands are asked to do is no different from what all believers are instructed to do in their relationships with one another. The marital context is simply the most intense and demanding example of that requirement.

Christ provides the model not only with regard to the depth of a husband's love but also to its practical outworking. The sacrificial element—"gave himself up"—points to the cross and to Christ's atoning sacrifice for sin. The extent of Christ's love is seen in his willingness to die—but not just any death. Who of us would be unwilling to jump into a lake to save our drowning child or to throw ourselves in front of a speeding car to save our wife? But Jesus allowed himself to be hung from a cross and to die the most excruciating and humiliating death possible to save us from eternal damnation. Moreover, he did this while we were still his enemies, in no way differentiated from the rest of sinful humanity. In this he provides an incredible model for husbands.

### The three purposes or goals of Christ's love for the church (5:26-27)

On one level the three elements listed in these verses deal purely with salvation, describing the effects of the cross on the lives of believers. On another, however, they could also be part of Christ's model for the husband-wife relationship. This is disputed, and most interpreters believe the second level was never Paul's intention. I'm not so certain, for the whole passage has relevance for defining the husband's role in marriage, as I believe this nuance does. Let's see how this works itself out.

(1) Christ gave himself on the cross "to make [his bride] holy, cleansing her by the washing with water through the word" (v. 26). This speaks of the process of sanctification, in which the believer is made holy, or set apart, for God. To be sanctified means to be cleansed or purified from sin. When we grow in holiness we grow in the strength to defeat sin in our lives. The power to do so is not inherent in ourselves but is given to us by the exalted Christ. This is the work of the Holy Spirit, whom we receive at conversion (Rom 8:14-17) and who

empowers, guides, and teaches us all we need in order to truly live for God (John 14:26–27; 16:13–15). When God justifies us, he declares us "right" with himself on the basis of the sacrificial blood of Christ. At that moment we begin the process of sanctification, in which God the Spirit makes us holy and launches us into spiritual growth.

In this verse it is the church as the corporate body of Christ that is set apart to be like him and to serve him; this includes every individual church member as the object of the Spirit's sanctifying work. So we are "sanctified in Christ Jesus and called to be his holy people" (1 Cor 1:2) by the process of being washed, sanctified, and justified in Christ's name (1 Cor 6:11). In Ephesians Paul states that the Spirit seals us (Eph 1:13–14; 4:30), gives us wisdom and insight (1:17), provides us access to the Father (2:18), mediates God's presence in us (v. 22), reveals the mystery of God (3:5), strengthens us (v. 16), makes possible unity within the church (4:3, 4), fills us (5:18), and enables us to use the armor of God with prayer (6:17, 18). All of this defines the way in which he sanctifies us.

"Cleansing her by the washing with water" is an image that connotes ritual cleansing. In the Jewish world ritual cleansing occurred in homes before meals—a preventative measure in case someone might have touched an impure substance (Mark 7:3–4). There were several pools in Jerusalem, called *miqvōt* (singular *miqvah*), that were used for ceremonial cleansing before going up to the temple. The likely Old Testament background for Paul's image here is Ezekiel 16:8–14, part of the metaphor of God forgiving his adulterous wife, Jerusalem, by entering into a covenant (of marriage) with her and then bathing and washing her, thereby forgiving her and restoring her as his wife. In Ezekiel 36:25–27 the metaphor was extended to depict a future cleansing involving the sprinkling of pure water, followed by the infusion of a "new heart" and a "new spirit." If we add to this the Jewish wedding ritual in which the bride on the wedding night takes a ritual bath, purifying herself for the wedding ceremony, it is viable to think that Paul might also be thinking of the husband in his imagery. As his bride purifies herself on the wedding night, it is the husband's privilege and responsibility to become a purifying agent in her life, the one who will perpetually seek to draw her nearer to the Lord in their relationship. As Christ presents his bride to himself holy and radiant (5:27), so the husband presents his bride to himself and becomes a sanctifying presence in her life.

For the early church cleansing was internal rather than external, taking place *en rēmati*—"by the word." In Titus 3:5 Paul speaks of "the washing of rebirth and renewal by the Holy Spirit." Many have suggested that the apostle here in Ephesians might be speaking of Christian baptism and that he has in mind a literal rather than a spiritual washing with water (as in 1 Cor 6:11; 12:13). While possible, that is unlikely, for 1 Corinthians 6:11 is likely metaphorical, and 1 Corinthians 12:13 uses the word "baptize" (not "washing with water," as here). The only mention of baptism in Ephesians occurs at 4:5 ("one baptism"), so that explanation seems improbable.

Paul is here referring to the inward cleansing of the Spirit in the process of sanctification. The pure water is the word of God that cleanses at conversion and purifies during the sanctifying process. As believers are immersed (pun intended) in the word of God, their lives are changed. There are two elements intended here: the proclamation of the gospel and the teaching of the church. The latter is especially in mind as the basis for Christian growth. When Paul spoke of pastors and teachers training the saints for ministry (Eph 4:11–12), this ministry in the word was the intended means for that training (see also Acts 2:42). In Ephesians 6:17 the word of God is called "the sword of the Spirit," the major offensive weapon for the church engaged in spiritual warfare (all the other pieces of armor in 6:13–17 are defensive).

(2) Christ gave himself "to present her to himself as a radiant church" (5:27a). The image is that of a lovely bride on her wedding day as she goes in procession to meet her groom. This

is reminiscent for me of Song of Songs 1:15: "How beautiful you are, my darling! Oh, how beautiful!" (see also Eph 4:7). Christ is the groom, the church his bride, and he has not only purified her but also made her radiant and striking. As above, the background is Ezekiel 16:10–14, where after God had cleansed Jerusalem, his bride, he gifted her with magnificent garments and jewelry so that she "became very beautiful and rose to be a queen," renowned throughout the kingdom for her loveliness. "The splendor I gave you," he declares, "made your beauty perfect" (Ezek 16:13, 14). This classic imagery of the bride, bathed and adorned in gorgeous garments, continued into the time of Paul.

The progression in Ezekiel reflects the "already and not yet" nature of Paul's **eschatology** (doctrine of the last things). As a result of Jesus' death on the cross, cleansing from sin took place and repentant sinners were forgiven and given a part in the bride of Christ. The "already" refers to the present beauty and splendor of the church as it is made holy by the Spirit day by day. Yet this passage especially has in mind the "not yet" of the final presentation at the end of this world, when Christ ushers his bride into heaven to enjoy the eternal radiance of his glory. Both present and future are in view here—but especially the future, when the church will be made radiant (*endoxos*: "glorious, filled with splendor").

(3) Christ gave himself so that his bride would be pure, "without stain or wrinkle or any other blemish, but holy and blameless" (5:27b). The bride will not only be beautiful but also perfect. In a sense she is transformed by the love of her groom to a perfection she could not otherwise have attained. It is obvious that only Christ could truly accomplish this, but this is still the ultimate goal of every believing husband as he lifts up his wife. As in 1 Peter 3:7, the husband "treats her with that respect" due her as his wife. The image is that of cherishing her, of considering her perfect in his eyes.

The goal is that she be "holy and blameless," recalling 1:4, where Paul declared that Christ "chose us in him before the creation of the world to be holy and blameless in his sight." We are back to the process of sanctification, the Spirit's setting us apart to be like Christ. In the imagery of Ezekiel 16 Jerusalem, like us, was horribly marred, to the point that she had stooped to prostitution. But God in his love cleansed her and restored her beauty to a glorious and perfect level that she could never have attained on her own. That is what Christ and the Spirit have done for us. We have been transformed from our ugly, rebellious old selves and elevated to a level of loveliness and splendor that was previously unimaginable to us. This is due entirely to the work of Christ and the Spirit in us.

## PAUL CULMINATES HIS EMPHASIS WITH REASONS FOR THE HUSBAND'S LOVE (5:28-30)

### To Love Your Wife is to Love Yourself (5:28)

In verse 22 Paul speaks of the wife submitting "as to the Lord," meaning that her acquiescence to her husband is part of her faithful submission to Christ. The same correspondence is true of the husband's love. He loves her for two reasons: first because of his own love for Christ, since she as his bride is part of his covenant with Christ (vv. 26–27). Second, he loves her because the two have become one flesh (v. 31) and she therefore is part of his very body. In loving her he is also loving himself in a new and more complete way. This is an extension of Leviticus 19:18: "Love your neighbor as yourself." If this can be the case with a neighbor, it is doubly desirable for the most intense human relationship of all.

When Paul says that husbands "ought" to do this, he means that they owe it to Christ and themselves to fulfill their duty to love their wives. There is a spiritual obligation to be faithful in marriage. The metaphor Paul chooses here is that of a man working out and training to maintain his strength and appearance. The same care, effort, and consideration are to be extended to caring for his wife. The obverse is also true. A husband who fails to care for his wife demonstrates that he does

not really care for himself, since he is ignoring "the better half"
of his own being.

## THE NEED TO FEED AND CARE FOR YOUR OWN BODY,
## YOUR WIFE (5:29)

Paul and the Ephesians both know that people take care of
themselves because they do not hate their own bodies. At my
stage of life my body has to some degree gone south on me
(I walk with a cane), and I cannot say I am enamored with it.
At the same time I work out several times a week and am trying hard to maintain what I have left. So this principle is still
true for me, and I'm confident it is for you as well. Husbands, it
goes without saying, are to extend the same degree of concern
to their wives, who in a real sense constitute their own bodies
(v. 28).

Husbands work hard to "feed and care" for their bodies, and
they are obligated to do the same for their wives. Two areas
of life that tend to receive our solicitous attention are our diet
and our appearance, and Paul implicitly calls on us as husbands to extend the same loving concern to our wives, making
every caring effort to meet their physical, emotional, and spiritual needs. The issue here has nothing to do with the outward
appearance of "trophy wives." Christian husbands should want
their wives to feel good about themselves, not just to look good
to others for enhancement of the husband's ego. I resonate with
the translation "nourishes and cherishes" (NKJV, ESV, compare
NRSV) with regard to the body; the immediate connotation is of
loving, tender care.

## WE ARE MEMBERS OF HIS BODY (5:30)

The husband's attentive care for his wife is individual; Paul
centers on people's love and concern for their own bodies. But it
is also corporate, focusing on the fact that husband and wife
are equally "members of his body" (v. 30). Since Christ is the
head of both husband and wife and equally cares for both, the

husband, as the channels for Christ's loving care for his wife, is obliged to embrace his privilege and duty.

The teaching about Christ and the church is more than a model for husband-wife relationships. We now see this area of the Christian life as the sphere within which the marital relationship develops and grows. Everything husbands and wives are and do is defined by the reality that they are part of a new humanity as members of the body of Christ. The man is at the same time both the husband of his wife and a part or member of the bride of Christ. Those two realities define not only who he is but also the decisions he makes.

The husband relates to his wife within the new community relationships that govern every action either takes. They are first members of Christ's body and only secondarily married to one another. They love each other on the basis of Christ's incredible love for them, and they care for each other as Christ has cared for them. This is why the husband exhibits submission along with his wife. His sacrificial love, both modeled after and tied in to the love Christ has for both of them, is manifested through a continuing series of submissive acts.

## PAUL CONCLUDES WITH THE NATURE OF THE HUSBAND-WIFE RELATIONSHIP (5:31–33)

### THE BASIS: THE TWO CONSTITUTE ONE FLESH (5:31)

All of Paul's arguments have stemmed from the reality of the husband-wife relationship as part of the new covenant of marriage—new in the sense that the spouses are now incorporated into the body of Christ. The basic reality stems from Genesis 2:24: "That is why a man leaves his father and mother and is united to his wife, and they become one flesh." The way Paul cites this passage, weaving the quote into the text without an introductory formula (such as "it is written"), is unusual for him. Reverting back to the Genesis account, God created the first woman from the side of the man (Gen 2:21–22). From that point on he would take a woman from her family and join her to a man in the covenant of marriage. The wife would become part of the husband's family. In both cases the two are recreated as one flesh.

In Ephesians the unity between husband and wife reflects that of the church (see Eph 2:14–18, 4:4–6). Oneness is the norm: oneness with each other, oneness with the church, and oneness with Christ. There is a double union, with each spouse joined to Christ and at the same time joined to the other. In this way the "one-fleshed" husband and wife become the key figure in the larger unity of the church. In the Old Testament the family was the heart of the clan, the clans made up the tribes, and the tribes constituted the nation of Israel. The same kind of progression is true of the church. Everything begins with the family, starting with husband and wife, who in a real sense together constitute one member within the family of God. Singles, also an intrinsic part of the church's family, should never be allowed to feel left out. It is vitally important for churches to integrate everyone within the family.

In fact, Paul is saying in verses 31–32 that the oneness of husband and wife does more than reflect the unity of the church. In Genesis 2:24 God established this coherence in marriage as a promise that anticipated the unity of Christ and the church. The relationship between the two is typological, signifying that there is a promise-fulfillment pattern between an Old Testament event or person (the "type," or promise) and a New Testament event or person (the "antitype," or fulfillment). In this instance marriage is the old covenant promise and the Christ-church union the new covenant fulfillment. Paul is saying that God gave the union couples find in marriage to prefigure the even greater union of Christ and the church. More on this will follow in the next section.

## THE GREAT MYSTERY OF MARRIAGE (5:32–33)

### The mystery: Christ and the church (5:32)

There has been extensive debate on the meaning of "this is a profound mystery" (Greek, "this mystery is great"). Catholics have long believed that "mystery" here refers to a sacramental view of marriage in which God's grace is poured out and the mystery becomes marriage itself. The problem is that no New Testament text understands either mystery or marriage in this way, making this a later interpretation interpolated after the fact onto this text.

At issue here is whether the "mystery" is the marital union (v. 31) or the Christ-church union (v. 32b). The problem with suggesting that the term refers to marriage is that Genesis 2:24 doesn't involve a mystery. The institution of marriage has not been hidden and is not being revealed here in Ephesians in a new way. The other passages in this letter that speak of mystery (Eph 1:9; 3:3, 4, 9; 6:19) clearly have in view the union of Jew and Gentile in Christ—a "new" story altogether!

The problem with inferring a reference to the Christ-church union is less evident. Certainly the union between Christ and the church is a new truth that had been hidden from the old covenant reality and is interconnected with the union of Jew and Gentile in Christ. However, Paul's use of "This," falling as it does immediately after the Genesis quote, would seem to hark back to it. So the inference that the mystery refers to the Christ-church union, though more likely, still seems inadequate.

Most likely the mystery is the typological connection between the husband-wife melding of Genesis 2:24 and the Christ-church union to which Paul refers immediately after the "This" statement. It would, as I have said, seem natural to construe the mystery as referring to the marital union of the previous clause, and that is probably why Paul adds "but I am talking about ...," as though he has gotten ahead of himself and needs to clarify his point. Paul is evidently saying that the place of the bride in marriage is fulfilled and brought to completion by the place of Christ's bride, the church, in the new union with Christ. Husband and wife become one flesh and take their place as the core of the one people, the church. Unity is the great mystery. Humanity, fractured and splintered by sin, is brought together to form the new humanity as God intended.

The original creation is renewed and completed in the new creation in Christ.

### The heart of the matter: love of the husband, respect of the wife (5:33)

Paul returns from the Christ-church union to that of husband and wife, summing up his teaching in this section. He stresses anew the responsibility of both spouses: the husband must sacrificially love his wife, and the wife must respect her husband. Note the emphasis on every married believer: "each one of you." This demonstrates the importance of this principle—every single husband in the church is to comply with these instructions. His privilege is to love his wife unconditionally, and her joy is to accept and reciprocate that love.

Paul reverses the order of his earlier discussion, mentioning first the requirement for husbands. In verses 28–31 he emphasized that the two are one flesh and that the wife thereby becomes part of the husband's own body. The stress here is on the husband loving his wife "as himself"—as part of his very being. He loves her not only "as he loves himself" (NIV) but as a part of himself. Being human involves a natural love of self, and since the wife completes the husband's self, his love is made complete in her.

The following injunction to the wife is difficult to interpret, for she is called to *phobeomai*, a term that connotes fear, respect, or reverence, depending on the context. Literally, she is called to "fear her husband." This hardly means that she is to be afraid of him. Paul is building an **inclusio** with "submit to one another out of fear of Christ" in 5:21. Thus verses 21–33 are framed with "fear of" passages, with the fear of the wife, here, paralleling our fear of Christ in verse 21. Both ideas relate to a sense of responsibility, a fear of failing to fulfill our obligation to the Lord. Still, there is a double meaning, since that responsibility is linked to the idea of "respecting" her husband as her head. Her respect for her husband is part of her obligation to obey Christ. As I have pointed out earlier, the authority is vertical, that is, it reflects the authority of Christ to both husband and wife. The husband's authority in the family is given by Christ, not held by the husband in and of himself. So the wife's "fear" reflects her responsibility to Christ in marriage, and her submission and respect are part of her walk with Christ.

This section moves from the general (the members of the body of Christ living worthy lives) to the specific (relations among the social groups that together comprise the Christian household), beginning with wives and husbands. Instructing the wife to submit to the headship of her husband as part of her Christian walk would not having sounded unusual in the first-century setting. The husband's responsibilities, however, would have been surprising and new for the first century. The husband is directed to love his wife sacrificially and to use his authority for her welfare rather than his own. The reason for this is that the marital relationship is not only modeled after but anchored in the Christ-church unity. The love of Christ transforming both sides of the marital relationship makes it a prime example of mutual submission within the church. The wife willingly and lovingly submits, even as the husband exercises his headship to magnify and glorify his wife.

The message of this extended discussion is as fresh and important for our day as it was for Paul's. Marriages have never been more under fire, and Satan is working overtime to disrupt the Christian family. There has never been a time when the family was more important: in our age of rugged individualism and the sense of narcissistic entitlement that drives most people, the sacrificial love and servant heart of the Christian family are essential. Without these safeguards our way of life would run the risk of going the way of the Roman Empire—into selfish oblivion.

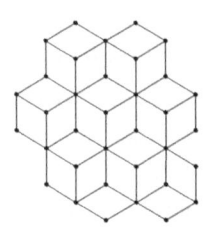

# SUBMISSION IN HOUSEHOLD
# RELATIONSHIPS, PART 2
## PARENT-CHILD AND MASTER-SLAVE
(6:1-9)

I t is natural that after dealing with husband and wife Paul
would turn his attention to parent and child (vv. 1–4) and then
to slave and master (vv. 5–9). In all three sections Paul speaks
first to the submissive member (wife, child, slave), following
conventional practice. Yet the greater responsibility is on the
authority figure, for each one is responsible to the Lord to love
their subordinate partner in Christ (implicit) and be considerate of their needs (explicit). Thus all three fall under the mutual submission command of 5:21, and none of these mandates
can properly be fulfilled until all the members have been filled
with the Spirit (v. 18). In fact, all the virtues called for as part
of the new self in 4:17–5:21[1] are necessary to live out these relational requirements.

---

1. These virtues include righteousness, holiness, true speech that builds
up others, proper work, kindness, compassion, goodness, forgiveness, and
wisdom.

# PAUL INSTRUCTS PARENTS AND CHILDREN (6:1-4)

## INSTRUCTIONS TO CHILDREN (6:1-3)

### Obey your parents (6:1)

Paul here instructs children to obey those whom God has placed in authority over them. The children he addresses are old enough to make choices while still young enough to remain in the household. In the first-century Jewish world a boy was considered a man at the age of thirteen, at which time he was called *bar mitzvah* or "son of the commandment," a term applied only since the Middle Ages to the initiation ceremony by the same name. When the boy came of age he entered an apprentice role, starting his career. With regard to Jews, then, Paul's command especially had in mind children up to the age of thirteen, though in the Gentile **Hellenistic** world his words might have applied to children up to their late teens. There were at times adult children living in a household who would also have come under this injunction, though to a lesser degree.

Wives were to offer their husbands voluntary submission, but Paul gave the children a stronger admonition, holding them to the standard of unwavering obedience. This stems from Torah injunctions against the disobedient child, emphasized throughout the Old Testament (for example, Deut 21:18; Prov 1:8; Isa 30:3). The sister passage in Colossians 3:20 commands minor sons and daughters to obey "in everything," and that is implicit here. Both Jewish and Roman writers did address situations in which disobedience might be called for, as when parental commands went against God's will (see Acts 5:29). But the general rule is stated here.

This obedience to parents was to be done "in the Lord," meaning that it was to be a part of the young person's walk with God. As with the submission of wives (Eph 5:22), children's refusal to heed parental rules and boundaries still today constitutes rebellion against God, not just against parents. God's word warns repeatedly that such disregard for parental authority will bring down divine wrath upon the perpetrators. A child's obedience is important not only because it is a critical aspect of their relationship with Christ but because it is "right"—fitting and proper for a Christ follower. For proper decorum in any home—Christian, Jewish, or pagan—the deference of children to their parents was expected. Still, for Paul the Torah regulation was uppermost (as in the next verse). Children obeying parents is right because it is commanded by God himself in his law.

*Honor your parents (6:2-3)*

Paul quotes the fifth commandment from Exodus 20:12 (from the **Septuagint**, the Greek translation of the Old Testament; see also Deut 5:16). The fact that this is the first command of the second table of the Decalogue (which deals with interpersonal ethics) shows the importance of the family and of obedient children in the Jewish world. In fact, disrespect and disobedience could be considered capital crimes that could lead even to the child's death (Lev 20:9). This command linked the vertical commands regarding relations with God to the horizontal commands regarding relationships among people, since the life of the people and their relationship to Yahweh were dependent on the harmony in their families.

The command to honor parents, as we have seen, covers adult children as well as young children. Younger children were to obey, and older children were to respect and care for their aging parents. A great deal has been said about the latter aspect in Jewish writings. Paul himself states in 1 Timothy 5:8 that those adult children who have failed to provide for their parents have "denied the faith and [are] worse than an unbeliever." Clearly the requirement to honor parents is lifelong, but it will be expressed differently at different stages of life. In fact, there is a reversal: the parents care for the child when she is young but the child for the parents when they are old. This commandment is often ignored even by Christian families!

Paul adds that this "is the first commandment with a promise." At first glance this seems incorrect, since the second commandment, against idolatry, also includes a promise (God's showing love to the obedient; see Exod 20:6; Deut 5:10). But in the second commandment the statement of divine love is not strictly a promise but a depiction of God's favor and mercy to his obedient people. So the fifth is indeed the first (and only) commandment linked to an actual promise. Paul's purpose was to demonstrate the overriding importance of children obeying their parents. He viewed this, in fact, as the single most critical aspect of human relationships, and the one that provides the basis for all the others.

There are two parts to the divine promise in Ephesians 6:3: divine blessings and a long life. In the Torah the promise of well-being centered on the promised land, but here it is in a sense Christianized and extended to embrace every area of life. This is not primarily a promise of material prosperity. While that is included, the promise deals not only with material benefits but with every other area of life—with physical, social, and religious well-being. In Old Testament wisdom literature this promise of prosperity was also connected to the advice of parents regarding life issues, since children who heeded that advice were likely to do better in life. While that aspect may be included here, Paul's primary thrust is God's blessings poured out upon his (and the parents') obedient children.

The blessing of a long life has sometimes been understood in terms of eternal life, but both in Exodus and here the context favors a lengthy earthly existence. After all, these are the children of earthly parents, and their obedience will most naturally result in a longer life on earth. By listening to their parents and thereby learning mistakes to avoid, they will have a much better chance, in terms of natural consequences, to enjoy both an improved and a longer life. Moreover, God will honor their respect and obedience to their parents by granting them a longer life.

## Instructions to Parents: Don't Provoke, but Build Up Your Children (6:4)

Children are to obey, but parents are also commanded to use their authority to build up rather than to anger their children. There is a distinct line of authority from God to parents to children, but all members of the family are responsible to recognize that God is sovereign over them and requires them to be faithful. Both in the Roman and the Jewish worlds fathers wielded unlimited authority—even life-and-death power—over their children. While Roman social codes centered around that aspect of patriarchal power over children, Paul here reverses the norm and focuses on the obligation of fathers to rule lovingly and to raise up their children rather than beating them down.[2]

Paul has earlier discussed the issue of anger (4:26–27, 31). Here he applies this to parents, instructing them not to provoke their children to anger. Again, this reverses the norm, for in the ancient world children were the ones told not to anger their parents through disobedience. Yet this unaccustomed injunction directed to fathers made a great deal of sense in the early church, which emphasized the responsibility of those in authority to use their power wisely and to improve the lives of those under their care. Still today parents are to make certain that the result of their discipline in the home is a stronger sense of self-worth and personal value on the part of their children. They are not to marginalize and diminish their children or make them bitter and angry through mistreatment, insensitivity, or unrealistic demands. In my years of ministry I have observed that too many people struggle with anger based on issues stemming from the way they were brought

---

2. In the Jewish world this was the father's duty, but mothers had authority over the children as well, and we in our day would extend this to both parents.

up. The church must challenge parents to be more positive in their homes.

The key, Paul says, is to "bring [children] up in the training and instruction of the Lord." Paul intends for this to apply on two levels: training in the practical disciplines necessary for everyday life and instruction in the Christian faith. Paul used *ektrephete*, the verb here translated "bring them up," in 5:29 of the husband "feeding" or "nourishing" his wife as his own body; that same quality of care is to be extended to dependent children. The parental (here primarily the patriarchal) task is that of bringing up children to be responsible adults, both in the things of life and in the things of the Lord.

The two nouns rendered here as "training" and "instruction," then, have application both for the lessons of daily life and for religious education. The first is the basic Greek word for discipline or instruction (*paideia*), from which the English word "pedagogue" is derived. It thus refers to the whole process of training a child, from infancy to maturity, including discipline. The second carries a somewhat negative connotation in the Greek, speaking of admonition or warning to help the child avoid bad decisions that will lead to harm. Together they connote the total training of the child. There is a difference of opinion regarding interpretation of the phrase "of the Lord." It could refer to looking to the Lord (1) as the One doing the actual training *through* the parents, (2) as the source of the training, or (3) as the sphere and content of the training. A combination of the first two makes the most sense. In the end all true preparation for life comes from the Lord, and it is he who guides and enables parents to do their job well.

## PAUL INSTRUCTS SLAVES AND MASTERS (6:5–9)

### INSTRUCTIONS TO SLAVES (6:5–8)

The institution of slavery was intrinsic to the ancient world from very early on, as seen in the fact that Hagar, the mother of Ishmael, was an Egyptian slave who belonged to Sarah and

Abraham (Gen 16:1). It has been estimated that by the first century AD as many as one-third of the people in the Roman Empire at any given time were slaves, and over half may have been slaves at one time or another. Slavery in the first century was in several particulars similar to slavery centuries later in the Americas. Slaves were bought and sold like cattle and had few rights. Their masters could punish them with impunity and force them do whatever they wished. While there was a range of treatment, and some masters were quite humane and even caring, there are numerous records of serious abuse.

Yet there are significant differences between first-century Roman slavery and its eighteenth- and nineteenth-century American counterpart. Slavery in the Roman Empire was never connected to any particular race or people group. Slaves were the product of military captivity or of debt (the latter being the primary source of slaves in the first century, since there were few wars). Moreover, slaves were often given some form of remuneration for services and could in some cases even earn their emancipation, frequently by the time they were thirty.

There were four types of slaves: agricultural field workers; domestic or household slaves; those who worked in their master's business; and specialized slaves trained as medical doctors, teachers, or scribes. Many slaves were prized for their education, often serving in high capacity in businesses and making a great deal of money for their masters. Many such high-profile slaves received better rewards for their service and thus were eligible to purchase their freedom at an earlier age. Some became bond slaves; the term applied to those who were offered freedom but preferred to remain as slaves because of their propitious situations.

Slaves were often considered to be part of the family or household of their owners, and in Christian worship household slaves would sit side-by-side with their masters and serve the church when their owners allowed. They were welcomed as full members of the church. There is no evidence to indicate that Paul sought to end the institution of slavery, although he and the other New Testament writers did transform the institution, as master and slave were considered brothers in the church and equally the slaves or servants of Christ. Slaves were expected to accept their lot and obey their masters, but masters were also enjoined to respect their slaves and treat them with kindness and fairness. God is Master over both, and ultimately both are to obey him.

*Obey with respect and recognize responsibility to Christ (6:5)*

Paul's command to the slaves resembles his directives to wives and children. Like children, they were to obey their masters, and like wives they were to respect them. While they belonged to their owners on an earthly level, they belonged to Christ on the heavenly plane, and this latter dimension was the basis for everything Paul asked them to do. Paul emphasizes that that during the slaves' earthly existence the master/slave relationship is entirely *kata sarka*, "according to the flesh." He addresses them here not primarily as slaves but, more importantly, as believers who have been purchased by an infinitely superior power: the blood of Christ. So their obedience to their earthly owner, while very real, takes a lower priority than their obedience to Christ, who is Master of both owner and slave.

Paul first enjoins these Christian slaves to obey "with respect and fear" (literally, "with fear and trembling," as in KJV, NASB, ESV, NRSV). In a pagan context this would have been assumed and construed in only one way: terror of severe punishment. On the surface Paul is referring to the respect due the masters and the fear of coming under their ire, but at the deeper level he has in mind the fear of failing in their responsibility to God, as in Philippians 2:12: "work out your salvation with fear and trembling" (see also 1 Cor 2:3; 2 Cor 7:15). Certainly both thrusts are present here, but the primary meaning stems from the governing passage in 5:21: "out of reverence [fear] for Christ." If they fail to give their masters their due respect, they will face not only the anger of their human masters but, more fearfully, the wrath of God.

Next, slaves are to obey "with sincerity of heart"; Colossians 3:22 adds "and reverence." This is not just referring to sincere obedience but depicts a single-minded person focused on his duties and carrying them out with deep-seated integrity. Sincerity refers to a complete absence of deceit or duplicity, along with attention to fulfilling all obligations. Such a person was highly regarded in Hellenistic as well as Jewish circles.

Slaves were, then, to carry out their responsibilities "as [they] would obey Christ" (literally, "as to Christ"). As we have seen elsewhere (5:22; also Rom 13:1, 2), this has a double meaning. Slaves were to obey their masters as they would obey Christ and were also to obey them because this was part of obeying Christ. Their primary duty was to Christ, and obeying their human master was tantamount to obeying Jesus. Also, they were to obey in the same way and with the same respect they were showing Christ.

### Obey as slaves of Christ (6:6)

Paul presents first negatively and then positively the kind of obedience slaves were to offer. Negatively, they were not to obey in order to win their masters' favor "when their eye is on you." The NIV "not only" is probably correct, for Paul's point is that they were to obey "not primarily" in order to please their masters but mainly to please the Lord, recognizing that both sides were part of the motivation. The Greek *opthalmodoulia* is composed of two words that together literally mean "eye-service." The term is not found elsewhere in Hellenistic writings, so Paul probably coined it to fit slaves who served in order to curry favor.

The slaves were to serve not as "people-pleasers" (Greek *anthrōpopareskoi*; NIV "to win their favor") but positively, as "slaves of Christ," recognizing their true Master who expects them to glorify God even in their difficult human situation. They ultimately serve Christ, a far more exalted figure than their human master, so in obeying their earthly lord they are in reality serving their heavenly Lord. They may be mistreated by their earthly owner, but they will be vindicated by the exalted Christ, and that will bring eternal glory and honor that will more than make up for their earthly dishonor.

In their temporary earthly situation they must "do the will of God from [their] heart," referring to the centrality of divine guidance and will in all human affairs. In Romans 12:2 the transformed life is defined by the command to "test and approve what God's will is—his good, pleasing, and perfect will." Also, in 1 Peter 4:2 the purpose of believers is defined as to "live the rest of their earthly lives … for the will of God." Slaves likewise were to give God's commands the ultimate place of authority, and part of that entailed serving and obeying their earthly masters. Moreover, they were to do so "from the heart," often translated "wholeheartedly" (REB) or "with all your heart" (NLT, GNT). There was to be no grudging service or grumbling or bitterness. In obeying their master they were actually serving God, and that afforded them the strength to be gracious and even joyous in their service.

### Serve as to the Lord—he will reward you (6:7-8)

The Greek at the start of this verse, *met eunoias*, means "with a good attitude" or "willingly" and connotes a positive disposition and sense of goodwill with which an action is done. A friendly, helpful attitude was to underlie slaves' service. Needless to say, such an attitude would have strongly endeared them to their owners. This disposition would have been very difficult to maintain when masters were cruel or overbearing, so Paul adds that their motivation was to be "as if you were serving the Lord, not people"—which, of course, was exactly the case. Their obedience was to apply even more with respect to their ultimate Master than to their earthly master. They were serving God by serving their human owner, so when that owner was unjust the Christian slave was able to maintain her equanimity and keep her attitude pure by focusing on God as the true recipient of her service. There may have been little or no reward in this life, but God would make it up to her with eternal reward.

This is spelled out in greater detail in verse 8. Paul appeals to the doctrine of rewards, pointing out that slaves could serve even unjust masters with goodwill "because you know that the Lord will reward each one for whatever good they do, whether they are slave or free." They might not expect just recompense, especially from bad owners, but from God they could be assured that every good deed will be rewarded. This is a frequent teaching in Scripture, as in Proverbs 24:12—"Will he not repay everyone according to what they have done?" (see also 2 Chr 6:23; Ps 28:4) or Revelation 2:23—"I will repay each of you according to your deeds" (also 1 Pet 1:17; Rev 22:12).

At the judgment seat of Christ we will all give account of our lives (Rom 14:12; 2 Cor 5:10; Heb 13:17) and receive our due based on the way we have lived. We will repent and receive forgiveness for our wrongs and will also receive reward for all we have done for God, the church, and others. Paul is applying this truth to slaves, reminding them that their eternal Master in heaven will repay the good they have accomplished in their attitudes and in their service. God is ever watching and knows every thought and deed, and Paul is promising recompense for every good. The slaves might never receive their due during this life, and injustice might be their lot. When that was the case, they were to remember that they were actually serving a much higher Master, and the reward from him would be eternal rather than temporary and earthly.

## INSTRUCTIONS TO MASTERS: FAIR TREATMENT (6:9)

As the slaves are responsible to respect and serve their owners with goodwill and grace, Paul charges the masters to demonstrate the same attitude and good deeds in the way they treat their slaves. As stated above, this was brand new material for an ancient treatise on master-slave relationships. The radical difference stems from verse 8, where divine recompense is promised to both slave and free. The masters have the same responsibility and are promised the same reward as the slaves because they answer to the same God for both their attitudes and their actions. All believers, including masters and slaves, have been freed from bondage of sin to become slaves of God (Rom 6:22). Both serve the same heavenly Master, and so both are responsible to live within the confines of their social circumstances in a manner that pleases God. The masters may receive a certain kind of temporary reward from misusing their slaves, but they will ultimately face God's displeasure and judgment. How much better to receive eternal reward for doing what is right!

This was obviously not complete equality, for the slaves were to obey their masters willingly and gladly, but it did mean that the masters were obligated to treat their slaves with the same regard the slaves showed to them. They were not to "threaten them" with punishment for an infraction; such threats were the norm in controlling slaves, but since the violence of many Roman slave owners was widely known, slaves were justifiably frightened by any threat. Owners had the freedom to use any punishment that came to mind, from beatings or whippings even to crucifixion, and slaves had no rights or recourse of appeal against mistreatment. Paul's point was that Christian masters were to treat slaves with love and loyalty rather than with intimidation, a radical concept for the first century.

The reason to refrain from threatening slaves was that Christian masters, too, had a heavenly Master whose authority trumped any they had from Rome. And unlike earthly, sinful masters, "there is no favoritism with him." Reward comes to free and slave alike (6:8), but so does judgment, as in 1 Peter 1:17: "Since you call on a Father who judges each person's work impartially, live out your time … in reverent fear." The social status of a wealthy owner brooked no favoritism with God, from whose heavenly vantage point one tiny ant is no different from another. Slave and master enjoyed the same status with God, and earthly zillionaires with their hundreds of slaves (as was the case with some ultra-wealthy Romans) would receive no preferential treatment. The masters needed to understand that while Rome allowed them to get away with the mistreatment of slaves, God would not, and they would pay for their sins.

There is a hierarchical relationship with both parent-child and master-slave, as child and slave are required to obey those whom God and society have placed over them. Parent and slave owner are responsible to God to lovingly care for those within their jurisdiction and to sacrifice their power position to serve and build them up. Thus, as is the case with wives and husbands, these two relationships fall under the universal rubric of "mutual submission" stemming from 5:21. Also, the parents and the slave owners are themselves slaves of Christ, and their responsibility toward their charges stems ultimately from the Lord. There is both a vertical and a horizontal component underlying their duty to use their authority wisely to build up those under their care.

In my commentary on Colossians in this series, I applied this principle to employer-employee relations (Col 3:22–4:1). Some think this trite, but the inclusion fits well. It goes without saying that there are many differences between the ancient and modern scenes. Slaves could not leave the master, and the master had life and death power over them. There are also many more laws protecting employees in our day, as well as a good deal of power in the employees' hands to effect change.

Still, the similarities are real and worth exploring. The truth is that in all too many businesses a negative relationship prevails between employers and employees. I worked in a factory during college, and the unions expected the workers to view management as the enemy. That is a sad state of affairs. Christ and Paul demand that workers and management look on each other as colleagues with the common goal of making the company successful and sharing the benefits. This is what the so-called American dream is supposed to be about.

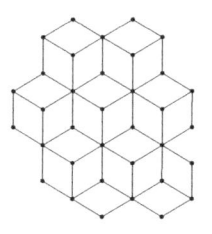

# PUTTING ON THE WHOLE ARMOR OF GOD

## (6:10-24)

This passage concludes the section of the letter on right Christian living (4:1-6:20). At the same time it concludes the entire letter, for both the doctrinal and the practical wrap up in this section on spiritual warfare and the need to learn how to use every weapon in God's repertoire. The emphasis on the battle against the cosmic powers is found throughout the letter (1:21; 2:2; 3:10; 4:27, compare 4:13). Satan in frustrated rage (Rev 12:12) has gone to war against God's people and wants to destroy them spiritually. He and his fallen angels use temptation and evil thoughts to sidetrack the saints in an effort to gain more and more control over their lives. The sources of these temptations are found in the vice lists of this book (4:17-19, 25-30, 31; 5:3-7, 11-12), and through them the evil powers keep believers bogged down with the world and spiritually defeated.

Believers need spiritual strength, which comes to them both vertically from the Lord and horizontally from fellow members of the body of Christ. The overcoming of the dividing wall (2:14) and the unity of the people of God in Christ's new creation (v. 15) cannot take place until the demonic forces are defeated, and that can happen only "in the Lord." The devil's strategies cannot be overcome without divine help. The pieces of the believer's armor come from God's own armor in Isaiah 59:17. God's people must employ every facet of the strength God gives in defeating their great enemy—Satan and his minions.

## PAUL GIVES AN OPENING ADMONITION TO BE STRONG IN THE LORD (6:10)

"Finally" translates an unusual phrase (*tou loipou*) that not only indicates the beginning of the final section but also means "from now on." Paul is saying that the battle that is starting now will be ongoing until the Lord returns. The whole letter, with its emphasis on the battle against the principalities and powers that is at the heart of the church and its work in the world, has been leading up to this closing admonition. The key to victory in the cosmic battle is spiritual strength, and the reason for the many problems in the church is the tendency of the finite, fallible beings who make up the church to engage the enemy in their own inadequate strength. They must turn to God and be infused by the Spirit so they can "be strong in the Lord and in his mighty power." The verb "be strong" is a present passive imperative, meaning that God must be the source and that his input must be ongoing. If we are to be victorious in our walk, we dare not stop relying on him and receiving his mighty power. Satan never rests, and so we dare not waver in our dependence on God's empowering presence in our lives.

"In the Lord" means that Christ is the sphere within which we find the inner strength to walk worthily (4:1).[1] There is no adequate power with which we can defend ourselves from the onslaughts of the demonic hordes apart from the enabling presence of the Lord and the Spirit. First Corinthians 10:13 expresses this perfectly:

> No temptation has overtaken you except what is common to mankind. And God is faithful; he will not let you

---

1. In Ephesians "Lord" always refers to "the Lord Jesus Christ" (1:3, 15, 17, and others).

be tempted beyond what you can bear. But when you are tempted, he will also provide a way out so that you can endure it.

The Triune Godhead is involved in our lives, providing the strength we lack to live victorious lives in a sinful world fraught with dangers. We experience this power through the unity between ourselves and Christ. In union with him we become "more than conquerors" (Rom 8:37).

The particular sphere within which we attain this spiritual victory is "his mighty power," stressing the greatness of what Christ has made available for his followers. Paul stresses the extent of God's strength in Ephesians 1:19–20, where we are told of "his incomparably great power" given to us. This is the same power God used to raise Christ from the dead and exalt him to his right hand. Paul is pulling out all the stops to help his readers understand what wondrous strength God has made available to them.

## GIVEN THE PRESENCE OF THE OPPOSING POWERS, PAUL STRESSES THE NEED FOR STRENGTH (6:11–13)

How do we fully use the divine power with which God infuses us? Paul turns to a powerful (pun intended) metaphor drawn from the Roman legions. Ephesians is one of the Prison Letters, and while Paul is writing he is looking at members of the praetorian guard (the elite guards of the palace and governmental apparatus in Rome) to whom he is chained in his apartment in Rome (see Phil 1:13). They wear their extensive armor only when going into battle, but their presence leads Paul to carefully choose the appropriate articles to describe the spiritual armor God has placed at our disposal. As noted above he builds on Isaiah 59:17, where God, the Divine Warrior, dons his armor to deliver Israel and defeat its enemies.

### The Danger: The Devil's Strategies (6:11)

Paul begins with a command to "put on the full armor of God," stressing the need for each individual piece in the midst of battle and including each item from the complete set worn by infantry soldiers as they went to war. If a soldier were to forget even a single item, he would be in grave danger, for in ancient battle the thrusts of swords and spears could come from any conceivable angle, and any flaw in the armor could prove fatal. Believers are to put on this armor like a new set of clothing (Rom 13:12; Eph 4:24; Col 3:10), thereby gaining the strength and protection that will ensure victory. "Of God" here could indicate possession (God's armor) or source (the armor from God). A growing number of scholars prefer the latter, as a designation that the same armor God wore in Isaiah 59 he now gives to his people.

This is similar to Ephesians 4:8, 11, where Christ is depicted as the Divine Warrior who defeats the cosmic powers and then turns over the spoils of victory to his people, the church. Also, in 2 Corinthians 10:3–5 Paul tells believers that we do not "wage war as the world does" but use a different set of weapons equipping us to "demolish strongholds"—the pretentious teachings of the world. These are the weapons of the Divine Warrior. Like Timothy, we "fight the battle well" (1 Tim 1:18) and refuse to "get entangled in civilian affairs," seeking rather to "please [our] commanding officer" (2 Tim 2:4).

The purpose of clothing ourselves with God's armor that this allows us to "take [our] stand against the devil's schemes." The hordes of Satan are the opposing army in the holy war, and Satan is a brilliant general with an incredibly well planned set of strategies that can easily lead to our defeat and destruction. Moreover, he does not fight according to the rules of the Marquess of Queensberry or the Geneva Conventions. He fights dirty and uses every trick in the book to gain the victory over us. The term "can" (*dynasthai*) means more than merely being able; it connotes having the power (from God) to do something. God does more than simply fight alongside us. He infuses us with his power as we fight. This parallels Isaiah 40:28–31, in which Yahweh, who never tires, suffuses his people with strength when they are ready to collapse. Their job is to put their "hope in the LORD" so that when they are about to stumble they will "find new strength"[2] and be enabled by God to "soar on wings like eagles."

The key to victory in ancient warfare was to remain standing through all of the battle situations one faced. Those who fell would die, for they would be helpless against the swords being brandished against them from every direction. Four times in verses 11–14 Paul cites the image of standing to connote final victory. His reference is to defensive tactics in verses 11, 13a, 14 (standing against Satan) and to offensive strategy in verse 13b ("after you have done everything, to stand"). We must endure the action of demons against us, while at the same time taking the battle to them and defeating them.

Most of all, we are to take our stand "against the devil's schemes." I prefer "strategies" as a translation of the Greek *methodeia*, as it makes the military imagery more specific. Paul used the same term when speaking of the false teachers with their "deceitful scheming," referring to the deceptive plans of heretics (and here the source of their plots, Satan) to trap unwary church members (Eph 4:14). The devil is the general leading the opposing armies and developing a brilliant military strategy to surround and destroy God's people (1 Cor 7:5; 2 Cor 2:11, 4:4; 2 Thess 2:9–10). He plans to lead the weaker members into a trap, strike them from every side, and so defeat them. His weapons are well known, and he specializes in tempting people through worldly enticements, fleshly pleasures, and material luxuries to forget God and live for self (Eph 2:2; 4:27).

### THE OPPONENTS IN THE WAR (6:12)

Paul here goes into more detail about the opponents conducting the unholy war against God's people. God must empower

---

2. "Find new strength" (NASB, NLT) is better than the NIV's "renew their strength." They don't *regain* their former human strength but rather are filled with the strength of the unfaltering God!

us with superhuman weapons because there are superhuman forces arrayed against us in tireless pursuit. Ours is a "struggle" against overwhelming odds, for we are fighting not against mere "flesh and blood" opponents but against the very powers of darkness. All of the world's horror movies taken together couldn't begin to approximate the reality we face, for these are the evil powers behind every terror this world has ever known!

If only it were just the Roman legions facing us in battle! (Has that ever before been said? It has now.) No wonder our spiritual resistance constitutes a struggle. Picture, if you will, a wrestling match between a super-heavyweight (the devil) and a flyweight (our self). The odds would seem hopeless were it not for one critical fact: God is fighting on our side. Both in ancient wrestling and in ancient warfare hand-to-hand combat determined the outcome. No quarter was given and none taken. The fight was to the finish: it was either victory or death.

This becomes especially true when we realize that the enemy force we face consists of "rulers," "authorities," and "the powers of this dark world." This is the closest the Bible comes to describing the military order of the demonic forces. What chance, we might ask in dismay, do we have against such cosmic powers? Paul frequently uses the first two terms (ruler and authorities) to depict the demonic realm (Eph 1:21; 3:10). The third is literally "world powers of this darkness," which describes their ruling function and power in the world of evil. While these beings were cast out of heaven into this world and are now imprisoned in it, they constitute the gods of this world and its rulers under their leader, Satan (John 12:31; 14:30; 16:11; 2 Cor 4:4; 2 Pet 2:4; Jude 6; Rev 12:7–9). In the Roman world the term "world powers" (*kosmokratores*) spoke of the absolute power of the Roman deities; here it denotes the evil "deities" over the spirit-world of darkness and evil.

The first three terms are summed up in the fourth description, "spiritual forces of evil in the heavenly realms." This is an umbrella term encompassing all of the fallen angels. They are spiritual forces arrayed against God and his people, and they both constitute and stand completely on the side of evil in all its forms. We live and function "in the heavenly realms" (2:6) and receive spiritual blessings (1:3) as well as fight against the evil powers (3:10; 6:12). Ours is a spiritual battle in a spiritual realm. But the exalted Christ is also at work there (1:20), and in him our victory is secure.

## THE WHOLE ARMOR: STANDING FIRM IN THE BATTLE (6:13)

In this verse Paul restates the main theme of the section— "put on the full armor of God"—but here he also uses the image to introduce the list of the items of armor in verses 14-17. "Because of this" (NIV "therefore") points back to what Paul has just stated: that we are engaged in a seemingly hopeless war against hostile forces of evil too great for us to endure in our own strength, and that we need serious help. Our only hope is the intervention of God and of the exalted Christ. At the same time we must remain cognizant of the relentless enemy arrayed against us and avail ourselves of the aid God provides.

The battle has been joined, and the forces of the enemy are in attack mode, coming at us fast and furiously. Paul changes his imperative from "put on" (clothing imagery) to "take up" (weapon imagery). This is a stronger verb, often used in a military setting, that speaks of an emergency situation in a battle that is already in process. The soldiers are arming themselves one piece at a time, but they are in a hurry lest the encroaching hostile forces catch them unprepared.

Paul's list begins with the defensive aspects of battle. The "day of evil" has arrived, and we must "stand [our] ground," resisting the onslaughts of the enemy. Picture the scene from the movie *Braveheart* of the Scottish forces in the valley, waiting for the British army to arrive on the hills surrounding them. The "day of evil" has been variously understood as a general reference to the difficulties we experience in the present age (the "evil days" of 5:16), specific periods of serious persecution and trials, or the troubles of the last days centering on the "man of lawlessness" or the antichrist of 2 Thessalonians 2:3-12 and 1 John 2:18. Likely Paul has in mind all of these and is referring to the spiritual battles of the present age that will culminate at the end of the age. As Hebrews 12:11 reminds us, all of these difficulties are painful and discouraging, but God clothes us with his armor and makes certain it will ultimately produce "the peaceful fruit of righteousness."

At the end of the day our goal is clear, "after [we] have done everything, to stand" in victory upon the field of battle. The word for "done everything" (*katergasamenoi*) may be translated "prepared." It refers to our thorough preparation for the battle, including instruction in how to use each piece of armor effectively and well. That includes a deep knowledge of God's word and of theological truths—knowledge at our disposal to use against Satan (as Jesus did in Matt 4:1-11).

## PAUL DESCRIBES THE PIECES OF ARMOR (6:14-17)

Many commentators believe that there is no close connection between the individual articles of armor and the spiritual qualities Paul lists. I disagree, as I will demonstrate in my discussion below. I believe that Paul, following Isaiah 59:17, carefully thought through which qualities would best fit the belt, the breastplate, and so on. As stated above at 6:11, he continuously had in his direct line of vision a Roman guard and no doubt thought deeply about the linkage with God's spiritual armor.

### The Belt of Truth (6:14a)

All of the pieces of armor are connected to the opening "stand firm," picturing the infantryman standing at attention as each piece is fastened to his body, providing the strength that will allow him to stand fast in battle. The belt that was "buckled" or "strapped around" the waist held the armor in place and allowed the soldier to fight without worrying about becoming entangled by his garments or armor. The sword was fastened to it and the tunic and breastplate held in place by it. For a soldier this would have been a sturdy leather belt that would have held all of these pieces in place (similar to Elijah's belt in 2 Kgs 1:8).

Paul is here alluding to Isaiah 11:5, which says of the messianic "branch" that "He will wear righteousness like a belt and truth like an undergarment" (NLT; also NET).

The foundation piece of the Christian armor is "truth," and Paul intends the term here both objectively and subjectively. On the objective side it refers to Christian revealed truth: the gospel truth along with the established doctrines of the church and the teachings of the word of God (Eph 1:13; 4:21). On the subjective side it refers to right Christian living (4:24, 25; 5:9; see the virtue lists of 4:25-30, 32; 5:1-2, 8-9, 18-21)—to a life of sincerity and honesty, truly dedicated to God and Christ.

### THE BREASTPLATE OF RIGHTEOUSNESS (6:14B)

Again building on Isaiah 59:17 ("He put on righteousness as his breastplate"), Paul next mentions this most important protective piece of the armor. The breastplate covered the chest, sides, and back. For the wealthy it was made of bronze or another strong metal, while for the poor it was often a thick piece of leather fashioned to cover the upper torso. Since sword thrusts in battle could come from any angle, it was essential that all of the vital organs be protected. The breastplate would fit over the head and be hinged at the sides with leather straps and metal bars and then fastened at the waist, often with a leather or metal apron to protect the groin region.

The concept of righteousness as a protective piece of spiritual armor is also both objective and subjective. Objectively, it relates to our justification by the blood of Christ (Rom 3:21-26), pointing to the atoning sacrifice of Christ, who became the ransom payment for our sin, leading to our redemption or purchase for God. God, the Judge of all, declared us to be right with him and innocent in his sight, leading to our salvation. Subjectively, righteousness results in our sanctification; through it we are made right by the power of the Spirit and enabled to live fittingly for him. This righteous living allows the believer to confront and expose evil, triumphing over the evil powers through Christ.

## THE SHOES: THE GOSPEL OF PEACE (6:15)

Paul alludes here to Isaiah 52:7: "How beautiful on the mountains are the feet of those who bring good news, who proclaim peace, who bring good tidings, who proclaim salvation." Roman military footwear was an incredible invention that gave troops a huge advantage over opposing armies. These boots were made of a supple leather and strapped up the leg. On the soles were metal studs that afforded stability for long marches and gripped, guaranteeing a firm foothold in battle. The Roman army marched twice as fast as other armies, and its enemies were often surprised at the speed with which the soldiers arrived, ready for battle.

Spiritual footwear is defined as "the readiness that comes from the gospel of peace." The noun *hetoimasia* has been understood by some to mean "steadfastness," a "firm footing" in the midst of battle. That would make sense here, but the noun and verb in both the Old Testament (as translated into Greek in the **Septuagint**) and the New Testament ordinarily means "preparation, readiness," and that is more likely what Paul has in view here. So the metaphor speaks of preparation for battle and the readiness that results. God's word makes us ready to engage the cosmic powers in spiritual warfare.

Two genitives follow: "of the gospel" and "of peace." The first might refer to the gospel as the source or means by which we are made ready to engage the enemy. More likely, however, it points to the goal or object of the action—that we are ready to proclaim the good news (as in Isa 52:7). Here Paul is not emphasizing the defensive side, as he did with the first two pieces of armor, but is turning to the offensive dimension of warfare. Armed with the gospel, we are taking the fight to the enemy. As in 2 Corinthians 10:4-5, we are fighting not with "the weapons of the world" but with God's weapons, which "have divine power to demolish strongholds." We march into battle shod with the readiness to wield the power of the gospel, the word of God (so also Rom 10:15, which quotes Isa 52:7).

Paul calls this offensive weapon "the gospel of peace," which at first glance seems incongruous in a section on warfare. But Isaiah 52:7 states that the divine messenger "proclaims peace," and three times in Ephesians 2:14–18 Paul points out that the breaking down of the wall of hostility brings peace and enables God's people to find unity as Christ's new creation. Christ himself declared it memorably in John 14:27: "Peace I leave with you, my peace I give you. I do not give it to you as the world gives." Christ's peace is both a peace with God and a peace between fractious human beings. Satan brings conflict and division, so to proclaim and bring peace constitutes a distinctive victory over the powers of evil. When a soldier is convinced that he cannot lose and goes into battle at peace with himself and his fellow soldiers, he is much less vulnerable than he might otherwise be.

### The Shield of Faith (6:16)

The KJV interprets the opening of this verse as "above all," seemingly identifying the shield as the most critical piece of armor. That, however, is unlikely, and it is perhaps better to translate this as "in addition to all this" (NIV), looking to faith as the fourth element of the Christian armor. The Greek word for "shield" here is *thyreon*, linked to the word for "door" (*thyra*). Paul has in mind not a small shield but the Roman "great shield," which was almost the size of a door and was often covered by a calf hide. Soldiers would use such shields to cover a company of men and to protect them from the enemy's arrows, which were frequently dipped in pitch and set on fire. Such a shield would both blunt the arrow and quench the fire. This picture is ideally suited to the imagery of Satan's fiery arrows in the second half of this verse.

As with the spiritual qualities above, there is both an objective and a subjective side to faith. Objectively, it is the Christian faith, as in "unity of the faith" in Ephesians 4:13, that shields us from Satan's lies and the deceptions on false teachers (v. 14).

There "faith" refers to the core collection of doctrines to which the true church unanimously holds. Subjectively, it refers to our active trust in and dependence upon Christ, as stressed in 1:15, 19; 3:12, 16–17; 6:23. It is our dynamic faith that enables us to clothe ourselves with and effectively use God's full armor as we struggle in an evil world to remain faithful to him. Faith turns our hearts and minds from relying on self to full surrender and continuous reliance on him.

Through this twofold faith we will find the strength in every battle to "extinguish all the flaming arrows of the evil one." Satan as a roaring lion wants to devour us (1 Pet 5:8). Paul reinforces his point with another picture, that of a destructive farm combine that wants to "sift [us] like wheat" (Luke 22:31). The metaphor of flaming arrows illustrates the terrible danger posed by the temptations, trials, and evil thoughts (in fact, all of the vices named in this letter) sent by Satan to demolish the spiritual bastions of the faithful. The skins or fur placed on the shields worked to quench the fiery arrows, and faith does the same against the schemes of the devil. The evil machinations of the evil one are smothered by an active faith.

## THE HELMET OF SALVATION (6:17A)

The helmet is another of the basic pieces of armor, this one intended to protect the head from injury. Wealthy soldiers had helmets of bronze, while poorer soldiers wore leather helmets. This is another direct allusion to Isaiah 59:17, where the Divine Warrior "put on ... the helmet of salvation" and went out to deliver his people and repay his enemies, including the faithless in Israel.

The emphasis on salvation is not so much about final salvation as it is about the present experience of salvation, helping the readers to understand the divine power and deliverance they have already received in Christ. In Ephesians 1:3 they have already received God's spiritual blessings (listed in 1:3–14), and in 2:6–7 they are already seated with God in Christ in the heavenly realm. They are a new humanity and part of Christ's new creation (2:14–15), and they have been saved by grace and raised from spiritual death (1:18–20; 2:8–9). It is now time for them to put this present salvation to work in their daily lives.

### The Sword of the Spirit: The Word of God (6:17b)

The final piece of armor is the primary offensive weapon in the arsenal of believers. Earlier Paul chose the great shield rather than the smaller shield commonly used in fighting. Here Paul reverses that choice, referring not to the large broadsword but to the short sword of the infantryman. This was another major invention that was key to Rome's might, for it was razor sharp on both sides and came to a penetrating point, in contrast to the swords of Rome's enemies, which were sharp only on one side. When the Roman army was advancing, scouts from the enemy camp would go from village to village, shouting, "The short swords are coming! The short swords are coming!"

Paul drew upon Isaiah 11:5 in verse 14, and now he draws on Isaiah 11:4: "He will strike the earth with the rod of his mouth, and with the breath of his lips he will slay the wicked." Christ the Divine Warrior will put to flight and destroy the powers of evil, and his followers will take part in his great victory through the Spirit. This sword is wielded and made available by the Spirit, and the one brandishing it is invincible because the Spirit has fashioned it and made it an unstoppable force for taking the battle to the enemy. The sword of the Spirit is the word of God. As we are reminded in Hebrews 4:12, it is "alive and active. Sharper than any double-edged sword, it penetrates even to dividing soul and spirit ... it judges the thoughts and attitudes of the heart."

Paul is undoubtedly referring both to the proclamation of the gospel and to the teaching of the word. As God's word is proclaimed and taught, the cosmic powers retreat and slink off in defeat. Today, sadly, it is somewhat rare to see the word taught in depth in churches. There seem to be fewer and fewer adult Bible study classes, though everywhere I go I encounter people wanting to be taught and hungry for more of the word, and groups like Bible Study Fellowship seem to be flourishing. Too many churches appear not to recognize people's hunger for biblical truth. I pray that this interest will produce a renaissance of serious Bible study.

The situation, however, is not all bad news. Evangelistic ministry is growing, and all over the world the gospel is being proclaimed with ever-increasing power. When that happens, Satan and his fallen angels are forced to retreat and lives are changed. It is exciting to observe local churches joining with organizations like InterVarsity and Cru (formerly known as Campus Crusade for Christ) to reach the lost.

## PAUL SPEAKS OF PRAYER AS THE BINDING FORCE OF THE ARMOR (6:18–20)

Paul's emphasis here on the critical importance of prayer is intimately connected to the armor of God passage that precedes it. The five weapons cannot be effective without prayer, which binds them together into a complete set or armor (a "whole armor"). Prayer is not a sixth piece of armor but the enabling force that governs the effectiveness of the entire set. The armor is bathed in and consecrated by prayer and draws its power from it. The key term is "all," which Paul uses four times to stress the all-embracing nature and force of prayer. Prayer is a foundation for all Christian activity, and especially for the holy war against the powers of evil. Prayer becomes a channel through which the presence of God is invited into a situation, and it enhances the almighty power of God that stands behind the individual pieces of armor as they are wielded in spiritual battle.

### PRAYING IN THE SPIRIT (6:18)

Paul enjoins believers to "pray in the Spirit," to seek the empowering presence of the Spirit undergirding our prayer and to immerse ourselves in him, allowing him to guide and strengthen us as we "fight the good fight" (1 Tim 6:12; 2 Tim 4:7). There may be a double meaning here, as we pray both "in" and "by" the Spirit.[3] Some construe this as a reference to praying in tongues, but Paul is usually more explicit when he intends that meaning. This may include that aspect of prayer but cannot be restricted to it.

Prayer is essential, and it must take place "on all occasions" (literally, "at all times"); compare Paul's call for Christians to "pray without ceasing" in 1 Thessalonians 5:17. In every kind of situation and in everything we do, we need prayer. Satan never takes a break in his warfare against us, so we dare never grow weary of covering all of our activities with prayer. Moreover, we are to approach God "with all kinds of prayers and requests." Paul may have in mind corporate and individual prayers, but "all kinds of prayer" might also be a reference to different categories of prayer, similar to what we see in the various types of psalms—for example, praise songs, worship songs, lament psalms, thanksgiving psalms, and imprecatory psalms. On all occasions and with every kind of prayer, we are called to train our sight and to depend utterly on our heavenly Father.

Paul goes on to encourage his readers to "be alert and always keep on praying"—a repetition for emphasis of the "at all times," above, adding the dimension of alertness or vigilance in prayer. The verb (*agrypnountes*), meaning "be on the watch," is reminiscent of Jesus' words to his disciples in Gethsemane ("Watch and pray so that you will not fall into temptation," Mark 14:38), or in the Olivet Discourse ("Be on guard! Be alert! You do not know when that time will come," Mark 13:33; see also Luke 21:36). And the verb behind "keep on praying" (*proskarterēsei*), meaning to "be devoted to" or "persist in" something, speaks of a zeal for prayer that leads to fervent intercession.

Finally, this persevering prayer is to be uttered on behalf of "all the Lord's people." True prayer will be comprehensive, enveloping the whole church and including all its needs.

---

3. For the Spirit as intercessor, see Rom 8:26–27. For the Spirit as teacher and guide, see John 14:26; 16:12–15.

Of course, this was easier in the ancient house church, with forty or fifty people, than it is in modern churches with hundreds or even thousands of participants. Still, the implication is that the saints are to be deeply concerned for each other and desire to be involved in each other's lives, and this includes interceding for the personal needs of those around us. A church characterized by oneness is a praying church. We grow spiritually both by the vertical involvement of the Spirit in our lives and by the horizontal involvement of our brothers and sisters in Christ encouraging us and bearing us up in prayer.

### PAUL'S PERSONAL PRAYER REQUESTS (6:19-20)

In verse 19 Paul concludes the sentence he began in verse 18, saying in effect, "And pray in the Spirit ... for all God's people, including me." Paul's prayer request is for intrepid boldness in proclaiming the gospel. In Ephesians 3:12 he spoke of approaching God with "freedom and confidence," and here he uses the same terminology to refer to fearlessness in proclaiming the gospel. The one leads to the other. "Given me" (*dothē*) is a divine passive meaning "that God may give me." Paul is not just asking for personal confidence as he preaches but for a divine infusion of strength and courage to make the good news clear and powerful in every circumstance. Most agree that Paul is not speaking generally of opportunities to witness but has especially in mind his situation as a prisoner in Rome. As a Roman citizen involved in a capital trial he had the right to defend himself before Nero and the highest Roman authorities. Thus Paul wanted the Spirit to give him fearless confidence, not just to make a good defense of his innocence but to make the gospel truth absolutely clear to the highest authorities in the land.

Paul frequently asked for prayer, both for himself and for his proclamation of the gospel (Rom 15:30-32; 2 Cor 1:11; Phil 1:19; Col 4:3-4; 2 Thess 3:1). This intercession was especially needed as he was on trial for his life—with obvious repercussions for Christians in general, since Nero's decision would set a precedent for the treatment of all Christians within the Roman

Empire. In his trial before Festus and Agrippa in Acts 26:24–29, he used the occasion to proclaim the truths of the gospel and sought "to make [Agrippa] a Christian." Here he asks for boldness to do the same with Nero. Paul does not want to yield to the pressure of the occasion and fail to witness to the gospel out of fear for his life.

Paul, in effect, wants his audience to put into practice Jesus' directive in Matthew 10:19–20: "When they arrest you, do not worry about what to say or how to say it. At that time you will be given what to say, for it will not be you speaking, but the Spirit of your Father speaking through you." Philippians 1:12–14 provides an example of how decisively this principle works: we read that "the whole palace guard" was evangelized and that Christians everywhere became bolder in proclaiming the gospel. In one sense Paul was in shame as a prisoner, but ultimately he was functioning as God's official ambassador to Rome.

Specifically, Paul wants to "fearlessly make known the mystery of the gospel." He wants to hold nothing back, to speak openly, clearly, and fearlessly about God's mysteries. Paul has spoken of mystery often in this letter (1:9; 3:3, 4, 9; 5:32), referring to the revelation of those divine secrets hidden in the past but now revealed through the gospel. Here he applies the term especially to the salvation found in Christ and to the union forged between Jew and Gentile by the breaking down of the wall of hostility between the two (2:14–18). At first glance we may find it strange for Paul to bring up this mystery here. However, it is worth noting that Paul was writing during a time of persecution and animosity against Christians. All differences are resolved through the salvation Christ brings, and the gospel is the mystery that erases all of the hatred and animosity between Jew and Gentile, Roman and Christian.

Paul is not simply another Roman citizen standing before his emperor defending his innocence. He is "an ambassador in chains" (6:20), a poignant metaphor implying that God has officially sent him as heaven's special representative to the Romans and has chosen to do this via the unlikely avenue of bondage and prison. Being an ambassador in chains would have been the ultimate disgrace for a Roman official. Nero himself in AD 68 chose suicide over exile. Yet God selected Paul's chains to allow him to proclaim the gospel to the governmental apparatus in Rome. Most ambassadors swept into the city in a special cortege of officials and luxurious carriages, but Paul had arrived on a prison ship surrounded by a phalanx of Roman guards. Still, Paul was an official envoy, sent out on a mission just as Jesus had sent his disciples in John 20:21–23.

Paul wants a special infusion and empowerment from the Spirit for this task. At the end of the verse he repeats his desire to "declare it fearlessly, as I should." He is under serious obligation to God to fulfill his ambassadorial duty in Rome, and he needs a great deal of prayer to enable him to do so boldly.

## PAUL CONCLUDES HIS LETTER (6:21–24)

Greek letters always included this kind of closing greeting. Verses 21–22 are a near copy of Colossians 4:7–8, demonstrating again that these are indeed sister letters, perhaps even sent with Tychicus at the same time.[4] As with Paul's other letters, his remarks commend the letter carrier, explaining why he is being sent, and then close the letter with a prayer-wish and a final benediction. Unlike his other letters, however, he doesn't include greetings and instructions, possibly because he had spent a great deal of time with the Ephesians on the third missionary journey (Acts 19) and now depended on Tychicus to convey those greetings.

### THE SENDING OF TYCHICUS (6:21–22)

Tychicus was from the province of Asia, where Ephesus was located, and had become a trusted associate at the end of Paul's third missionary journey. He had been among the seven (Acts 20:4) representing the Pauline churches in the collection

---

4. See "Author" and "Date" in the introduction.

for the poor in Jerusalem. As Paul's personal envoy he bore the letter to Colossae as well as Ephesians, perhaps at the same time, and he updated both churches on Paul's situation.[5] Later he would be sent to Crete (Titus 3:12), and then to Ephesus, possibly with the second letter to Timothy (2 Tim 4:12), written shortly before Paul's death. So he appears to have been with Paul for the last several years of his life and to have functioned as Paul's personal representative to the churches.

Paul commends Tychicus as a "dear and faithful servant in the Lord." The term "dear" is actually "beloved brother" and emphasizes his extremely close relationship to Paul as his coworker and friend. Most likely he was traveling with Onesimus, Philemon's returning slave, whom Paul also called "a dear brother" in Colossians 4:9 and Philemon 16. If so the two, who had become trusted associates, personally carried the three letters back to the province of Asia. Paul wanted them to bring these churches up to date on his "circumstances" (NIV "everything"), which he summarized as "how I am and what I am doing," specifying his personal situation and the state of his ministry in Rome.

Paul restates this in verse 22, in which he spells out Tychicus's true purpose. Paul was sending Tychicus and Onesimus not only as letter couriers but to personally convey their firsthand knowledge of Paul and his team in Rome and to "encourage" the Ephesian Christians with the triumph of the gospel in Rome (see Phil 1:12–14). As they saw the power of the gospel manifested through the "ambassador in chains" and learned how it continued to flourish in all the known world, they would be encouraged to realize anew the power of God and the victory of the saints of whom they were a part.

---

5. This is seen in "so that you also may know," probably pointing to the Colossian letter also sent with Tychicus.

## THE CLOSING BENEDICTION AND PRAYER-WISH (6:23–24)

Paul has asked for prayer for all the saints (v. 18) and then for himself (vv. 19–20) and now closes his letter with two prayers for the Ephesians (vv. 23–24). Peace has been one of the themes of this letter, enabling these disparate believers to overcome their inveterate hostility toward one another (2:11–13) and find unity and peace in Christ (vv. 14–18), centering on the reality that Christ "himself is our peace" (v. 14). In Ephesians 6:15 Paul identifies one of the pieces of the Christian's armor as "the gospel of peace"—as he has reminded us in this letter, the bringing of oneness and peace to conflicted humanity is a major victory over Satan. Through Christ racial divides are nullified and people can overcome their deepest failure and be made right with both God and their fellow human beings.

Peace produces "love with faith." Ordinarily faith, hope, and love form the Christian triad (as in 1 Cor 13:13; Gal 5:5, 6), but here Paul emphasizes peace based on the centrality of the issue of unity in this letter. Love (the love of Christ) is central to the prayer of Ephesians 3:18–19 and to the ethical mandate of 5:1–2 (the love of Christ producing love within the community). Divine love (1:4; 2:4) must always be lived out in love among the saints (1:15; 4:2, 15–16).

To be truly effective, love must be combined with faith. Faith brings us to salvation (1:13; 2:8) and defines our spiritual growth (1:19; 3:12, 15, 17), and the "shield of faith" (6:16) provides major protection against the evil powers. It is this mixture of love and faith that empowers Christian victory and defines Christian maturity. The source is "God the Father and the Lord Jesus Christ." Love and faith are trinitarian gifts, however, and Paul elsewhere identifies them as Spirit fruit, as we see in Galatians 5:22–23. The compassionate love of our Father and the sovereign grace of our Lord make possible our possession of both of these key Christian traits.

Finally, Paul provides the typical prayer-wish (6:24) with which he closes most of his letters (1 Cor 16:23–24; 2 Cor 13:14; Gal 6:18; Phil 4:23, and others). Paul began this letter with his customary "grace and peace to you," and now he closes it with "Grace to all who love our Lord Jesus Christ." The letter is framed, then, by the unmerited grace of God and Christ. For Paul it is divine grace that has brought God's salvation to humanity and made it possible for us to inherit eternal life.

"With immortality" (NIV "with an undying love") is the final phrase of the letter, and its meaning is disputed. Depending on which term it modifies, the phrase could be translated "the immortal Lord Jesus" or "with undying [or sincere] love" (most versions) or "may grace be experienced for all eternity." Since the prayer-wish centers on God's gift of grace, the third is preferable, as recognized by several recent interpreters. Paul wanted his readers to understand that God's grace is not something they have experienced at conversion but that is no longer operative in their lives; the reality is that they will know the grace of the Triune Godhead through all eternity. Through the endless ages we will never exhaust the limitless resources of his grace. This is made all the more precious by the love relationship we share with Jesus.

In this final section of Ephesians we realize anew the seriousness of the Christian life. At stake are both present peace and eternal joy. Satan and the fallen angels know that they have one final chance to wreak havoc on God's plans and to defeat his followers, and it would appear today that they are waging war against us as never before. We have absolutely no chance of attaining victory unless we rely entirely upon divine power as we enter the fray. Yet he has made that power available and has clothed us in his "whole armor" to equip us for accomplishing the task. When we avail ourselves of all that God has made available to us, we cannot lose; indeed, we are "more than conquerors" (Rom 8:37) as the Divine Warrior goes to war with us and infuses us with his strength. Our task is both vertical (through prayer) and horizontal (through the faith and love of the saints) as we put the strength of the Godhead to work on our behalf.

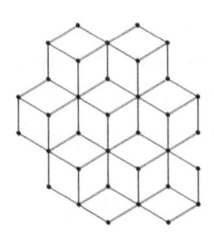

# GLOSSARY

**apocalyptic** Refers to truths about the coming of the last days, which God has hidden from past generations and is now revealing to his messianic community.

**christological (adj.), Christology (n.)** Refers to the New Testament's presentation of the person and work of Christ, especially his identity as Messiah.

**eschatology (n.), eschatological (adj.)** Refers to the study of the last things or the end times. Within this broad category, biblical scholars and theologians have identified more specific concepts. For instance, "realized eschatology" emphasizes the present work of Christ in the world as he prepares for the end of history. In "inaugurated eschatology," the last days have already begun but have not yet been consummated at the return of Christ.

**eschaton** Greek for "end" or "last," referring to the return of Christ and the end of history.

***Haustafeln*** German for "house table." A social code that provides instructions for relationships within a household.

**Hellenistic** Relating to the spread of Greek culture after Alexander the Great (356-323 BC).

**Holiness Code** A common name for the laws contained in Leviticus 17-26.

**inclusio** A framing device in which the same word or phrase occurs at both the beginning and the end of a section of text.

**Septuagint** An ancient Greek translation of the Old Testament that was used extensively in the early church.

**Shekinah** A word derived from the Hebrew *shakan* ("to dwell"), used to describe God's personal presence taking the form of a cloud, of ten in the context of the tabernacle or temple (e.g., Exod 40:35-38; Num 9:15-17; 1 Kgs 8:10-12).

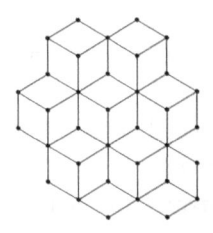

# BIBLIOGRAPHY

Arnold, Clinton E. *Ephesians*. Zondervan Exegetical Commentary on the New Testament. Grand Rapids: Zondervan, 2010.

Barth, Markus. *Ephesians*. 2 volumes. Anchor Bible. Garden City, NY: Doubleday, 1974.

Best, Ernest. *A Critical and Exegetical Commentary on Ephesians*. International Critical Commentary. Edinburgh: T&T Clark, 1998.

Bruce, F. F. *The Epistles to the Colossians, to Philemon, and to the Ephesians*. New International Commentary on the New Testament. Grand Rapids: Eerdmans, 1984.

Hoehner, Harold W. *Ephesians: An Exegetical Commentary*. Grand Rapids: Baker, 2002.

Hughes, R. Kent. *Ephesians: The Mystery of the Body of Christ*. Wheaton, IL: Crossway, 1990.

Lincoln, Andrew T. *Ephesians*. Word Biblical Commentary. Dallas: Word, 1990.

Morris, Leon. *Expository Reflections on the Letter to the Ephesians*. Grand Rapids: Baker, 1994.

Snodgrass, Klyne. *Ephesians*. The NIV Application Commentary. Grand Rapids: Zondervan, 1996.

Stott, John R. W. *The Message of Ephesians: God's New Society*. Downers Grove, IL: InterVarsity Press, 1979.

Thielman, Frank. *Ephesians*. Baker Exegetical Commentary on the New Testament. Grand Rapids: Baker Academic, 2010.

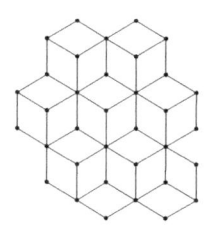

# SUBJECT AND AUTHOR INDEX

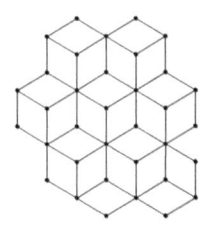

# INDEX OF SCRIPTURE AND OTHER ANCIENT LITERATURE

## Old Testament